P9-DYD-614

13 HOURS

Also by Mitchell Zuckoff

13 HOURS

THE INSIDE ACCOUNT OF WHAT REALLY HAPPENED IN BENGHAZI

—

MITCHELL ZUCKOFF

with members of the
Annex Security Team

TWELVE

New York · Boston

This book is a work of fiction. Names, characters, places, and incidents are the product of the author's imagination or are used fictitiously. Any resemblance to actual events, locales, or persons, living or dead, is coincidental.

Copyright © 2014 by Truth & Courage L.L.C.

All rights reserved. In accordance with the U.S. Copyright Act of 1976, the scanning, uploading, and electronic sharing of any part of this book without the permission of the publisher is unlawful piracy and theft of the author's intellectual property. If you would like to use material from the book (other than for review purposes), prior written permission must be obtained by contacting the publisher at permissions@hbgusa.com. Thank you for your support of the author's rights.

Twelve
Hachette Book Group
1290 Avenue of the Americas
New York, NY 10104

www.HachetteBookGroup.com

Twelve is an imprint of Grand Central Publishing.
The Twelve name and logo are trademarks of Hachette
Book Group, Inc.

The Hachette Speakers Bureau provides a wide range of authors for speaking events. To find out more, go to www.hachettespeakersbureau.com or call (866) 376-6591.

The publisher is not responsible for websites (or their content) that are not owned by the publisher.

Printed in the United States of America

Originally published in hardcover by Hachette Book Group
First oversize mass market media tie-in edition: November 2015

10 9 8 7 6 5 4 3 2 1
OPM

ATTENTION CORPORATIONS AND ORGANIZATIONS:
Most HACHETTE BOOK GROUP books are available at quantity discounts with bulk purchase for educational, business, or sales promotional use. For information, please call or write:

Special Markets Department, Hachette Book Group
1290 Avenue of the Americas, New York, NY 10104
Telephone: 1-800-222-6747 Fax: 1-800-477-5925

For JCS, SPS, TSW, and GAD
Veritas et Fortitudo

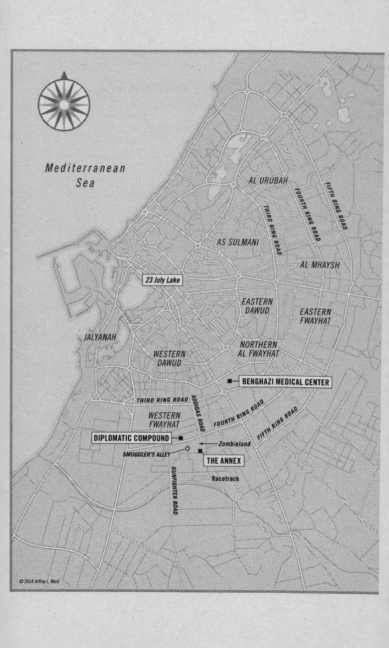

BENGHAZI, LIBYA

0 Miles   1   2

0 Kilometers   2

Airport

AL FUWAYHA

SPAIN

ITALY   GREECE   TURKEY

TUNISIA   *Mediterranean Sea*   CYPRUS

★ Tripoli   • Benghazi

ALGERIA   LIBYA   EGYPT

NIGER

0 Mi.   400   800

0 Km.   800   CHAD   SUDAN

CONTENTS

CONTENTS

A NOTE TO THE READER

This book documents the last hours of an American diplomatic outpost in one of the most dangerous corners of the globe. Based on exclusive firsthand accounts, it describes the bloody assault, tragic losses, and heroic deeds at the US State Department Special Mission Compound and at a nearby CIA base called the Annex in Benghazi, Libya, from the night of September 11, 2012, into the morning of the next day.

It is not about what officials in the United States government knew, said, or did after the attack, or about the ongoing controversy over talking points, electoral politics, and alleged conspiracies and cover-ups. It is not about what happened in hearing rooms of the Capitol, anterooms of the White House, meeting rooms of the State Department, or green rooms of TV talk shows. It is about what happened on the ground, in the streets, and on the rooftops of Benghazi, when bullets flew, buildings burned, and mortars rained. When lives were saved, lost, and forever changed.

The men whose experiences comprise the soul and spine of this book are well aware of the political storm surrounding Benghazi. They recognize that the word itself has become unmoored, no longer simply the name of a dusty Mediterranean port city on Libya's northeastern coast. They know that some Americans use Benghazi as shorthand for US government malfeasance or worse. They also understand that their explanations and revelations will be used as evidence to fit arguments and accusations in which they have chosen not to participate.

It's not that they don't care about those issues. It's just not their purpose. Their intent is to record for history, as accurately as possible, what they did, what they saw, and what happened to them—and to their friends, colleagues, and compatriots— during the Battle of Benghazi.

———

Although written as a narrative, this is a work of nonfiction. No scenes or chronologies were altered, no dramatic license was taken, and no characters were invented or created from composites. Descriptions from before, during, and immediately after the battle came from the men who were there, from verified accounts, or both. All dialogue was spoken or heard firsthand by primary sources. Thoughts ascribed to individuals came directly from those individuals.

The main sources of this book are the five surviving American security force contractors, known as "operators," who responded to the surprise attack on the Benghazi diplomatic Compound, spearheaded the counterattack, and carried out the rescue of State Department personnel and residents of the CIA Annex. Several names have been changed or withheld for privacy or security reasons, but all descriptions and information included about individuals is true. Classified details were omitted, in keeping with standard nondisclosure agreements among clandestine government employees and contractors. Those changes and omissions had no material effect on the story and did not misrepresent the known facts. The individual accounts of the operators were fundamentally in sync, but occasionally they diverged on details, such as when a particular radio call was sent. Whenever possible the narrative reflects the varying perspectives, which can be attributed to the fast-moving nature of events, the fog of war, and team members' overriding concerns about remaining alive rather than keeping track of chronologies.

Secondary sources include additional interviews, photos and videos, the voluminous record of public documents, congressional reports and testimony, and media reports. Those sources, credited where appropriate in the text and cited in the Select Bibliography, were used to provide context, fill gaps during periods when the primary sources weren't present, and to confirm or elaborate upon the participants' recollections. Further discussion of sourcing can be found at the end of the book, in "A Note on Sources" (page 345).

Previous accounts of these events, in books, magazines, and other media, have disturbed and even disgusted the men whose story is told here. Versions with fictionalized dialogue, imaginary incidents, false or exaggerated claims, and sensationalized allegations serve no purpose other than to inflame and obfuscate. The goal of the real security team members is to recount the Battle of Benghazi through as transparent a lens as possible. They and the family of a sixth operator have a financial stake in this book, but their only editorial demand was that the story be told truthfully.

It would be folly to think that this or any other account would be the last word on events with such wide-ranging implications. But after so many words have already flowed, with many more to come, consider it the first word directly from the battlefield, from men who know from hard experience and seared memories what actually happened during those harrowing thirteen hours.

—Mitchell Zuckoff

CAST OF CHARACTERS

THE ANNEX SECURITY TEAM:

Dave "D.B." Benton—A thirty-eight-year-old former Marine sergeant and SWAT team officer, D.B. was a scout sniper whose specialties included hostage rescue, direct-action assaults, surveillance, reconnaissance, and close-quarters battle. Before Benghazi, he'd been honored for contract security work in Iraq, Afghanistan, and elsewhere. Taciturn and thoughtful, a married father of three, D.B. frequently partnered in Benghazi with his good friend Kris "Tanto" Paronto.

(Courtesy of Dave Benton)

Mark "Oz" Geist—At forty-six the oldest member of the team, the laid-back Oz spent a dozen years in the Marine Corps, including work in an intelligence unit, then became the police chief in the Colorado town where he grew up. After running a private investigation company, in 2004 he became a security contractor to the State Department in Iraq. Twice married, Oz had a son with his first wife and a teenage stepdaughter and an infant daughter with his second wife. *(Courtesy of Mark Geist)*

Kris "Tanto" Paronto—A former member of the Army's 75th Ranger Regiment, the voluble Tanto had a personality as colorful as the many tattoos on his muscular body. At forty-one, he'd spent a decade working as a contract security operator— a job he considered part of a battle between good and evil— in countries throughout the Middle East. Tanto held a master's degree in criminal justice, owned an insurance adjusting

business, and had a son and a daughter with his second wife. *(Courtesy of Kris Paronto)*

Jack Silva—A former Navy SEAL, Jack spent a decade in the service, carrying out missions in Kosovo and the Middle East. Introspective and smart, Jack left the SEALs to spend more time with his two young sons and his wife, who learned while Jack was in Benghazi that she was pregnant. At thirty-eight, Jack divided time between contract security work and real estate, buying, reno-

vating, and selling properties. Jack often partnered with fellow former SEAL Tyrone "Rone" Woods.

(Courtesy of Jack Silva)

John "Tig" Tiegen—Tig was thirty-six, a former Marine sergeant from Colorado who spent several years as a security contractor for Blackwater. He worked for the company in Afghanistan, Pakistan, and Iraq, before going to work for the CIA's Global Response Staff. Quiet and precise, the married father of infant twins, Tig was in the midst of his third trip to Benghazi for GRS, making him the team member with the most experience in the city. He often teamed with Mark "Oz" Geist.

(Courtesy of John Tiegen)

Tyrone "Rone" Woods—Rone was forty-one, a powerfully built former Navy SEAL who'd spent

two decades in the service before returning to civilian life in 2010. During his SEAL years, Rone had served in Somalia, Afghanistan, and Iraq, where he earned a Bronze Star with a "V" for valor. Twice married, the father of three sons, Rone was a nurse and a paramedic. Eager to spend more time with his family, Rone had decided that Benghazi would be his last trip with the GRS.

(Courtesy of the Woods family)

OTHER KEY PARTICIPANTS:

J. Christopher Stevens—The American ambassador to Libya was a youthful fifty-two, a never-married, California-born, career Foreign Service Officer who dedicated himself to improving relations between the United States and Arab countries.

Sean Smith—Smith was a State Department communications officer by day, a well-known online gamer by night. Thirty-four, married with two young children, Smith worked for the State Department for ten years after serving in the Air Force.

Glen "Bub" Doherty—A former Navy SEAL, the affable Bub was a member of the Tripoli-based GRS team that flew to Benghazi after the attack began. Forty-two, divorced with no children, Bub was a charismatic blend of discipline and bonhomie. He was old friends with Rone and Jack from the SEALs, and newer friends with Tanto from their work together in Tripoli.

"Bob"—A CIA staffer, Bob was the agency's top officer in Benghazi. He oversaw all intelligence activities and personnel at the Annex, including the security operators.

"Henry"—A civilian in his sixties, Henry worked as a translator at the Annex and accompanied the security team on its rescue mission to the diplomatic Compound.

Alec Henderson—The highest-ranking State Department Diplomatic Security agent in Benghazi, Henderson was inside the Tactical Operations Center when the attack began. He sounded the first alarm and called the Annex and the Tripoli embassy for help.

David Ubben—Ubben was a Benghazi-based Diplomatic Security agent who'd spent time in the

US Army. When the attack began, Ubben and two Tripoli-based DS agents who traveled to Benghazi with Ambassador Stevens ran to their quarters to collect their rifles and body armor.

Scott Wickland—Wickland was a Benghazi-based Diplomatic Security agent assigned to protect Ambassador Stevens. A former rescue swimmer in the US Navy, Wickland led Stevens and computer expert Sean Smith into the villa's safe haven when the attack began.

13 HOURS

Prologue

A BLOODTHIRSTY MOB BORE DOWN ON THE UNITED States' poorly defended diplomatic post in Benghazi, Libya. Besieged American envoys and staffers withdrew to a locked room as fires set by the attackers drew closer. The Americans prayed and appealed for rescue, calling home to Washington and to nearby allies. If no help came, they feared one of three fates: They'd be killed by the invaders, suffocate from smoke, or be roasted alive. In the meantime, they'd fight.

The date was June 5, 1967.

War had just begun between Israel and Egypt, and morning radio reports in Benghazi were filled with false claims that US military planes had provided air cover for Israeli attacks or had bombed Cairo, less than seven hundred miles away. Hundreds of Benghazans swarmed into the streets and rallied at the consulate of the United Arab Republic, as Egypt was then called. The demonstrators' ranks swelled with some of the two thousand Egyptian construction workers then in Libya to build an Olympic-style stadium. Soon they turned violent. The throng grabbed cobblestones from the torn-up streets and headed toward a former Italian bank building that housed the American consulate.

A handful of Libyan guards fled their posts. The attackers barraged the building with stones and broke through the barred windows and the heavy front door. As the horde approached, the eight American men and two women inside the building frantically burned sensitive documents. The consulate workers were well armed, but the officer in charge, John Kormann, recounted in a memoir that he ordered that no one shoot, lest they enrage the mob further. The Americans tossed tear gas grenades to slow the onslaught. Cornered, they met their enemies with rifle butts and ax handles, then retreated up a wide marble staircase. They took refuge in a second-floor vault used as the consulate's communications hub.

Unable to reach their quarry but unwilling to leave, the attackers pillaged the building and set it aflame. Kormann feared that the invaders would splash gasoline under the vault door to burn or suffocate the Americans. He kept that thought to himself as fire engulfed the consulate. One consolation for Kormann and his colleagues was that the intense heat and thick smoke drove back the mob. The Americans shared five gas masks as they destroyed top-secret files and disabled cryptographic machines.

Several climbed up to the roof to continue burning documents, but returned inside when a group of men dropped a ladder down from an adjoining roof and rushed toward them. Unable to reach the consulate workers, the attackers cut the halyard that hoisted the American flag on a rooftop pole, allowing it to hang limp down the front of the building. A US Army captain asked Kormann's permission to re-raise the flag. Kormann refused, but later he relented. "I had been a combat paratrooper in World War II," he wrote. "I knew what defiance and a bit of bravura could do for soldiers under mortal stress. A display of courage can be infectious and inspiring, just as an act of cowardice can be demoralizing." Dodging rocks hurled from below, the captain dashed onto the roof and restored the Stars and Stripes to its rightful place.

State Department officials in Washington discussed rescue options, including sending a Marine unit and using paratroopers. But executing those plans would take more time than the Americans had. Meanwhile, the trapped Americans got sporadic phone calls through to their British counterparts, who had a battalion stationed outside Benghazi under a treaty arrangement. Four attempts to reach the Americans by fifty British soldiers were repulsed or delayed, and the mob set fire to a British armored car.

With no rescue in sight, Kormann took down from the wall a photo of President Lyndon Johnson and his wife, Lady Bird Johnson. He broke it from its frame, flipped it over, and wrote on the back that, whatever happened, they had done their duty. Everyone in the smoky vault signed the farewell note.

As night approached, a garbled message gave State Department officials the misimpression that the Americans were near death. Secretary of State Dean Rusk appealed again to the British. Two hours later, a British armored column made another attempt. This time, the British broke through to the consulate and brought all ten Americans to safety.

———

Forty-five years later, on September 11, 2012, the American diplomatic outpost in Benghazi again came under sudden siege by a murderous mob. Again the attackers couldn't reach their prey, so they plundered buildings and set fires with deadly intent. But this time, no British or other friendly troops were close enough to attempt a rescue.

With fires raging, gunmen swarming, State Department security officers taking cover, and the US ambassador missing, a call went out from one of the overwhelmed Americans: "If you don't get here soon, we're all going to die!"

Heeding that call was a band of elite warriors who'd left the United States military and had joined a clandestine organization that protected American covert intelligence operatives abroad. They had come to Benghazi as security officers for American diplomats and CIA agents, but now they'd need to rely on their past training, two as

Navy SEALs, one as an Army Ranger, and three as Marines. They knew that they'd be vastly out-numbered, but they also knew that they were their fellow Americans' only hope.

This is their story.

ONE

Benghazi

———

JACK SILVA LEANED FORWARD IN HIS WINDOW SEAT aboard the Turkish Airlines jet as it approached Benghazi's Benina International Airport. He looked outside at the plane's shadow racing across the caramel-colored desert below. Jack believed deeply in yin and yang, the Chinese concept that a connection exists between seemingly opposing forces, like dark and light, life and death. So it was unsurprising that two conflicting thoughts entered his mind. First was excitement: *I wonder what adventures this place is going to bring.* Then came its counterbalance, worry: *I wonder if I'll ever see my family again.*

It was August 2012, and Jack was about to join the Benghazi team of a secretive US government organization called the Global Response Staff. Created after the 9/11 attacks, the GRS consisted of full-time CIA security staffers, supplemented by former military special operators like Jack, who

were hired on a lucrative contract basis. GRS officers served as bodyguards for spies, diplomats, and
other American personnel in the field. The more
dangerous a posting, the more likely GRS operators were nearby in the shadows, protecting America's envoys and covert intelligence gatherers. Few
if any postings were more dangerous than Benghazi, Libya.

As a former Navy SEAL, Jack was a natural fit for
the GRS. At thirty-eight years old, self-possessed
and darkly handsome, he stood six foot two and
carried 210 pounds on his muscular frame. In his
usual attire of a black T-shirt and khaki shorts,
Jack looked like a strapping construction worker.
On the plane, though, wearing dress slacks, brown
leather shoes, and a tucked-in button-down shirt,
he might be mistaken for an American businessman seeking import-export opportunities ten
months after the death of deposed dictator Muammar al-Gaddafi. At least that was Jack's hope as the
jet's wheels touched down.

Jack's arrival marked his first visit to Libya and
the start of his sixth trip as a GRS operator; his
previous trips had taken him to the Middle East
and elsewhere. For official purposes in Benghazi,
Jack would simply say that he'd be working as a
security staffer for US government personnel. Men
who protect spies don't advertise that fact.

Before leaving the plane, Jack slipped off his
gold wedding band and tucked it into a small box
for safekeeping. He'd picked up the habit years
earlier, after deciding that he didn't want his

enemies to know that he had a family: a wife and two young sons waiting for him back home in the Pacific Northwest.

Jack stepped onto the tarmac and felt the bone-dry afternoon heat of the Libyan summer. His aviator sunglasses were modest protection from the harsh white glare of the North African sun. Entering the run-down terminal building, Jack pushed through doors to a room with a luggage carousel and more than a hundred people packed inside a space that would have felt crowded with half as many. His fellow luggage-seekers, most of them men, shouted in Arabic and gestured wildly as they fought to claim bags. The air was thick with flies and the nauseating stench of baked-on body odor. Jack took short breaths through his mouth in a futile effort to keep both at bay.

He'd been on guard from the moment he left the plane, a reflex reaction whenever Jack arrived in hostile territory. Hyper-aware, his jaw set, his every movement grew deliberate, measured to convey in body language that he wasn't looking for trouble but wouldn't flinch from it, either. Jack felt the stares of strangers upon him and knew that at least some were armed. He also knew that everyone watching him had reached the same instant conclusion: American. He suspected that at least some wished him dead.

As he waited for his bags, Jack caught sight of a burly, bearded man standing with his back against a wall at the periphery of the scrum. The man's eyes scanned the crowd while his body remained as still as a lizard on a tree limb. He wore khaki cargo pants and a navy-blue button-down shirt, untucked, Jack knew, to conceal a gun in his waistband. Their eyes met for an instant. Jack returned his gaze to the luggage carousel, and the bearded man remained expressionless, glued to the wall.

When Jack grabbed his bags, the man pushed away from the wall and turned toward the exit door leading to Customs. Jack followed a short distance behind. By the time Jack stepped outside the terminal building, he and the bearded man had closed the distance between them and fallen into step with each other. Still they didn't speak as the man led Jack toward a white Toyota pickup truck caked in dust.

Jack tossed his bags in the back and slid into the passenger seat. The bearded man got behind the wheel. In a single, practiced motion, the man reached down and grabbed a pistol.

"It's loaded," the man said.

He held it out, butt-end first.

Jack relaxed as he took the gun. He reached out his right hand and returned a powerful handshake offered by his fellow former SEAL and GRS colleague Tyrone Woods, whose radio call sign was "Rone."

"How's it going, brother?" Rone said, a bright smile emerging from his thick salt-and-pepper beard.

As Rone started the truck, they caught up on each other's lives and families, then set aside those thoughts like wedding rings slipped into boxes.

Rone drove toward the airport exit, bound for an upscale neighborhood called Western Fwayhat. Their destination was a CIA-rented property known as the Annex, which was the agency's secret headquarters in Benghazi. Less than a mile from the Annex was the United States' public presence in the city: a walled estate known as the US Special Mission Compound, which served as a base for State Department diplomats.

As their talk turned to business, Rone filled Jack in about the peculiarities of the treacherous place where they'd be working to keep other Americans safe. Rone's overriding message was that they'd be kept busy, and they'd have to remain alert, but there was nothing about Benghazi they couldn't handle. In a strange way, Rone said, he almost liked the place.

Still, something about how his old friend described Benghazi—a lawless city where no one was in control, where lines between America's friends and enemies shifted and blurred, where they could trust only each other—gave Jack the distinct impression that Rone considered this to be their diciest assignment yet.

Jack had landed in a country most Americans know only from disturbing headlines. A North African nation roughly the size of Alaska, Libya is a vast desert with a tiny fringe of fertile soil at its northern coast. To its west are Tunisia and Algeria, to its east is Egypt, and to its south are Niger, Chad, and

Sudan. The country is divided into three regions: Tripolitania, to the west, with Tripoli as its capital; Cyrenaica, to the east, with Benghazi as its capital; and Fezzan, to the arid south. A majority of the six million Libyans live in or around Tripoli and Benghazi, at the edge of the Mediterranean Sea. Some 97 percent of the population is Sunni Muslim.

A brief history of Libya is an inventory of invasions by outside powers. If an empire had ships and armies in the Mediterranean, its to-conquer list included Libya's two major ports, Tripoli to the west and Benghazi to the east, separated by the Gulf of Sidra. Over the millennia, occupiers included the Phoenicians, the Persians, the Romans, the Byzantines, and the Ottomans. Sometimes competing empires split the baby. The Greeks claimed the area around Benghazi in 630 BC, while the Romans settled near Tripoli. Historians say the Greeks even named Libya, using it as a term to describe all of northern Africa west of Egypt.

By 74 BC, the Romans had conquered eastern Libya, temporarily uniting east and west. Then came the Vandals, a Germanic tribe that drove out the Romans and earned their namesake reputation by plundering the east. The Ottomans invaded Tripoli in 1551 and ruled Libya for more than three centuries, with limited success controlling the ever-restive eastern tribes around Benghazi.

While successive conquerors were vanquishing and bleeding Libya, two Arab tribes flowed onto its sands from Egypt. Starting in the eleventh century, the Bani Hilal tribe settled near Tripoli, while the Bani Salim tribe settled in the east. The Bani Salim freely mixed with and married the native Berbers around Benghazi. As generations passed, the result was a homogeneous ethnic and religious region, what one historian called the "total Arabization" of eastern Libya.

During the 1800s, the Ottoman Turks gave up hope of controlling Benghazi. The Turks allowed eastern Libya to exist as a semi-independent state ruled by the Senussi Muslim sect, which preached a pure form of Islam under which followers conducted all aspects of their lives by the teachings of the Prophet Muhammad. While Tripoli and western Libya matured into a relatively modern region, eastern Libya retained its old ways, governed by tribal bonds and religious laws. That divide made it impossible to understand present-day Libya without contrasting Benghazi with its larger, richer, better-looking, and worldlier sister, Tripoli.

In 1912, the exhausted Ottoman Empire signed a secret pact that gave Italy control of both west and east Libya. Tripoli adapted to Italian rule, but eastern Libya fought colonization, especially by a Christian nation. By 1920, the Italians had had enough. Drained by the First World War, Rome ceded autonomy over eastern Libya to Idris al-Senussi, head of the strict Senussi religious order.

When Benito Mussolini rose to power in Italy two years later, the fascist dictator wanted Benghazi to be part of his empire. Years of fierce fighting followed. In September 1931, Italian forces finally captured and hanged the leader of the opposition guerrillas, Omar al-Mukhtar, a Senussi sheikh who became a martyr to Libyan independence. Even with Mukhtar gone, Mussolini set out to destroy any entrenched opposition around Benghazi. He built a two-hundred-mile fence along the border of Egypt and by some estimates deported one-third of eastern Libya's civilian population to concentration camps. He executed twelve thousand more.

With Benghazi under Italian control, waves of workers arrived from across the Mediterranean. The Arab natives were forced into menial jobs, deprived of schooling, and excluded from politics. World War II made matters worse, as Benghazi was bombed hundreds of times as the Axis and Allied powers traded control over the rubble. British pilots adapted a popular song to reflect the carnage, with a lyric that included the line, "We're off to bomb Benghazi." Like a long-abused animal, Benghazi grew mean and wary.

After World War II, Libya was divided among the British, French, and Americans. Oil had yet to be discovered, so no one wanted colonial responsibility for an impoverished, bombed-out Arab sandbox. In 1951, the Allies helped to establish the United Kingdom of Libya, an independent, constitutional monarchy ruled by the Muslim leader Idris al-Senussi. The title was better than the job: King Idris had dominion over the world's poorest country and one of its least literate.

That changed radically in 1959 with the discovery of immense oil reserves, enough to eventually account for 2 percent of global supplies, or more than a million barrels exported daily in 2012. Suddenly King Idris had money to lavish on friends and pet projects in his native east, leaving Tripoli and Libya's west to decay. In east and west alike, the elite grew rich while everyone else remained poor.

In 1969, while the eighty-year-old King Idris was abroad, the timing was ripe for a bloodless coup led by a power-hungry twenty-seven-year-old army officer: Muammar al-Gaddafi. Over the next forty-two years, the erratic, brutal, egomaniacal Gaddafi earned the sobriquet bestowed on him by Ronald Reagan: "[M]ad dog of the Middle East."

From the start, Gaddafi worried about Benghazi's rebellious bent and its ties to the exiled King Idris. So he squeezed the region dry. Previously, the Libyan capital had alternated between Tripoli and Benghazi; Gaddafi made Tripoli the permanent capital. He moved the National Oil Corporation from Benghazi to Tripoli, despite the fact that most of the country's oil is in the east. He relocated a memorial that had been erected in Benghazi to honor Omar al-Mukhtar, fearing that Benghazans would rally behind the rebel martyr's legacy, as eventually they did.

As hospitals, schools, and the standard of living rose in Tripoli, Benghazi suffered oppression and neglect while its oil paid Tripoli's bills. Benghazans seethed as they watched Gaddafi celebrate himself in countless statues and endless tributes. The bitter separation between Benghazi and Tripoli wasn't just political and cultural, but physical. No railway or highway connected the two cities, only narrow roads that snaked through more than six hundred miles of desert.

Through all the turmoil, one comfort for Benghazans was their local soccer club, Al-Ahly Benghazi SC, whose name translates as "The People's Club." Gaddafi favored rival Tripoli soccer clubs and despised Al-Ahly Benghazi. That hatred deepened after the Benghazi team won the 1974 league championship, a victory that coincided with the anniversary of Gaddafi's coup. Benghazi fans flooded the streets to celebrate their club's triumph, ignoring the milestone of Gaddafi's rule. He wouldn't forget or forgive.

Years later, Gaddafi's soccer-playing son Saadi became owner, manager, and captain of a soccer club called Al-Ahly Tripoli. Saadi raided Al-Ahly Benghazi for its best players, and bribed or bullied referees to ensure victories. By the summer of 2000 Al-Ahly Benghazi was on the verge of disgrace: One more loss and it would fall from the country's top soccer division. Saadi Gaddafi came to Benghazi to luxuriate in his rivals' agony.

As the referees made dubious calls, the crowd grew restless. When a loss seemed inevitable, something snapped. The humiliation of their cherished soccer club became a symbol of all that Benghazi had endured under Gaddafi, from public executions to relentless poverty amid spectacular oil wealth. Al-Ahly Benghazi's head coach shoved the referee. Fans stormed the field then spilled into the streets. They torched the National Soccer Federation building and hurled stones at monuments to Gaddafi's regime.

The penalties were predictably severe: eighty arrested, thirty sent to Tripoli to stand trial, and three sentenced to death. On September 1, 2000, on the thirty-first anniversary of Gaddafi's coup, his security forces stormed the Al-Ahly Benghazi clubhouse. They smashed furniture, memorabilia, and trophies, then bulldozed the building. The club was suspended indefinitely.

Benghazi got its revenge a decade later, in 2011. After suffering countless more indignities and witnessing the Arab Spring revolutions in Egypt and Tunisia, the city became the cradle of the Libyan Civil War that ended Gaddafi's rule and his life.

━━━

Jack's arrival in Benghazi was the latest chapter in the adventurous life of a modern gunfighter. He grew up in Northern California, the only child of immigrants who worked long hours to send him to private school. As a boy Jack spent as much time as possible outside, building forts and imagining what it would take to survive if America's enemies invaded his hometown. He excelled at science and math, but after a single day of college decided that he'd had enough formal education. Jack enlisted in the Navy with a single goal: to become a SEAL.

Jack was nineteen and had completed boot

camp when he was sent to a ten-week Navy vocational training program. There Jack badgered his
instructors to arrange a screening test for admission to the Navy's Basic Underwater Demolition
School, the first step in the yearlong process to
become a SEAL. But when the opportunity arrived
without notice, Jack had been enjoying himself so
much in vocational classes during the day and partying at night that he'd let his physical training slip.

The screening test was only a fraction of what
it took to become a SEAL, but it was tough
enough to weed out candidates with no chance
of making it. Jack's friends considered the chis-
eled young sailor a shoo-in. He made it through
the five-hundred-yard swim in the required time.
Jack climbed out of the pool and far exceeded the
required number of push-ups, completing more
than eighty in two minutes. Next were sit-ups, and
he exceeded the standard there, too. Then came
pull-ups. The screening test required applicants to
do eight perfect, dead-hang pull-ups with virtually
no rest between exercises. After weeks of slacking,
Jack did six, then willed himself to a seventh. His
muscles screamed. His lungs ached. His arms were
on fire. Jack made it halfway up on the eighth but
couldn't get his chin over the bar.

Jack hung there, refusing to let go but lacking
the strength to pull himself higher. The veteran
Master Chief SEAL giving Jack the test prod-
ded him: "If I light a fire under your ass, can you
get over the bar?" Jack tried again but couldn't.
When he dropped to the ground, his eyes filled

with tears. Jack returned to his room and told his shocked friends that he'd failed.

He'd remember it as one of the most traumatizing and motivating moments of his life. Instead of going through the legendary SEAL training program and becoming an elite special operator, Jack spent the next two years as a Navy airman on an aircraft carrier. When his next chance came, Jack destroyed every category of the SEAL screening test. By the time he finished SEAL training, Jack came to appreciate the yin and yang of what he'd experienced the previous two years. The humbling failure and its consequences gave him the strength and willpower to push through the brutal selection process and earn his Trident, the prized SEAL insignia, while scores of other would-be warriors quit.

Jack didn't talk much about his exploits, but during a decade in the service he spent time in more than twenty countries and carried out missions in Kosovo and the Middle East. He left the SEALs to spend more time with his growing family and to try his hand at business. Jack bought and sold real estate, renovating and flipping properties while working to stay one step ahead of the tumultuous market.

By the time Jack and Rone joined forces as GRS operators in Benghazi, the two former Navy SEALs had been friends for nearly a decade. They'd met when both served as instructors at the Naval Special Warfare training facility in Niland, California. One night not long after they met, Jack spent a night drinking at a local bar and didn't want to drive home. He walked to Rone's nearby condo, planning to crash there until morning. Not knowing who was at his door, Rone climbed out a window wearing only boxer shorts and carrying a pistol. He moved tactically around the corner to the front door, gun raised, to outflank the presumed intruder. When he saw it was a drunken Jack, Rone lowered the gun and laughed.

When Rone wasn't pointing a gun at him, Jack considered Rone to be smart and effective, a natural leader, and perhaps the most motivated and hardest-working person he'd ever met, no small praise among Special Operations veterans.

Rone was forty-one, a twice-married father of three sons. A former high school wrestler, he liked fast motorcycles and muscle cars, especially Ford Cobra Mustangs. Rone had a weightlifter's broad chest, light-brown hair, a meaty chin, and forearms like pile drivers. He'd earned his SEAL Trident in 1991 after twice going through Hell Week, a five-and-a-half-day torture test of mental and physical toughness, pain and cold tolerance, teamwork and determination, all on fewer than four hours of sleep. As a SEAL, Rone had served bravely in Somalia, Afghanistan, and Iraq, where he received a Bronze Star with a "V" for valor. The citation described his "heroic achievement, extraordinary guidance, zealous initiative, and total dedication to duty" in al-Anbar province of western Iraq. He was a healer as well as a warrior, having become a registered nurse and a paramedic. Rone retired

from the SEALs in 2010 with twenty years of service. He bought a bar called The Salty Frog in
Imperial Beach, California, and helped his wife in
her dental practice.

———

While Rone and Jack were adapting to civilian life,
US government agencies began increasing their
reliance on Special Operations veterans willing
to provide security to Americans in the world's
hottest spots. Jack and Rone each heard through
the SEAL grapevine about openings at GRS for
accomplished former operators. Both saw a chance
to return to the camaraderie and the purpose
they'd loved as SEALs. And then there was the
money. Each trip by a GRS contractor generally
lasted several months, and even with generous
downtime between trips, contract operators typically earned more than $150,000 a year.

If challenge and money were the yin, danger was
the yang. They worked undercover in small teams,
in places where some locals saw the very presence
of armed Americans as provocation. In December
2009, three GRS operators were among the seven
Americans killed in Khost, Afghanistan, when a
Jordanian triple agent working for al-Qaeda deto-
nated a suicide bomb at a CIA compound.

Jack, Rone, and scores of other former special
operators balanced the risk and rewards, then
chose to join the GRS. Among them was another
of Jack's close friends in the SEALs, a high-
spirited, fun-loving operator named Glen "Bub"

Doherty. Jack and Glen had become SEALs the same year, and now Glen also was a contractor for the GRS in Libya, working in Tripoli. Not surprisingly in the tight-knit world of former SEALs, Glen and Rone had also become friends.

More than fifteen years after Jack became a SEAL, he remembered a warning from one of their instructors: "Look around the room. In twenty years, half of you guys will be gone. Guys sitting next to you are going to be killed in training accidents or in combat or whatever." The longer he remained an operator for hire, Jack knew, the more likely that prediction would come true. Maybe for himself, maybe for Glen or Rone, or maybe for them all.

———

At the dawn of the Libyan revolution, Benghazans expressed thanks to the Americans in their midst for the United States' help in the fight against Gaddafi. In May 2011, *The New York Times* published a story that described how cab drivers, translators, and cafés refused payment from Americans. Benghazi youths waved the American flag alongside rebel banners. Some parents of newborn girls reportedly named their children Susan, in honor of Susan Rice, the Obama administration's ambassador to the United Nations, for her support of a no-fly zone that grounded Gaddafi's warplanes.

"Americans and, for that matter, all Westerners are treated hereabouts with a warmth and gratitude rarely seen in any Muslim country...in probably half a century or more," the *Times* story gushed. "People smile and go out of their way to say hello to them, and are almost shockingly courteous."

But the cheerful story ended on a discordant note. The last paragraph described a bullet whizzing over the head of a foreign jogger, presumably the reporter: "The sound of the rifle's report came a second later, as it would with a high-velocity round. Whoever fired it was not about to show himself, at least not yet." It foreshadowed what lay ahead.

Little more than a year later, the Benghazi through which Rone and Jack drove in the pickup wasn't waving American flags or offering them free meals.

After Gaddafi was dragged from a drainage ditch, sodomized, and killed by rebel fighters in October 2011, heavily armed militias that toppled the regime sought to expand their roles in a post-revolutionary Libya. With the approval of Libya's weak transitional government, and in the absence of a strong military or police force, local militias shifted from revolutionary fighters to national guardsmen, ostensibly to prevent Benghazi from spiraling into chaos.

Some militias remained outwardly grateful to America. Members of one militia, the large and well-armed 17 February Martyrs Brigade, were hired to provide security and act as a Libyan "Quick Reaction Force" to protect the US State Department's Special Mission Compound in Benghazi.

Financed by the Libyan Defense Ministry, the 17 February militia had established bases and training facilities, assembled an arsenal of light and heavy weapons, and enrolled as many as thirty-five hundred members organized into battalions.

The United States' relationship with and reliance on the 17 February militia was a classic example of how the quirks of Benghazi led to strange bedfellows. The militia took its name from an incident on February 17, 2006, during which Libyan security forces killed roughly a dozen people during a violent protest at the Italian consulate in Benghazi. The protesters, who set fire to the consulate building and several cars, were enraged by an Italian government minister who wore a T-shirt displaying controversial cartoons depicting the Prophet Muhammad. The militia's name also referenced February 17, 2011, the start of the revolution to overthrow Gaddafi.

Questions lingered about how much the United States' diplomatic corps could trust the 17 February militia, at least some of whose members were suspected of fierce anti-American sentiments. No such questions existed when it came to several other Benghazi militias, which were outright enemies of the United States.

The city harbored at least two hard-line Islamist militias, aligned ideologically with al-Qaeda, that openly despised America and the West. One virulent anti-American militia was called the Ansar al-Sharia Brigade, whose name meant "Partisans of Islamic Law" and whose members believed that democracy is un-Islamic and that all authority is derived from the Prophet Muhammad.

Some members of Benghazi's radical Islamist militias had fought against American troops in Iraq after the US invasion in 2003. Not only were these jihadis-turned-militiamen highly motivated to kill Americans, they had the means to do so: After Gaddafi fell, Benghazi was awash in weapons left over from the revolution.

Personal ownership of firearms had been outlawed since Libya gained independence. But when Gaddafi's soldiers were driven from the city, rebel fighters raided the armories where the regime had stockpiled thousands of AK-47s and more powerful weapons. After the revolution, anyone who didn't already have a gun could simply shop for one at a large outdoor market called al-Funduq. Beyond flea market fare, past food stalls with eggs, spices, and poultry, arms merchants threw open their car trunks to display pistols, assault rifles, grenades, mortars, rocket launchers, and heavy machine guns ready to be mounted on pickup trucks. The result of the free flow of guns could be seen on the blood-soaked gurneys of Benghazi's only hospital equipped for major surgery: 1,761 gunshot wounds in 2011, up from an average of 41 during the previous two years.

The abundance of weapons, the absence of a working Libyan government, and lingering anti-Western sentiments among certain militias led to increasingly brazen incidents during the spring and summer of 2012. On April 2, a British armored diplomatic vehicle was attacked after driving into a local protest. On April 6, a homemade bomb was thrown over a wall of the US Special Mission Compound. Four days later, another homemade bomb was lobbed at the motorcade of Ian Martin, the UN Special Envoy to Libya. In May, a rocket-propelled grenade struck the Benghazi offices of the International Committee of the Red Cross. A previously unknown organization, the Omar Abdul Rahman group, claimed responsibility and issued a threat against the United States on social media sites.

The attacks escalated on June 6, when an improvised explosive device blew a hole in the wall around the US diplomatic Compound. No one was injured, but the vulnerability of the Compound property was evident. A pro-al-Qaeda group took credit, calling it retaliation for the death of al-Qaeda commander Abu Yahya al-Libi, a native of eastern Libya killed in a drone strike in Pakistan. Five days later, on June 11, 2012, attackers fired a rocket-propelled grenade at a car carrying Sir Dominic Asquith, the British ambassador to Libya, as it drove through Benghazi. Asquith was unhurt, but two members of his security team were injured. The attack took place a half mile from the US diplomatic Compound. American operators responded and brought their injured British cohorts to the hospital. The next day, the UK closed its Benghazi consulate and evacuated its staffers.

A US government review of events in Benghazi during the spring and summer of 2012 found "a general backdrop of political violence, assassinations targeting former regime officials, lawlessness, and an overarching absence of central government authority in eastern Libya."

On June 25, America's ambassador to Libya, J. Christopher Stevens, sent a cable to Washington quoting local sources who said "Islamic extremism" appeared to be rising in eastern Libya, and that al-Qaeda's black-and-white flag "has been spotted several times flying over government buildings and training facilities."

On August 2, even as Jack was en route to join the GRS team in Benghazi, Stevens sent another cable to Washington seeking more bodyguards. The ambassador warned that "the security condition in Libya...[is] unpredictable, volatile and violent."

━━━

Two years before meeting at the Benghazi airport, Jack and Rone unexpectedly ran into each other in the lobby of an East Coast hotel. Both had signed up to undergo screening and training to become GRS operators. By coincidence, their friend and fellow former SEAL Glen "Bub" Doherty was there, too.

Several times since entering the GRS, Rone and Jack had been assigned to the same hazardous places. Rone usually landed first, then cryptically told Jack via e-mail what to bring and what to expect. That was the case in Benghazi, where Rone had arrived a month earlier on his second trip to the city. Jack felt like a new kid in school with a savvy older buddy waiting to show him around. But that would soon change. Rone told Jack that the summer in Benghazi would be his last job for the GRS. His contract was set to expire in early September, and he wanted to spend more time with his wife and to help raise their infant son.

As Rone drove from the airport and Jack scanned their surroundings, they steeled themselves for what lay ahead. The airport was outside the city, thirteen miles east of downtown Benghazi. Rone plotted an indirect course with twists and turns to make sure they weren't being followed.

Before flying to Benghazi, Jack had used Google Earth maps to learn the basic layout. His map study showed a city roughly the size of Atlanta, designed like one half of a target, with the port as its bull's-eye. Radiating outward from the port were five curved, half-moon-shaped ring roads, named First Ring Road through Fifth Ring Road. Straight roads that moved traffic closer or farther from the port intersected the ring roads. From the air, Benghazi looked like a spider's web.

Minutes into the drive, Rone and Jack came upon a checkpoint, little more than a bullet-pocked cement building that straddled the road's median. Rone slowed to a stop as two young men approached the pickup carrying AK-47s and dressed in a mix of ragged military uniforms and civilian clothes. Off to one side, another young Libyan man stood in the bed of an improvised military vehicle known as a "Technical": a pickup truck with a mounted heavy machine gun in back.

Rone had good reason to be cautious. Several weeks earlier, he and another GRS operator were driving from the airport with a truckload of supplies when members of a radical Islamist militia stopped them at gunpoint. Rone and the other operator believed that their antagonists were from the extremist Ansar al-Sharia Brigade. The heavily armed militiamen told Rone that the supplies now belonged to them.

Rone and the other GRS operator raised their assault rifles and declined the offer to be robbed. Rone radioed for backup from his fellow GRS operators still at the Annex. But the CIA's top officer in Benghazi, a man known publicly only as "Bob," instead promised that he'd alert the 17 February Martyrs Brigade and have the ostensibly friendly militia serve as a Quick Reaction Force.

Hearing Rone's call for help, other GRS operators at the Annex had grabbed guns and gear and rushed to an armored car. But Bob, the CIA base chief, ordered them to stay put. After fifteen tense minutes, during which several GRS operators argued with Bob, Rone radioed that he'd talked his way out of the standoff without firing a shot. Had it escalated, the outnumbered and outgunned Americans would have stood little chance. No "friendly" 17 February militiamen ever arrived to help.

Weeks later, the GRS operators were still fuming. Festering tensions with the CIA's Benghazi chief became an ongoing issue. Some of the more vocal operators wrote Bob off as spineless, or as one put it, "a chickenshit careerist" focused on retirement and a cushy government pension. Another possibility was that Bob's primary concern was not blowing the CIA's cover, even if it meant leaving the operators to fend for themselves.

When Rone and Jack were stopped on the drive from the airport, Rone knew that they'd encountered a relatively benign, quasi-official checkpoint. Rone calmly held up a document that identified him as a US government employee. The young men scanned it and waved them on. Rone told Jack about the gunpoint confrontation the previous month, warning him about makeshift roadblocks that militia groups threw up unexpectedly. Some GRS operators called the rogue militias "gangs with guns," filled with twitchy young men amped up from chewing leaves of khat. If Rone and Jack crossed paths with those militiamen, they'd likely need to fight, flee, or both.

━━━

Driving west along barren stretches of the highway that Rone called "Airport Road," Jack saw undernourished horses scrounging for garbage, scraggly sheep, and walls marked with Arabic graffiti. As they approached more densely populated areas, the landscape shifted to ramshackle strip malls with Internet cafés, hookah shops, and fabric stores, flanked by roadside stands where vendors hawked tomatoes and melons. No rain falls in Benghazi from June through August, so desert dust covered everything from the cars to the stores to the people in the streets.

Most of the men Jack and Rone passed wore Western clothing, though some dressed in loose-fitting cotton clothes the operators called "man jammies." Women were scarce in the streets, and the few Jack spotted wore black abayas and hijabs, the traditional Muslim cloaks and veils. Children and feral cats roamed unpaved alleys off the main streets, and Jack saw boys five to seven years old playing with a discarded tire. Jack and Rone talked about bringing their sons to a Third World country, to show them how fortunate they were.

As Rone continued his circuitous drive, Jack noticed Benghazi's most common architectural style: the unfinished, scaffold-wrapped concrete building. He smelled diesel fuel, roasting meat, rotting fruit, and cutting through it all, urine and feces. The city of more than seven hundred thousand residents had one badly outmatched sewage treatment plant. Waste flowed into the streets, the ground, and the 23 July Lake, a lagoon between downtown and the port where families picnicked.

As Jack's tour continued, he learned that the city's infrastructure was broken or nonexistent. Electricity went on and off at random. Dry fields featured bumper crops of plastic bags. If motor vehicle laws existed, no one seemed to know or care. Every other car seemed to have broken brake lights. Traffic routinely choked up at even minor intersections. Technicals were more common than police cars. Jack saw a burning car on a side street but not a person in sight, only a pack of wild dogs foraging for food.

Yet beyond the filth and chaos were touches of natural beauty, from green mountains beyond the city limits, to soaring palm trees at the edge of white sand beaches, to the sparkling blue Mediterranean. If the breeze was right, fresh salt air cut through the city's stink. Grapevines and guava trees graced stately old homes. Impressive ruins from past civilizations dotted the region. Dreamers who squinted and held their noses imagined that Benghazi had the raw makings of a beach resort.

Rone drove along the Fifth Ring Road at the outer reaches of the city to avoid temporary barricades and checkpoints. He cut across to the Fourth Ring Road, then wended his way to the Western Fwayhat neighborhood. The area was Benghazi's best address, home to decent restaurants and pricey stores, where the remaining foreign envoys clustered in estates surrounded by walls of cinderblock, mud, and stone topped with razor wire and broken glass. Although the neighborhood was better than most, it was still Benghazi.

As they approached the CIA Annex, Rone taught Jack the names that the GRS operators used for the local streets, like Racetrack, Gunfighter, and Adidas. Not far from their destination, Rone radioed the front gate so he and Jack wouldn't be vulnerable while waiting for someone to let them in. Soon Jack would meet the other contract operators at the Annex, men he'd come to know as Tanto, Tig, D.B., and Oz, along with a CIA staffer who was the GRS Team Leader.

In his radio call, Rone reported that he had minimal control of the pickup, meaning that he had left the vehicle for a period of time while at the airport. An agency staffer who oversaw Annex security would need to inspect under the hood, around the wheels, and everywhere else someone who hated Americans might have planted a bomb.

Rone and Jack pulled up to a steel gate in a ten-foot-high concrete-and-brick wall. Security cameras looked down on them. Although it was supposed to be a secret location, or at least a discreet one, Jack immediately realized that they weren't fooling anyone. Even a casual observer would have noticed the tight security, not to mention the carloads of Americans driving in and out, day and night.

The gate to the CIA's Benghazi Annex compound swung open. A guard raised a steel traffic arm and waved Rone and Jack inside.

TWO

The Annex

———

RONE AND JACK PULLED INTO THE CIA ANNEX, A LUSH, walled oasis in the rough desert of Benghazi. Originally built by a wealthy Libyan hotel owner as a multifamily compound, the property was nearly square and covered more than two acres of land. Its generous size, perimeter walls, and multiple houses, but most of all its proximity to the State Department's Special Mission Compound, made it an ideal base of operations for the US covert intelligence service. For a price, the hotel owner was happy to rent it to the Americans and move his family elsewhere.

The Annex's main features were a guard post, a gardener's shack, and four comfortable one-story houses, each with about three thousand square feet of living space. Large, well-tended lawns stretched behind each house to the surrounding walls. The houses were repurposed as combination work and residential quarters for roughly twenty

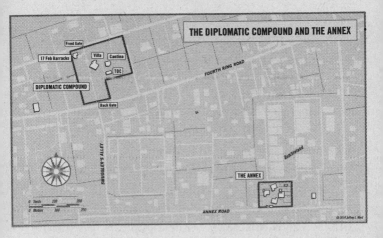

Americans on-site, including the Benghazi CIA base chief, Bob; his deputy; male and female case officers; analysts; translators; specialists; and GRS operators. A wide driveway cut diagonally through the Annex property. At its center was a small triangular courtyard where four turtles wandered in the shade of a picnic table.

After the pickup was checked for explosives, Rone drove Jack to the farthest house from the gate, which the Americans called "Building C." The Annex's command center, Building C contained the most secure intelligence area, the Sensitive Compartmented Information Facility, or SCIF (pronounced *skiff*), accessible only through a heavy steel door with a cipher lock.

Building C also housed a kitchen that had been transformed into a medical area, two bedrooms, and a room where Annex security staffers watched monitors from the video cameras mounted on the perimeter walls and throughout the property. As Jack and Rone walked through the building, Rone introduced Jack to the security team, an inter- preter, several case officers, and CIA chief Bob.

Also in Building C was the GRS Team Room, the operators' Command Post, with a broken-in couch and a wall of wooden cubbies that looked like high school lockers without doors. The cub- bies overflowed with the operators' assault rifles, night-vision goggles, helmets, body armor, ammu- nition, and everything else they needed to keep other Americans safe. Some operators personal- ized their cubbies, hanging photos of their wives and children. Along another wall were desks with computers and a whiteboard that recorded the operators' schedules for the week. A second white- board contained notices and classified intelligence updates.

Whenever a CIA case officer planned a meeting with a source to gather intelligence, he or she ide- ally gave the GRS operators at least a couple days' warning, to plan for their safety. If they didn't know the area well, the operators headed to their computers and used special mapping software developed for the military. Then, if time allowed, they'd get a feel for the place and familiarize them- selves with the people who frequented it. But Rone told Jack that scenario was rare; the case officers in Benghazi seldom gave them much time, so he'd need to be ready to scramble at a moment's notice. Everything in Benghazi was on a short fuse, Rone explained, making it difficult for the operators to feel comfortable about providing adequate security.

On the east side of Building C were generators and a swimming pool shaped like a shark's tooth, with swampy, greenish-brown water and a half

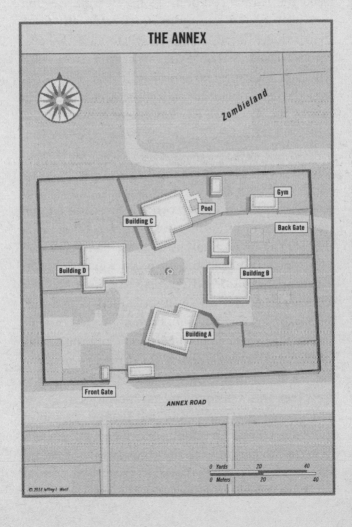

dozen or so goldfish named for several of the operators. The operators built a filtration system, partly covered the pool with a wooden deck, and called it "the pond."

At the back of Building C were glass doors that faced the Annex compound's north wall. Beyond that wall was an enormous stockyard with more than a dozen large, rectangular, tin-roofed sheds. Annex residents could hear sheep heading for slaughter bleating and whining inside. Rone told Jack that the operators called the area north and east of the Annex walls "Zombieland," because it looked like the set of a movie about the undead. On the far side of the Annex's east wall was an acre of scrub and trees, and beyond that stood a compound with a single-story home. To the south, across Annex Road, were other homes and a four-story concrete building under construction. Farther south, about a half mile away, was a dirt oval horse track. Every Thursday night was race night, featuring high-spirited Arabian stallions. To the west of the Annex was another walled compound, with a single large concrete home.

The diplomatic Special Mission Compound was located to the northwest of the Annex, across the Fourth Ring Road, only a half mile away as the crow flies and within ten minutes on foot.

The operators had embedded broken glass atop the Annex walls for added security, but the walls were no protection from the thick smell of manure and the swarms of flies drawn to the neighborhood by the stockyard, the racetrack, and the pond.

Buzzing veils of insects made life miserable for the GRS operators. Flies landed on their sweaty faces and rattled in their ears when they lifted weights at a makeshift workout area they called their "prison gym," located under a carport roof to the east of Building C.

Rone continued showing Jack around the property. Building A, closest to the front gate, housed four bedrooms and the main dining area, where an American chef prepared meals with the freshest local ingredients he could muster. Chicken and rice were staples, but they sometimes feasted on thick steaks. The chef earned the GRS operators' affection by keeping the refrigerator stocked with leftovers for nights when they returned late to the Annex. Building B, on the east side of the Annex, provided housing and work space, as did Building D, on the west side, where Rone led Jack with his bags.

Jack had three basic standards for a GRS workplace: good food, a good workout area, and his own room. Rone assured him that the food would be fine, but otherwise Benghazi was a bust. The workout area was a flyspecked mess, and Jack would be sharing a room. A heavy curtain strung down the middle provided a fig leaf of privacy. At least Jack would get along with his roommate, a GRS operator named John "Tig" Tiegen.

———

Tig was a laid-back thirty-six-year-old former Marine. He had brown hair, a close-cropped goatee, and a wary expression that he'd occasionally relax into a smile. He stood five foot eleven, weighed two hundred rock-solid pounds, wore wire-rimmed glasses, and sported a pair of dragon tattoos, one on each side of his chest. Tig grew up in Colorado in the sort of situation that typically leads nowhere or worse: a fractured family that included a father who disappeared before Tig's third birthday. He developed an attitude toward school that ranged from clownish to bored, making it easy for teachers to ignore him, which was fine with Tig.

When Tig was an aimless high school freshman, he stopped by the home of a friend's girlfriend one night when steaks were on the grill. "You want one?" the girl's father asked. When Tig answered yes, the man said: "Go mow the lawn." The connection between hard work and reward, discipline and order, had never been part of his life. Earning the steak satisfied Tig in a way he couldn't quite describe. He barely knew his friend's girlfriend, but within a month he moved into a bedroom that her father built for him in the basement. With help from his surrogate father, Tig set himself on a new path. He enlisted in the Marines before his eighteenth birthday because it was the toughest place he could find to prove himself.

Tig left the Marines as a sergeant but didn't want to stop doing military work, so in 2003 he signed up as a contract operator. After a year at the Army's Camp Doha in Kuwait and some time back home, Tig joined the private military company

Blackwater. Security stints followed in Afghanistan, Pakistan, and Iraq, where avoiding mortar fire became part of his daily routine. On paper Tig didn't meet certain GRS operator qualifications, but his experience and persistence won him a shot at the screening program. He earned his way in. On his first trip to Benghazi, in February 2012, Tig returned home early when his wife, a former diesel mechanic in the US Army, gave birth two months prematurely to twins, a boy and a girl.

When Jack arrived, Tig was on his third stay in the region, which made him the most experienced GRS operator in Benghazi. Tig had a hard edge, and he wasn't a big talker, but his fellow operators learned to appreciate his sardonic wit and his dark humor. One day he found a disabled flamethrower in Benghazi and used it to create a series of staged photos in which he looked like an action movie hero setting fires as he marched alone down an abandoned street. None of the other operators doubted that they could count on Tig if the action became real. Tig considered loyalty to be his greatest strength but also his main weakness: "I'm loyal to people who've tried to screw me over."

The operators were slaves to the assignments posted on the Team Room whiteboard, which was usually maintained by Rone, who was the highest-ranking contractor and the Assistant Team Leader. Endless tasks awaited Benghazi's CIA case officers, from gathering intelligence throughout the restive city to developing local sources. Generally, they were engaged in highly classified activities typical of Western spies in unstable countries. Like all case officers in Muslim countries, one of their tasks was to constantly plumb the depths of al-Qaeda sympathy and affiliation.

Twenty-first-century CIA case officers, or COs, were more likely to be Ivy League valedictorians than licensed-to-kill Jason Bourne types. That meant they needed GRS operators, even if the COs often acted as though they'd handle danger fine on their own. The Benghazi operators felt that the COs treated them as excess baggage, slowing them down and getting in the way. Yet every operator in Benghazi had a story about young, inexperienced case officers walking blithely into trouble or failing to perceive a threat, only to be steered clear of danger by a GRS escort.

One night not long after Jack arrived, he and Rone teamed up to protect a case officer on an intelligence-gathering operation in the heart of the city. Rone and Jack conducted countersurveillance to make sure the CIA staffer wasn't being followed. Jack watched unseen as two Arab men began trailing the case officer, who was oblivious as he strolled toward Rone's car. Jack tried to call Rone to inform him about the tail and to set up a new meeting place, so Jack's cover wouldn't be blown when he returned to the car. That proved impossible, so Jack got in the passenger seat and told the case officer in back, "You're being followed." The unknown men jumped into a car and began driving close behind the Americans. Rone hit the gas, expertly avoiding the usual traffic snarls and roadblocks. Eventually Rone lost the tail and returned them safely to the Annex.

Benghazi GRS operator Kris "Tanto" Paronto described the case officers' failings in the salty vernacular of a gung-ho former Army Ranger: "They're not combat COs, they're intel collectors. They're fucking glorified desk jockeys, that's what they are. They're smart people, but smart doesn't outsmart a bullet. They don't want us there, until something bad happens." Tanto had felt a similar attitude among certain CIA staffers earlier in his GRS career, but he considered none worse than Bob, the Benghazi CIA base chief: "As far as he's concerned, we're Walmart security guards."

No one on the GRS team, and perhaps no one in Benghazi, had a bigger personality than Tanto. The basic outline of his life could describe any number of people: forty-one years old; five foot nine; 175 pounds; brown hair; hazel eyes; the middle child of a college football coach and a first-grade teacher; gifted athlete; fishing enthusiast; twice married; devoted father of a boy he called "Bubba" and a girl he called "Princess"; former member of the Army's 75th Ranger Regiment; holder of a master's degree in criminal justice; owner of an insurance adjusting business.

A more vivid picture of Tanto emerged from his candid self-assessment: teenage vandal; adrenaline junkie; onetime steroid dealer; "loose cannon"; go-too-far practical joker; "a bit of an egomaniac";

take-a-bullet friend, warrior, and teammate; "worst student-body president" in his high school's history; serially imperfect husband; contract operator who rolled through Kabul blasting the Ricky Martin song "La Bomba" with his windows open. A brief version of his life philosophy: "If you're going to die, go down laughing. Laughing and fighting."

Tanto's other distinguishing characteristics were tattoos on his muscular body. One on his rib cage made it appear as though his skin was being ripped open to reveal an American flag within. One on his shoulder displayed the Army Rangers' tab and scroll insignia. Another, covering his back from shoulder to shoulder, was a customized version of the iconic painting by Raphael of St. Michael vanquishing Satan. Instead of Raphael's wooden spear, Tanto told the tattoo artist to give the saint a Crusader shield and a spear made from a crucifix. The design reflected Tanto's desire for God to help him destroy the demons in his life, demons that ended his first marriage and interrupted his military career. "It also symbolizes my job," he'd say. "You feel yourself as an avenging angel. You're killing or destroying or pushing back the evil in this world. There's a lot of it that's out there, and people still don't understand that. People think they can reason with it. You can't. They're evil and they will kill you."

"I don't wish the Crusades would come back," added Tanto, who'd spent a decade working as a contract operator, much of it in Muslim countries. "But I sometimes feel that they *should* come back. The tattoo is more or less a Christian warrior emblem, which a lot of us think that we are and believe that we are. We believe that we're warriors for the US, warriors for each other, but also warriors for God. Same as the terrorists, I guess. Warriors for God. It's just, I don't blow up and kill little girls. I don't go blow myself up and kill women indiscriminately. I've never shot anybody that hasn't been shooting at me."

Another Tanto-ism: "The last thing in the world that you're going to have when the money runs out or everybody leaves you is your word. Your balls and your word. If you can't say that you have stuck those out there and done everything you can to protect people, you ain't got anything. If you're not honest and willing to give your life for your brother, you're not worth your weight in piss." Tanto had a special place in his heart for the Ranger Creed, particularly the fifth stanza, which begins: "Energetically will I meet the enemies of my country. I shall defeat them on the field of battle for I am better trained and will fight with all my might. Surrender is not a Ranger word."

Tanto kept things lively at the Benghazi CIA Annex.

The garrulous Tanto usually partnered with his good friend and roommate, the taciturn Dave "D.B." Benton. At thirty-eight years old, D.B. had black hair, brown eyes, and a compact, muscular build. A middle child born to mixed-race parents, D.B. grew up in Pennsylvania, where he hated school, loved the outdoors, and idolized a grandfather who taught him "respect, integrity, courage, humility, empathy, and discipline." Above all, "He taught me how to win, and he taught me how to lose."

A military career seemed a natural inheritance: D.B.'s father served as a corpsman in the Navy and his uncles served in the Army and Marine Corps. His older brother preceded D.B. in the Marines, and the two served together from 1993 to 2000. During his years as a Marine sergeant, D.B. served as a member of a Maritime Special Purpose Force, a Special Operations–capable unit trained for everything from hostage rescue to direct-action assaults. D.B. was a scout sniper whose specialties included surveillance, reconnaissance, and close-quarters battle.

After leaving the Marines, D.B. joined a police SWAT team in Georgia, but after 9/11 he felt compelled to return to military service. He'd already been in contact with a Marine recruiter when a friend told him about an opportunity to work for the State Department as a contract personal security specialist. Since then, D.B. had collected multiple awards for performance under fire in hot spots including Iraq, Afghanistan, and Haiti. One of those awards came in Iraq in 2004, when D.B. worked for the State Department under a contract with Blackwater. He was the Team Leader in a five-vehicle convoy ambushed while driving through Baghdad after escorting Secretary of State Colin Powell to the airport. As the driver of the lead vehicle sped toward safety, D.B. calmly kept the rest of the convoy updated on what was happening, allowing them to respond to the insurgents and escape the ambush without casualties, according to the citation he received.

Married to his high school sweetheart, D.B. had a son and two daughters. His biggest worry was that he might let someone down who relied on him, so he remained on permanent guard to prevent that from happening. His favorite author was Joseph Campbell, who wrote famously about mythmaking and the hero's journey. D.B. considered one of Campbell's maxims especially apt: "A hero is someone who has given his or her life to something bigger than oneself."

D.B.'s friendship with Tanto was sealed when they worked together for the State Department in Baghdad in 2004. At the end of a workday, they were relaxing atop a Humvee when a Russian-made Katyusha rocket flew over their heads into a tent with more than thirty military contractors inside. D.B. knew that a natural reaction for some people would be to run the other way. But he and Tanto simultaneously had the opposite response, sprinting side by side into the smoke-filled tent to see who needed help. In the years that followed, both felt they'd developed a sixth sense that allowed each to know how the other would react when all hell broke loose.

———

Trips beyond the Annex walls, called "moves," could happen at any time, day or night. Though

Benghazi was unsafe for most Westerners, the operators prided themselves on knowing the city like natives and on being comfortable and confident enough to move by car or on foot almost anywhere they chose. The engines of their cars and SUVs were meticulously maintained, while the exteriors were invariably beaten up. Cars without dirt and dings in Benghazi revealed their owners as rich people, Americans, or both.

Growing beards and wearing local clothes, the operators tried to blend in, or at least not to stand out quite so much. They ate in restaurants, frequented coffee shops and hotels, shopped in stores and bazaars, and even walked like tourists through a small art museum located in an ancient palace near the port. Tanto's travels formed his impression of Benghazi as a seedy, savage city, ruled by dangerous militias and fueled by oil, guns, and "the almighty dinar."

Still, the operators knew that their lack of Arabic language skills and their distinctly American way of carrying themselves could put targets on their backs. So they took pains to attract as little notice as possible.

Usually the operators traveled armed with concealed knives and pistols. Some had custom leather holsters that allowed them to hide their guns without conspicuous bulges. Jack developed a quick-draw technique—lifting his shirt with his left hand, grabbing his pistol with his right—that an Old West gunfighter would have envied. Their cars carried their long guns, lethally dependable assault rifles.

Depending on the perceived danger of a move, the operators might drive armored vehicles and wear body armor with bullet-stopping inserts they called "chicken plates." Just as often they'd use locally purchased cars, which they called "soft-skinned" vehicles, and eschew personal armor to avoid calling attention to their movements. Sometimes they found greater safety in stealth than armor.

Occasionally the entire Global Response Staff team would be on duty for a move, but more often they worked in small units, with Jack and Rone frequently assigned together. Jack's roommate, Tig, usually partnered with contractor Mark Geist, whose call sign was "Oz."

Beefy and self-assured, at forty-six Oz was the oldest member of the team. A shade under six feet tall, weighing more than two hundred pounds, Oz had thick blond hair, sharp blue eyes, and a country boy's way about him. In junior high school and high school, Oz rode bulls in rodeos and broke wild horses. Since childhood he'd dreamed of becoming a soldier, a police officer, a cowboy, or a firefighter. He'd achieved the first three.

The grandson of a World War II tank commander, Oz had youthful memories of stacking hay, saving a calf during birth by turning it around in its mother's womb, and plucking the feathers off chickens whose necks had been wrung by his grandmother. He had a half-inch scar across his upper lip from being kicked in the mouth while branding a calf. Oz had joined the Marines when he turned eighteen. After a dozen years in the service, including time in an intelligence unit, Oz left to become a deputy sheriff and a police investigator. Later he became chief of police in the small town in eastern Colorado where he grew up, then started a private investigation business where he did bail bonding and bounty hunting.

Before going to work as a GRS operator, Oz did contract security work for the State Department in Iraq, starting in 2004. He'd also trained Iraqi SWAT teams and provided personal protection for a former prime minister of Iraq while working for another American contracting firm. Oz's unusual résumé included security work on a contract basis for Russian and Ukrainian airlines. Twice married, Oz had a son with his first wife and a teenage stepdaughter and an infant daughter with his second wife.

Working with Rone, Jack, Tig, Tanto, D.B., and Oz was a young CIA staffer. He didn't have the military background or training of the contract operators, but agency rules made him the Benghazi GRS Team Leader. His identity was confidential, so the other GRS operators usually called him by his radio call sign or referred to him by his title, abbreviated as "T.L."

Several of the six contract operators were old friends, like Jack and Rone, and Tanto and D.B. Some had worked alongside each other before, like Tig and D.B., in Benghazi or elsewhere, while some were on their first GRS trip together. Regardless of whether they knew one another before arriving in Benghazi, all were connected through networks of former special operators and security contractors. For instance, Jack and Tanto had never worked together prior to Benghazi, but they were linked through a third operator. While working on a contract basis in Tripoli, Tanto had become friends with Jack and Rone's old SEAL buddy Glen "Bub" Doherty, who continued to work on the GRS security team in the Libyan capital.

Some GRS security teams coexisted but never meshed, which wasn't surprising given the number of testosterone-fueled alpha males among the operators and their different service backgrounds. Some grew surly and withdrawn in the harsh and stressful conditions under which they worked. The GRS team in Benghazi during September 2012 certainly could have gone that way. Yet they jelled. They trusted one another in tight situations, and they liked working and hanging out together. When the chef had a night off, they'd make runs into the city for trunkloads of pizza and shawarma. Sometimes at night, when the work was done, they'd build a fire in a fifty-five-gallon drum and sit around the "pond" talking, smoking a hookah pipe, and making each other laugh. All were in their late thirties or forties, all had been around, and all had wives and kids they loved and could support more easily with their GRS pay. Their comfort among each other factored into the equation when Rone, Tanto, and D.B. were scheduled to return home at the beginning of September. Instead, all three extended their time in Benghazi, to help with an upcoming visit by the US ambassador.

━━━

When they weren't working or planning their next moves, the GRS operators cleaned their weapons, practiced shooting, updated their mapping software and other computer tools, and maintained their vehicles. Day and night, whenever they were in the Annex they understood that they constituted a Quick Reaction Force: If anyone from the Annex or the State Department's Special Mission Compound was in danger, they'd respond.

While on standby, most played video games. A voice would ring out over the radio, ordering operators to report for "tactical training." The GRS guys knew that was code for a *Call of Duty* tournament on Xbox in Building B. During the fiercely competitive games, Tanto and Oz engaged in brutal trash-talking that inevitably began with the phrase, "Your momma," and ended with anatomically impractical suggestions.

As a running joke, during meals or just walking through the Annex, one would randomly call out the cliché line from every bad horror or war movie: "I've got a bad feeling about this." They read, talked, watched pirated movies on CDs purchased from local shops, called and sent e-mails home, worked out, ran, and napped. Jack called his bed a "time machine," because every hour of shut-eye transported him one hour closer to returning to his family. That desire became more intense following a Skype session with his wife shortly after Jack arrived in Benghazi: She surprised him with news that she was pregnant. His excitement was tempered by the thought of another mouth to feed, another college education to plan for, and above all, another person relying on him to get home safely.

Jack's nonwork routine also included regular visits to a large olive tree next to Building D that was home to a neon-green praying mantis almost as big as his hand. The tree had a flytrap with a one-way opening on top, so flies lured to the bait couldn't get out. Jack watched up close as the giant mantis perched motionless above the opening, blending with the leaves. The moment its prey landed, the mantis would strike, snatching the fly with its spindly front legs, then devouring it. The mantis had a bulging stomach, testament to its speed and the endless food supply. Between flies, the mantis often turned its triangular head and calmly watched Jack watching it. After the mantis had eaten three or four flies, it would leave its spot at the flytrap buffet and climb higher into the tree. The mantis fascinated Jack, who considered it like a pet. Yet, in a hostile city where Americans made ripe targets for radical extremists who could blend effortlessly with their surroundings, Jack also could identify with the flies.

While Jack studied the mantis, Tanto had a different way of killing time between moves. Walking through the Annex, he'd pass a security camera and break into a wild dance, then resume walking as though nothing had happened. Tanto also enjoyed getting to know the Libyans they hired as local guards. One regularly hit him up for candy bars, so Tanto nicknamed him "Snickers." Tanto kept his new pal well supplied, then watched as the formerly skinny guard grew a spare tire. "You try to befriend them so at least they're a damn speed bump if we get attacked," he'd say. "It's a hearts and minds thing."

Tanto had strong opinions on most things, none stronger than his views on the best kind of operators in a place like Benghazi: "Guys that are ramped up all the time are not good GRS operators. They won't last at the job. You have to be able to associate, go to a restaurant and be out in town, go walk and order a paper, go order a coffee. If you're always looking like you're about ready to get in a fight, the locals will pick that up quicker than shit. But also you can't be so low key that when the shit hits the fan you can't turn that light switch on and go a hundred miles an hour." Tanto prided himself on being able to go "from zero to a hundred in five seconds, if not quicker."

Usually every Friday, American security team members from the Special Mission Compound drove to the Annex for a status update and to talk about the week ahead. The visitors were members of the Bureau of Diplomatic Security, known as the DS, the law enforcement and security arm of the State Department. Congress created the bureau in 1985, as part of a response to the 1983 bombing of the US Embassy and Marine Corps barracks in Beirut. Another impetus was the 1979 abduction of Adolph Dubs, the US ambassador to Afghanistan. Dubs died during a rescue attempt. No American ambassador had been killed in office since then.

Inside the United States, more than two thousand DS officers worked for the Diplomatic Security Service, to safeguard the Secretary of State and visiting dignitaries, everyone from Yasser Arafat to the Dalai Lama. On US soil, those DS agents also issued security clearances, conducted cybersecurity investigations, and battled passport and visa fraud. The larger and usually dicier role for Diplomatic Security agents fell beyond American borders.

Globally, some eight hundred DS staff agents, supplemented by more than thirty thousand security contractors, oversaw the safe conduct of American foreign policy. Their job was to protect personnel and sensitive information at roughly 275 diplomatic outposts in 157 countries. The job was endless. Between 1998 and 2012, one government study found, US diplomatic facilities and personnel came under "significant" attack 273 times, not including almost constant assaults on the US Embassy in Baghdad since 2004.

DS agents assigned a threat level to every diplomatic outpost, based on six categories: international terrorism, indigenous terrorism, political violence, crime, human intelligence, and technical threat. The threat levels were low, medium, high, or critical. The last two were defined as having "serious" or "grave" impact on American diplomats. During 2012, more than half of all American diplomatic posts around the world were considered "critical" or "high" for the threat of terrorism. However, only fourteen were considered dangerous enough for the DS to deem the threat level "critical" or "high" in every category. Two of those were in Libya: Tripoli and Benghazi.

For the DS agents in Libya, one of the biggest events in the summer of 2012 was a five-day visit to Benghazi, starting September 10, being planned by Ambassador J. Christopher Stevens, who normally was based at the embassy in Tripoli.

To help the DS agents in advance of Stevens's visit, the Annex's GRS operators conducted a security assessment at the Special Mission Compound, where Stevens would stay. During the review, Tanto asked the DS agents how many security team members they'd have on hand when the ambassador visited, not including local militiamen or other Libyans hired as guards. Five, they told him, each armed with an M4 assault rifle, a mainstay weapon of the US military. Tanto learned that the DS agents collectively had about a dozen years of military experience. He knew that the Annex operators had closer to one hundred years of collective military and contracting experience, much of it on elite security teams. The GRS team also had larger and more powerful weapons.

"If you guys get attacked by any big element," Tanto told them, "you're going to die." Realizing that he'd come across stronger than intended, Tanto reassured the DS agents: "If you need assistance, we're going to help you."

——————

During the first week of September, with the ambassador's visit just days away, Rone put his nursing and paramedic training to use by offering a refresher medical course for all Annex staffers. He walked them through the proper field response to gunshot wounds, explosion injuries, and other traumas. After a classroom session in Building D, Rone set up a practical exercise outside, using Jack as the "victim" in a scenario in which he supposedly was hit by a grenade. Ketchup substituted for blood on Jack's bare leg. Rone instructed everyone how to properly use a tourniquet and to safely evacuate a victim.

Another day, Rone and Jack drove to the diplomatic Compound with Bob, the Annex base chief. While Bob attended a meeting, Jack and Rone sat at an outdoor table under a covered patio with two DS agents, David Ubben and Scott Wickland. Ubben was a big guy, about six foot four and 250 pounds, with dark hair and a handlebar mustache that he was growing as part of a competition among the State Department security agents. Wickland stood about five foot ten, with a medium build, sandy-brown hair, and light eyes. The wispy fuzz on his upper lip suggested that Wickland was compcting in the cheesy mustache competition, too. Jack and Rone were ready to declare Ubben the winner.

The four men talked about their families and their prior military careers, Jack and Rone as SEALs, Ubben in the Army, and Wickland as a Navy rescue swimmer. Wickland and Ubben confided in the operators that they'd repeatedly requested more Diplomatic Security personnel at the Compound because they were short-staffed. Those requests had fallen on deaf ears, they told Jack and Rone, and they couldn't understand why.

In an effort to help, the operators arranged a drill to teach the DS agents ways to respond to a terrorist attack. The scenario called for an enemy force to attempt to overrun the Annex, but the operators explained that the same principles would apply if the target were the diplomatic Compound. They rehearsed how to respond to "active shooters" inside the walls, and how to keep track of all personnel who needed protection, above all the ambassador, a practice the operators called "accountability." The operators demonstrated the protocols they used for such events, to simultaneously repel an attack and ensure the safety of the staffers they called "non-shooters." By the time the drill ended, Jack concluded that their small numbers and their lack of special-operator military training would put the five DS agents who'd be guarding the ambassador at an extreme disadvantage if the Compound came under attack.

Sitting around together over morning coffee,

Jack and Rone frequently discussed flaws in security at both the Compound and the Annex. As contract operators, they were powerless to change the security system. But that didn't stop them from identifying holes in the defensive shield, anticipating ways terrorists might exploit them, and brainstorming potential responses. Some of the weak points they discussed were structural, involving the Annex and Compound properties' designs. Some perceived problems focused on staff levels and training. The macabre scenarios ranged from a truck bomb parked outside the Annex wall to a large force of attackers overrunning the Compound.

As the anniversary of the 9/11 attacks approached, coinciding with the ambassador's planned visit, Rone taped an eight-by-ten sheet of paper to a whiteboard in the GRS Team Room. On it was a printed warning that the GRS operators felt certain had come from somewhere higher up the chain of clandestine services in Washington. As several operators recalled, the intelligence cable warned: *Be advised, we have reports from locals that a Western facility or US Embassy/Consulate/ Government target will be attacked in the next week.* If those weren't the exact words, that was the unambiguous message the operators took from the cable.

As a precaution, the operators moved their body armor, long guns, ammunition, night-vision goggles, and other tactical gear into their bedrooms, so they could more quickly "jock up," as they called preparing for battle. Discussions had been under way for some time about "co-locating" the Compound and the Annex on the same property, so Bob the Annex chief suggested a trial run. He urged the Diplomatic Security team at the Special Mission Compound to move to the Annex during the ambassador's visit, for added layers of protection. The offer was declined.

In the days after Rone posted the intel cable, GRS team members signed their initials on the paper to show that they'd read it. It remained on all of their minds, but none were unnerved by it. When Oz read it, he concluded that it lacked a specific date or location, so he took no special action: "Other than just being extra vigilant, as always, it's nothing to worry about."

When Tanto saw that everyone on the team had initialed the cable, he peeled it off the whiteboard and shredded it. The date was September 11, 2012.

THREE

The Ambassador

—————

UNDER A BLAZING LIBYAN SUN, CHRIS STEVENS flashed his toothy smile, gripped a pair of scissors, and approached a ceremonial red ribbon like he meant business. But before putting blade to satin, Stevens pulled a signature move: He invited an official from the Libyan Ministry of Foreign Affairs, Abdurrahman al-Gannas, to join him for the honors. With their right hands clasped together on the scissors, Stevens and al-Gannas snipped the ribbon, triggering applause from US Embassy workers and Libyan officials, as a clutch of journalists recorded the scene.

The occasion was the August 26, 2012, reopening of the visa-granting Consular Section of the US Embassy in Tripoli. Including al-Gannas in the ribbon ritual was classic Stevens. As the American ambassador to Libya in the post-Gaddafi era, Stevens considered it essential to promote and protect US interests by working hand in hand, literally and figuratively, with the nascent Libyan government and the people it was supposed to represent. Trust-based bonds and personal connections, Stevens believed, led to successful diplomacy.

"The reopening of our Consular Section will create new opportunities for deepening ties between our two countries," he told the gathering. "Relationships between governments are important, but relationships between people are the real foundation of mutual understanding. That's why the reopening of our Consular Section is such an important milestone in relations between our two countries. So, my message to Libyans today is *ahlan wasahlan bikum*. You are welcome to visit America, and there's the door!"

The ceremony was one of the more public ways Stevens carried out his role as ambassador to Libya. Outside the view of reporters, he met with fellow diplomats and Libyans of high and low station, from government ministers to local officials, powerful businessmen to small shopkeepers, always with the goal of providing Washington policymakers with essential information about the North African hotspot. Often Stevens's contacts grew so comfortable in his presence that they dispensed with titles altogether and used his first name. The informality pleased Stevens, and the way Arabic speakers said "Chris" tickled him so much that he signed e-mails to friends by gently mimicking the pronunciation: *Krees*.

Stevens knew that much work remained. When the Consular Section ceremony ended, he returned to the nonstop chores of hands-on diplomacy. In the coming days he'd hold lengthy suit-and-tie meetings, but he'd also sit barefoot on the floor of a traditional underground Berber house and use his hands to eat a messy plate of barley dough, braised lamb, and tomato stew called *bazeen*. For a brief respite, he'd fly to Stockholm for a friend's white-tie wedding, and from there to Vienna for a two-day getaway. Two weeks after the ribbon cutting, Stevens would make a homecoming of sorts: his first visit as ambassador to the city where the Libyan revolution began, Benghazi.

———

There are generally two kinds of American ambassadors: high-profile business or civic leaders sent to glamour spots like France or Britain as payback for contributions or political support, and workhorses sent to hostile places like Libya as a reward for experience and know-how. Chris Stevens exemplified the latter.

Born John Christopher Stevens, he was fifty-two, never married, trim and long-limbed, with a high forehead crowned by puffy blond hair turning gray. His blinding smile drew people's attention, but his expressive blue eyes held it. They could flash anger when needed but more often displayed Stevens's true nature: thoughtful, inquisitive, empathetic, resolved, and patient.

Raised in Northern California, Stevens was a saxophone-playing son of a lawyer father and a cellist mother. He graduated in 1982 from the

University of California at Berkeley with a history degree. He spent two years in the Peace Corps, teaching English in the remote Atlas Mountains of Morocco, where he fell in love with the region and found his calling. In 1989, he received a law degree from the University of California's Hastings College of the Law in San Francisco. Later, he received a master's in national security studies from the National War College. For two years after becoming an attorney, Stevens practiced international trade law in Washington, DC, but his heart was set on the Foreign Service.

His focus was the Middle East, and upon joining the State Department he won stints in Saudi Arabia, Syria, Egypt, and Israel, where he worked on Palestinian issues during the second intifada. He became fluent in Arabic and developed a taste for the strong, syrupy tea over which relationships in the region are forged. Between foreign postings, Stevens worked on Middle Eastern policy at the State Department headquarters in Washington and served as a Pearson Fellow with the Senate Foreign Relations Committee.

In 2007, Stevens was appointed Deputy Chief of Mission, later chargé d'affaires, at the US Embassy in Tripoli. Within a year of his arrival in Libya, Stevens became a footnote to one of the many strange stories about Gaddafi. A diplomatic cable disclosed by WikiLeaks showed that in August 2008, Stevens tactfully warned Secretary of State Condoleezza Rice that the Libyan leader had his lecherous eye on her. "A self-styled intellectual and philosopher," Stevens wrote to Rice, "he has been eagerly anticipating for several years the opportunity to share with you his views on global affairs." During Rice's visit to Libya in September 2008, Gaddafi confessed that he had a crush on her. Rice later called the attention "weird and a bit creepy."

Stevens returned to Washington to run the State Department's Office of Multilateral Nuclear and Security Affairs. But when the Libyan revolution began in early 2011, the Obama administration wanted an experienced hand to reach out to the rebels. In March 2011, Stevens became the United States' Special Representative to the anti-Gaddafi rebels' umbrella political organization, the Libyan Transitional National Council, the TNC, based in Benghazi.

With no commercial airlines flying into the war zone, Stevens arranged for a Greek cargo ship to sail from Malta to Benghazi carrying him, ten DS agents, and a political attaché. The ship's hold bulged with armored vehicles, communications equipment, and supplies needed to establish a temporary diplomatic station. They arrived on April 5, 2011, spent a night aboard ship, then set up shop in rooms at the downtown Tibesti Hotel. Rebel leaders in Benghazi frequently met at the Tibesti, which also housed the Italian and Qatari envoys, United Nations officials, and foreign journalists covering the war.

The embassy in Tripoli had suspended operations and evacuated all Americans six weeks earlier, so Stevens's arrival made him the highest-ranking

US diplomat in Libya. He and Political Officer Nathan Tek immediately scheduled an endless stream of meetings with TNC officials and civic and business leaders, to provide US policymakers with information about the rebellion and to develop relationships in anticipation of a post-Gaddafi Libya. As Stevens told a State Department magazine in a story published in December 2011, they also funneled nonlethal aid to the TNC and created a program in cooperation with the rebel council to collect shoulder-launched anti-aircraft missiles called MANPADS.

On June 1, 2011, an explosion in the Tibesti Hotel parking lot destroyed two cars and blew out windows hundreds of feet away. A rebel spokesman described it as an attempt by Gaddafi loyalists to show they could still strike at will. Soon after, Stevens's security team learned of what US officials described as "a credible threat" against the Special Envoy mission and raced to find safer lodgings.

On June 21, 2011, Stevens and his Special Envoy team moved to a walled sanctuary of blooming guava and palm trees, wide swaths of emerald-green lawns, rows of gnarled vines heavy with purple grapes, and abundant flowers. Located in the Western Fwayhat neighborhood, the property opened onto a gravel street. Its rear wall bordered the Fourth Ring Road.

Among its convenient charms, the property was across the street from an upscale restaurant called the Venezia, which was popular with well-heeled Libyans and the multinational diplomatic corps. Throughout the summer, the onetime private compound was renovated for increased security. By August 2011 it was dubbed the United States' Special Mission Compound in Benghazi.

The Compound covered nearly eight verdant acres. One appeal of the property to the Diplomatic Security staff was that the main buildings were set back far enough from the surrounding walls to protect inhabitants against car bombs. In addition, the DS team arranged for sections of the walls to be reinforced and raised to nine feet, though some areas remained eight feet high. A barbed-wire crown topped most of the wall's length.

Inside and outside the property's three gates, rows of concrete Jersey barriers were arranged in serpentine patterns to prevent truck or car bombers from crashing through to the Compound. Steel traffic bars were installed to control vehicle entrance to the property, which occurred primarily through an imposing main gate in the north wall topped with spikes and known as Gate C1. To the side of the main vehicle gate entrance was a narrower pedestrian gate. A secondary gate, farther east along the same wall, was called B1, or Bravo gate. The third gate to the Compound, in the wall opposite the main gate, was called Gate C3 and opened out to the Fourth Ring Road. Other enhanced security measures on the property included sandbag fortifications, high-intensity

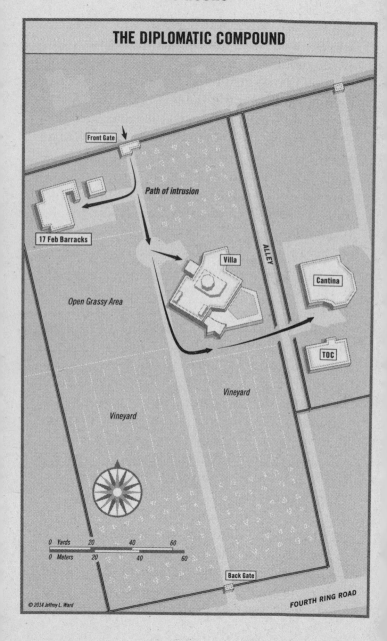

THE DIPLOMATIC COMPOUND

Front Gate

Path of intrusion

17 Feb Barracks

ALLEY

Villa

Cantina

Open Grassy Area

TOC

Vineyard

Vineyard

0 Yards 20 40 60
0 Meters 20 40 60

Back Gate

© 2014 Jeffrey L. Ward

FOURTH RING ROAD

lighting, explosive-detection devices, and an Internal Defense Notification System—known as a drop-and-cover alarm—in case the Compound came under attack.

All the buildings were reinforced with security measures, starting with the largest structure on the property, a split-level yellow concrete building known as Villa C. Stevens's working and living quarters were there, and it eventually gained an affectionate nickname, "Château Christophe." Part of Villa C, in the area where several bedrooms were located, was fortified as a safe haven, with locked metal grilles on the windows. At the interior entrance to the safe-haven area stood a heavy metal gate with double locks that looked like the door to a jail cell. Exterior wooden doors were hardened with steel. For added protection, the safe-haven area contained a last-refuge safe room, essentially a windowless closet that contained water, medical supplies, and other necessities.

A second structure, on the east side of the Compound, was Building B, also known as the Cantina, which contained bedrooms and a dining area. Next door to the Cantina was a third building, the Tactical Operations Center, known as the TOC, which served as the security and communications headquarters for DS agents based at the Compound. The fourth and final building on the property was a guesthouse by the front gate that had been converted into a barracks. It typically housed four armed Libyan security guards, all members of the 17 February militia.

Supplementing the militiamen were other locally hired guards, unarmed, who were provided under a contract with a British security company called Blue Mountain Libya.

To the uninitiated, the precautions might have seemed impressive. But in the realm of modern diplomatic protection, the Special Mission Compound in Benghazi was only modestly secure. Some might even say insecure, in light of recent history and relative to other American diplomatic outposts in hostile places.

After the 1983 bombings of the American Embassy and Marine Barracks in Beirut, and the 1998 bombings of the US embassies in Nairobi and Dar es Salaam, Congress established and strengthened security standards for embassies and consulates. Buildings needed to be engineered to withstand attacks by rocket-propelled grenades, and properties required deterrents to prevent hostile forces from entering en masse. The buildings also had to be invulnerable to fire.

But the Special Mission Compound in Benghazi was never an embassy or a consulate. Leased at a cost of about a half-million dollars a year, it was officially only a temporary residential outpost for American envoys and their DS protectors. The strictest security standards mandated by Congress didn't apply, so the fortifications at the Compound were essentially judgment calls. In hindsight, those calls were grossly inadequate. A December 2012 government review concluded that the Compound "included a weak and very extended perimeter, an incomplete interior fence, no mantraps and unhardened entry gates and doors. Benghazi was also severely under-resourced with regard to weapons, ammunition, [nonlethal deterrents] and fire safety equipment, including escape masks."

▬▬▬

Less than six months after Stevens and his team moved into the Compound, Gaddafi was gone and the US Embassy in Tripoli was reestablished under Ambassador Gene Cretz. Stevens returned to Washington, and the Special Envoy post remained unfilled.

In December 2011, a month after Stevens left Benghazi, a memo circulated around the State Department arguing for a continued US presence in Benghazi. One reason for maintaining the Compound, the memo argued, was to reassure residents of eastern Libya that the United States would object if the new Tripoli-based government neglected or abused them as Gaddafi had. Although no new Special Envoy was chosen to replace Stevens, the Benghazi Compound did remain open, overseen by a rotating cast of State Department employees who stayed brief periods and, while there, held the title "Principal Officer."

In early 2012, Cretz was nominated to become ambassador to Ghana, and Stevens was a natural choice to replace him. At his confirmation hearing before the Senate Foreign Relations Committee, Stevens struck a note of optimism: "There is tremendous goodwill for the United States in Libya now. Libyans recognize the key role the United States played in building international support for their uprising against Gaddafi. I saw this gratitude frequently over the months I served in Benghazi— from our engagements with the revolution's leadership to our early work with civil society and new media organizations."

When Stevens was confirmed as ambassador, the State Department featured him in a video that reintroduced him to Libyans. He talked about his upbringing, his education, and his experiences, as photos from his earlier days in Libya and other parts of the Arab world flashed on the screen. "Now I'm excited to return to Libya to continue the great work we've started," Stevens says on the video, "building a solid partnership between the United States and Libya to help you, the Libyan people, achieve your goals." He closed by promising that the two countries would "work together to build a free, democratic, prosperous Libya." Stevens's priority would be to win trust rather than points, to gain long-lasting respect rather than superficial concessions. He would defy the stereotypical image of the self-important American ambassador; instead, Stevens would radiate humility.

Armed with his new title, Ambassador Stevens arrived in Tripoli on May 26, 2012. He spent the next three months reestablishing relationships from his earlier posting in the capital. But his optimism was tested from the start by instability and violence.

From his office in Tripoli, Stevens observed firsthand the deteriorating security situation in

Libya during the late spring of 2012. Beyond his concerns about the fledgling Arab democracy, Stevens worried about his staff and himself. In early June, he sent an e-mail to a State Department official in Washington asking that two six-man Mobile Security Detachments, known as MSD teams, of specially trained DS agents be allowed to remain in Libya through the national elections being held in July and August. Stevens wrote that State Department personnel "would feel much safer if we could keep two MSD teams with us through this period [to support] our staff and [provide a personal detail] for me and the [Deputy Chief of Mission] and any VIP visitors." The request was denied, Stevens was told, because of staffing limitations and other commitments.

A month later, on July 9, 2012, Stevens and the embassy's security staff, led by DS agent Eric Nordstrom, asked the State Department to extend the presence of a Site Security Team, or SST, that consisted of sixteen active-duty military special operators. The Defense Department's Africa Command, which oversaw the unit, was willing to extend the team's stay in Tripoli. But State Department officials decided that DS agents and locally hired guards could do the job, and that the SST operators weren't needed. In the weeks that followed, General Carter Ham, head of Africa Command, twice asked Stevens if he wanted the SST to remain in Libya. Despite his earlier request to extend the team's stay, Stevens wouldn't buck the decision of State Department officials in Washington. He declined Ham's offers and the SST left Libya, even as Stevens moved forward with plans to visit the restive city of Benghazi.

However worried he might have been about security, to his staff Stevens remained outwardly upbeat, even inspirational. He posed for so many photos with Libyan children, grandmothers, local officials, and shopkeepers that embassy staffers half wondered whether anyone in Tripoli *didn't* have a picture of himself with the American ambassador.

On the day in late August 2012 that Stevens sat on the floor for dinner in a Berber home, his companion was a young Foreign Service Officer named Hannah Draper. Several weeks earlier, she'd written a starry-eyed blog post about him: "Ambassador Stevens is legendary in Libya for spending almost the entire period of the revolution in Benghazi, liaising with the rebels and leading a skeleton crew of Americans on the ground to support humanitarian efforts and meeting up-and-coming political leaders. Several Libyans have told me how much it means to them that he stayed here throughout the revolution, losing friends and suffering privations alongside ordinary Libyans. We could not ask for a better Ambassador to represent America during this crucial period in Libyan history."

If Draper sounded like an awestruck underling, her blog post reflected a widely held belief among diplomats and officials in Libya and Washington: Chris Stevens had the brains and courage that made him the right man for a monumental job. A dangerous job, too.

Two days before Stevens and Draper ate their meal of *bazeen*, the State Department issued a severely worded travel warning for Libya, cautioning that "political violence in the form of assassinations and vehicle bombs has increased in both Benghazi and Tripoli.... Inter-militia conflict can erupt at any time or any place in the country."

Still, Stevens refused to abandon his optimism. "The whole atmosphere has changed for the better," he wrote in an e-mail to friends and family in the summer of 2012. "People smile more and are much more open with foreigners. Americans, French, and British are enjoying unusual popularity. Let's hope it lasts." At least that was his view from Tripoli.

———

When Stevens arrived in Benghazi on September 10, 2012, more than nine eventful months had passed since he'd last set foot in the city. The public highlight of his visit was scheduled to be yet another ribbon cutting, this one at a local school. The ceremony would celebrate the opening of an "American Corner," a US-government-sponsored "friendly, accessible space" stocked with bilingual books, magazines, films, posters, guidebooks, and other materials for Libyans to learn about the United States. The Libyan man who ran the school had rescued an American F-15 fighter pilot who ejected from his doomed plane when it was shot down during the 2011 revolution.

Outside public view, Stevens intended to reconnect with old friends and contacts, and to solidify relationships with local government officials, business leaders, and fellow foreign diplomats in Benghazi. He seemed to have a clear-eyed view of the dangers he faced. "Militias are power on the ground," he wrote in his diary on September 6, according to *The New York Times*. "Dicey conditions, including car bombs, attacks on consulate," Stevens continued. "Islamist 'hit list' in Benghazi. Me targeted on a prominent website (no more off compound jogging)."

For security, two DS agents accompanied Stevens from Tripoli. Three other DS agents were already stationed at the Special Mission Compound, bringing the DS contingent in Benghazi to five.

Also at the Compound to greet Stevens was a State Department political officer named David McFarland, who'd been serving temporarily as the Benghazi Principal Officer. With Stevens's arrival, McFarland would return to Tripoli early the next morning. The final American at the Compound was a State Department computer expert who'd arrived a week earlier to ensure that the ambassador would enjoy secure communications. His name was Sean Smith, though many of his friends knew him best as "Vile Rat."

At thirty-four, Smith had been a State Department employee for a decade, after spending six years in the Air Force. Married with two young children, he had a close-cropped goatee, a wry smile that turned his eyes into narrow slits, and a legendary reputation in a far corner of the online gaming community.

Smith was a master player in EVE Online, a

science-fiction video game in which characters pilot customized spaceships through thousands of digital galaxies. Although the futuristic fantasy is ostensibly about mineral mining throughout the universe, EVE is a game within a game: The most intense action flows from the political machinations of tens of thousands of paying subscribers arranged into alliances. Smith's online persona and call sign was "Vile Rat," a diplomat and spy who manipulated complex relationships on behalf of his alliance, called GoonSwarm. In his real life, Smith was soft-featured, clever, and humble. In his fantasy life, his gaming avatar was cunning and looked like Smith's evil doppelgänger, with a hawkish nose and a perpetual scowl. The one thing Smith and his avatar had in common was a shaved head. To fill his downtime while in Benghazi, Smith kept in regular touch not only with his family but also with his fellow EVE players.

In addition to the seven Americans, also on the Special Mission Compound were three members of the 17 February militia who lived in the guesthouse/barracks near the front gate. A fourth militiaman who normally lived among them had been absent for several days, citing a family illness. The guards' trustworthiness was suspect, at best. During the months prior to the ambassador's visit, a US government review revealed, the Compound "had been vandalized and attacked...by some of the same guards who were there to protect it."

In addition, on-site was a rotating cast of unarmed Libyan guards supplied under the contract with

Blue Mountain. Five were on hand at any given time, working on-and-off eight-hour, around-the-clock shifts. They opened and closed the gates, operated the metal detector, and checked bags at the entrance gate. Their most important role was to patrol the grounds, to provide early warning in the event of an attack.

Upon Stevens's arrival at the Compound, the resident DS agents showed him the improvements and security enhancements at Villa C since he'd last been there nine months earlier as Special Envoy. The tour by Stevens's personal security escort, DS agent Scott Wickland, also gave the ambassador a chance to reacquaint himself with the layout of his temporary home in Benghazi.

The main area of the spacious villa had an open floor plan of perhaps two thousand square feet. Beyond the entrance foyer were a modern kitchen and formal dining room to the left, a large entertaining or living room in the center, and a breakfast nook area toward the right. The well-appointed residence was decorated in a modern, if stodgy, Middle Eastern style, with cushy upholstered chairs and couches, and thick Persian rugs spread out on sparkling beige-and-black marble floors. Oil paintings and ornate sconces graced the walls, and fancy crystal chandeliers hung from the ceiling. Heavy, walnut-colored drapes framed the windows, complementing polished dark-wood tables and other expensive furnishings. Out back was a swimming pool and a cabana, remnants of the Compound's former incarnation as an upscale home.

Ultimately Wickland led Stevens to the most important part of the villa: the safe-haven area. While there, the DS agent instructed the ambassador how to unlock and open the emergency escape windows in his bedroom.

Afterward, the DS agents drove Stevens the short distance to the CIA Annex, where everyone on the property crowded into Building D's living room to meet the ambassador. Stevens launched into a standard talk about the political and security status in Libya, the progress being made, and the challenges ahead. Jack and several other GRS operators said hello to the ambassador then zoned out. They found him affable and approachable, friendlier than many of the stiff diplomats and government officials they'd encountered. But they didn't need to be told how unstable Benghazi was or to be reassured that the situation would eventually improve. When the meeting ended, Stevens and the DS agents returned to the diplomatic Compound.

At that moment, Benghazi was home to nearly thirty Americans in official capacities: seven at the Special Mission Compound and the rest at the CIA Annex.

━━━

That night, Stevens was scheduled to meet with Benghazi's mayor and city council at the El Fadeel Hotel. The meeting was supposed to be private, but council members were so excited by Stevens's presence that they alerted local reporters. That multiplied the security threat exponentially. One of the DS agents protecting Stevens called the Annex for backup, telling the operators that the DS didn't have enough agents on hand to protect Stevens at such a high-profile public event.

The need for added security from the Annex operators was especially acute. At the time of Stevens's visit, the 17 February militiamen at the Compound were staging a partial work stoppage. The disgruntled militiamen had refused to accompany the American diplomats' vehicle movements through the city, to protest low pay and long working hours. Nevertheless, US officials still officially considered the 17 February Martyrs Brigade to be a Quick Reaction Force in the event of an attack on the Compound. A memo dated one day before the ambassador arrived in Benghazi outlined the understanding between the US diplomatic post and the militia. "In the event of an attack on the US Mission," according to the document, obtained later by *The Washington Post*, the Americans "will request additional support from the 17th February Martyrs Brigade." The document said the militiamen would be paid the Libyan equivalent of about twenty-eight dollars per day, and militia fighters would provide their own weapons and ammunition.

With the militiamen refusing to protect the ambassador as he moved through Benghazi, Rone and Jack volunteered to accompany Stevens to the

September 10 hotel meeting. Their only condition was that they'd act as a shadow security detail, out of sight of reporters and cameramen. Even if they weren't publicly identified as CIA contract operators, a photo of them in a local newspaper would potentially make them targets afterward.

It occurred to Jack that if al-Qaeda sympathizers or a radical Islamist militia wanted to kill the ambassador, neither he nor Rone would make much difference. It wouldn't be a gunfight, Jack thought, but a massive explosion that would take out the El Fadeel Hotel and everything else within a half-block radius. But Jack's fears proved unwarranted, and the event went smoothly.

Afterward, Stevens ate dinner with a prominent hotelier and caterer named Adel Jalu. Then the ambassador and his protectors returned safely to their respective lodgings in the Compound and the Annex.

Before turning in, Stevens jotted a few notes in his diary, excerpts of which were later published by the special-operator website SOFREP.com. In his lefty scrawl, Stevens wrote: "Back in Benghazi after 9 months. It's a grand feeling, given all the memories." Of the officials he met at the El Fadeel, Stevens wrote: "They're an impressive and sincere group of professionals—proud of their service on committees, all working as volunteers.... There was a little sourness about why it had taken so long to get to Benghazi, and about ambassadors who came to talk but didn't do anything to follow up. But overall it was a positive meeting."

Stevens also noted an exchange of "heated words" between his dinner companion Adel Jalu and the ambassador's friend and translator, Bubaker Habib, director of the English Language Skills Center in Benghazi. The subject of the dispute was the Muslim Brotherhood, the political organization determined to see Arab states ruled by strict Islamic law, or Sharia. Stevens didn't tell his diary where he stood on the matter during the dinner debate.

━━━

Late that same night, September 10, 2012, Jack and Rone sat together in the living room of the Annex's Building D, watching the spears-and-sandals movie *300* on a big-screen TV. The GRS operators enjoyed repeated showings of the blood-soaked story of fearless King Leonidas and his tiny force of Spartan soldiers, outnumbered ten thousand to one by the Persian army at Thermopylae in 480 BC.

Jack noticed the sculpted beard sported by the actor Gerard Butler, who played the warrior king: closely cropped on the sides, long and full at the chin. He looked at Rone, then at the screen, then back at Rone.

"You're trying to grow the *300* beard, aren't you?" Jack asked.

Rone kept his eyes on the screen but smiled broadly: "Yup."

FOUR

September 11, 2012

━━━━━

IN THE FIRST HOURS OF TUESDAY, SEPTEMBER 11, 2012, Benghazi stirred from sleep as the muezzins' call to the *Fajr* prayer echoed across the ancient city. "*Allahu Akbar!* [God is Supreme!]," they proclaimed. "*Ashadu anna Muhammadan Rasool Allah!...Hayya 'ala-s-Salah!* [I bear witness that Muhammad is the messenger of God!...Come to prayer!]" The first of five daily devotions by pious Muslims resounded then faded. Soon after, the sun edged over the horizon. Minutes later, at 6:43 a.m., three men in a car with Libyan police markings slowed to a stop on the gravel street on the north side of the US diplomatic Compound.

One man, dressed in a police uniform, climbed to the second floor of a half-finished building next door to the Venezia restaurant that overlooked the Compound. His uniform bore the insignia of the Libyan Supreme Security Council, known as the SSC, a coalition of militias that organized a rudimentary police force for the rough city. The other two men waited inside the idling car. The car displayed SSC emblems, in the red, black, and green colors of the Libyan rebel movement.

The elevated vantage point of the construction site gave the uniformed man a clear view over the wall and into the Compound. He could see the buildings and fortifications, including Château Christophe, the villa where Ambassador Chris Stevens slept. The man also could see a flagpole where the American flag would fly throughout the day at half-staff, to honor the eleventh anniversary of 9/11. The man recorded what he saw with a cell phone camera.

In the days before the ambassador's visit, DS agents had asked that a marked SSC car be posted outside the Compound around the clock when Stevens was on the property. Normally, when they arrived at the Compound, SSC officers would check in with the locally hired guards. Yet neither the Libyan guards nor the American DS agents had been told that anyone from the SSC would be visiting the Compound that morning, much less surreptitiously taking photographs of the layout.

Operators have two words to describe unknown persons photographing secure locations without warning or permission: "surveillance," to gain information, and "reconnaissance," to gain tactical advantage. Surveillance of an American diplomatic site was worrisome, to be answered at a minimum by countersurveillance to determine the observer's identity and intent. Reconnaissance was worse, as it anticipated offensive military or militant action.

A Blue Mountain Libya guard working the early shift spotted the photographer and went outside the Compound gate to speak with him. Confronted by the unarmed guard, the man in the SSC uniform denied wrongdoing, returned to the car, and left with his two companions and his photographs.

Even before the suspicious photographer showed up, Stevens had intended to spend the day inside the Compound walls, to avoid making himself a tempting target to anyone with al-Qaeda sympathies or other anti-American sentiments on the anniversary of 9/11. The ambassador's agenda included discussions at Villa C with a local appellate court judge; the owner of a shipping company whose brother had political aspirations; and a political analyst. His final scheduled meeting of the day would be with the Turkish consul general, Ali Akin, who had helped the Americans when Stevens first landed in Benghazi in April 2011.

The Blue Mountain guard's report about the photographer sent the American DS agents into high alert. Two agents asked the guard to show them where he saw the uniformed man, to determine what the photographer had been able to observe. A DS agent also informed officials at the CIA Annex of the suspicious incident, as part of their longstanding arrangement to share security information in the event that the GRS operators needed to be called in as a Quick Reaction Force.

In addition, a DS agent spread word about the photographer among 17 February militia commanders presumed to be friendly to the Americans. The 17 February militia leaders told the DS agents that they would complain on the Americans' behalf to the local office of the SSC.

Separately, Stevens reviewed a draft of a complaint about the incident that he wanted delivered to local police authorities. "Early this morning," read the draft, as reported by *Foreign Policy* magazine, "one of our diligent guards made a troubling report. Near our main gate, a member of the police force was seen in the upper level of a building across from our compound. It is reported that this person was photographing the inside of the US Special Mission." Another complaint, intended for the Benghazi office of the Libyan Ministry of Foreign Affairs, began with a protest that requests for police protection at the Compound during Stevens's visit had been ignored. "We were given assurances from the highest authorities in the Ministry of Foreign Affairs that all due support would be provided for Ambassador Stevens' visit to Benghazi. However, we are saddened to report that we have only received an occasional police presence at our main gate," it read. "Many hours pass when we have no police support at all."

September 11 was a typical half day of work at Libyan government offices, where bureaucrats had perfected the art of late arrivals, long lunches, and early departures. By the time Stevens approved the final drafts, no Libyan officials were around to receive them. The complaints would have to wait at least another day.

In late morning, Stevens sent cables to Washington that included a weekly report of security incidents. He described Libyans' "growing frustration with police and security forces." Previously, a local SSC official had acknowledged to Stevens that they were too weak to keep the country secure.

Also on September 11, Stevens approved a cable, later reviewed by *The Daily Beast*, that raised the disturbing possibility that two leaders of ostensibly friendly Libyan militias in Benghazi had soured on the United States. The cable said the militia leaders believed that the United States was supporting one of their rivals in his bid to become the country's first elected prime minister. If the rival leader won a vote scheduled for the following day, September 12, 2012, in the Libyan Parliament, Stevens wrote, the two disgruntled militia leaders warned that they "would not continue to guarantee security in Benghazi, a critical function they asserted they were currently providing."

Between sending cables, attending meetings, and doing paperwork, Stevens received an unsettling text message from Gregory Hicks, the Deputy Chief of Mission at the embassy in Tripoli, which made him Stevens's second-in-command among US diplomats in Libya.

"Chris," Hicks wrote, "are you aware of what's going on in Cairo?"

Stevens responded that he wasn't, so Hicks explained that protesters had stormed the US Embassy in the Egyptian capital. Stevens shared the news with a member of his security team and went on with his day.

Separately, one of the DS agents in Benghazi, Alec Henderson, heard about the Cairo protests from a counterpart in Tripoli. From his post in the Compound, Henderson called the Annex to be sure that all the Americans in Benghazi were aware of the escalating unrest seven hundred miles away in Egypt.

By all accounts, the Cairo demonstration was sparked by Egyptian media reports about an amateurish movie trailer posted on YouTube for an anti-Islamic film called *Innocence of Muslims*. The video, made by a Christian Egyptian-American with a history of bank fraud and multiple aliases, defamed the Prophet Muhammad by depicting him as a bloodthirsty, womanizing buffoon, a homosexual, and a child molester.

Fueling the anger among Egyptian Muslims, erroneous reports suggested that the US government was somehow involved in producing the film. The US Embassy in Cairo might have unwittingly contributed to that impression by issuing a noontime statement awkwardly disavowing the video. As Gregory Hicks told Ambassador Stevens, the Egyptian protesters had scaled the embassy wall and burned the American flag. They replaced it with a black jihadist flag with white lettering in Arabic that read: "There is no God but Allah and Muhammad is His messenger."

━━━

September 11, 2012, began as a typical day for the GRS operators at the Annex. For the first move of the day, Tig accompanied Bob the base chief, his deputy, and a case officer to a 9:00 a.m. meeting with Libyan contacts at an office on the Fourth Ring Road, almost directly across from the back gate of the diplomatic Compound. While there, Tig heard Bob and the other staffers discussing how Libyan officials had asked about the location of the Annex. Afterward, Tig provided security as the CIA officers went to the Compound to inform the ambassador and the DS agents that the Libyans they'd met with had warned them about a threat to local government buildings that day. Tig listened as Stevens said he wasn't concerned because he intended to remain inside the walls of the Compound, and because the threat apparently was made by one group of Libyans against another.

After a breakfast of oatmeal and eggs, Oz ran into Rone outside Building A. They sat together enjoying coffee, conversation, and the warm morning breeze. Oz had been reading *No Easy Day*, a memoir by a former SEAL Team Six member about the raid to kill Osama bin Laden. For days he'd been needling Rone—"Hey, is writing books part of SEAL training?"—knowing that

Rone had mixed feelings about a SEAL discussing his work.

"I finished that book," Oz said. "You can have it now—I know you're wanting to read it."

"Yeah, fuck you," Rone answered, returning to his coffee.

Oz had a light daytime schedule of *Call of Duty* games, a workout, a nap, an afternoon snack, and a shower. At night he was scheduled to escort a female case officer to a dinner with a prosperous Libyan businessman and his wife. Oz and the case officer, who had grown friendly with the Libyan couple through work contacts, left the Annex around 6:00 p.m. They stopped at an Internet café for coffee, then drove by the beach on their way to their hosts' upscale home. During the drive, the case officer idly wondered whether the Annex needed quite so many security officers and GRS operators. Oz assured her that they needed every last one. As sunset approached shortly before 7:00 p.m., nothing seemed out of the ordinary. The evening was clear and Benghazi was its usual bustling, boisterous self.

Oz, the case officer, and the Libyan couple sat down over a traditional North African meal of lamb kebab, dates, and dessert pastries made from delicate layers of phyllo dough with pistachios and honey. They talked about politics and life in their respective countries. After dinner, the hosts poured tea and brought out a hookah pipe, but it was missing the upper bowl that holds the tobacco. Using his combat knife, Oz hollowed out a pear and fashioned it into an improvised hookah bowl. Their host admired his skill and his knife, so Oz surprised him by making it a gift.

━━━

During late afternoon, Tig and Rone began looking ahead to the next morning, when they were scheduled to protect the ambassador during a planned visit to the offices of the Benghazi-based Arabian Gulf Oil Company. The DS agents at the Compound were unfamiliar with the oil company's neighborhood, as they normally relied on a local driver to get them around. But Tig and Rone knew the area well, so they agreed to serve as the advance team.

As night fell, the two operators drove to the oil company's offices to scope the place out and to be sure they knew where to take Stevens the next day. On the way back to the Annex, at around 8:30 p.m., Rone and Tig drove past the Compound. All was quiet. Rone called the DS agents on his cell phone.

"Hey," Rone told a DS agent, "we figured out where the place is. Do you want us to come over now, to tell you where it's at, or do you want us to wait?"

The DS agent told Rone they should wait until morning. As they drove back to the Annex, Rone and Tig talked about how troubling they found it that the DS agents were so unfamiliar with their surroundings that they had to rely on a local driver to get them around Benghazi.

In general, all the GRS operators worried that the ambassador's visit was rife with vulnerability. Highest on their list of concerns was the planned American Corner ribbon cutting because it had been announced in advance. But as they talked among themselves, the operators concluded that Stevens could be targeted at any time and at any place during the five-day visit because the State Department security team was so lightly staffed.

Back at the Annex, at around 9:00 p.m., Tig left Rone and the GRS Team Leader in the Building C Team Room. He walked next door to the room he shared with Jack in Building D.

When Tig arrived, Jack was getting ready to hit the rack. They said goodnight then retreated to their separate sides of the heavy curtain they'd hung for privacy. Jack undressed and took out his contact lenses, placing them on a shelf for easy access. He carefully arranged clean clothes on a chair next to his bed and stuck his wallet, empty except for cash and a government ID, in a pocket of the pants he'd laid out. As always, he left his boxed wedding ring in a dresser, along with a mesh bag containing his credit cards, driver's license, and other personal items. The valuables would remain tucked away for the duration of the trip. Jack placed his holstered pistol at the head of his bed, so he'd be armed for a fight at a moment's notice.

Jack glanced over to an open gear locker. Like

the other GRS operators, he'd arranged his assault rifle, body armor, and other gear close by in response to the intel cable about a possible attack on an American target. Jack slid his two-way radio into a charger on a nightstand next to his bed. All the operators kept the handheld radios within reach around the clock, so they'd be instantly available in case of emergency. His setup complete, Jack was living up to the title of "commando": He sat naked on his bed, reading e-mail on his laptop computer. He began to mentally compose a message to his wife.

———

Tanto had spent part of the day working on the computer mapping software, alerting Annex case officers to known terrorist locations in Benghazi and the city of Derna, some 150 miles to the east. As night fell, Tanto and D.B. were on call as the Quick Reaction Force. They relaxed with coffee as they watched the mythological action movie *Wrath of the Titans.* During a break, D.B. called home to his family. They returned to the movie as they waited for Oz and the case officer to return from dinner.

———

As the protests continued at the US Embassy in Cairo, media reports described turmoil spreading to other Muslim countries throughout the region. The GRS operators had been told about the events in Egypt, but they neither saw nor heard anything to suggest that anyone in Benghazi was upset about an offensive YouTube video clip from an anti-Muslim movie. From all appearances in the quiet neighborhood around the Compound and the Annex, September 11, 2012, would soon pass into history as an unremarkable day in Benghazi.

———

Over at the Compound, at 7:40 p.m., Stevens and one of the DS agents escorted Turkish Consul General Ali Akin outside the main gate. The sun had set nearly an hour earlier, so it was dark as they stepped into the empty gravel road. Stevens said goodbye to Akin, then returned to Villa C.

A half hour later, a British security team dropped off vehicles and communications equipment at the Compound, a routine arrangement following the closure of the British consulate three months earlier. Nothing seemed out of the ordinary when the ambassador went outside the gate with Akin, or when the British team left at around 8:30 p.m.

By 9:00 p.m., the seven Americans at the Compound were settling down for the night. Communications specialist Sean Smith was in his room in Villa C, where he'd been chatting online with a friend from EVE. Earlier in the evening, when the friend said that they'd be in contact again soon, Smith answered ruefully: "assuming we don't die tonight. We saw one of our 'police' that guard the Compound taking pictures."

Three DS agents sat together outside the villa, talking under the stars near the swimming pool.

One was Scott Wickland, Stevens's personal security escort. Also outside was Wickland's fellow cheesy-mustache competitor, David Ubben. Relaxing with Wickland and Ubben was one of the two DS agents who'd accompanied Stevens from Tripoli. The other DS agent who'd traveled with Stevens sat on sentry duty inside Villa C, watching a video on the flat-screen television in the living room.

The fifth and highest-ranking DS agent in Benghazi, Alec Henderson, was in the building known as the Tactical Operations Center, the TOC. His shift was over, so normally the video security monitors inside the TOC would be unmanned, an established practice under which the Compound relied on the local guards to keep watch over the perimeter when no agents were on duty. The idea was that those unarmed Libyan guards would radio the DS agents if trouble arose. But Henderson wanted to finish some paperwork, so he'd gone to the TOC before turning in.

All five DS agents carried only their pistols, as usual when they were within the Compound walls. Their "kits" of body armor, helmet, radio, M4 assault rifle, other weapons, and ammunition were stashed in their individual bedrooms. Wickland's and Henderson's kits were in Villa C, Ubben's was in the TOC, and the kits belonging to the two Tripoli agents were in the Cantina building, across from the TOC.

After bidding goodnight to the Turkish diplomat, Stevens retired to his room in the villa to unwind. A recent issue of *The New Yorker* magazine awaited him, but first he recorded his thoughts. "It is so nice to be back in Benghazi," Stevens wrote in his diary on a page dated September 11, according to SOFREP.com. "Much stronger emotional connection to this place—the people but also the smaller-town feel & the moist air & green & spacious compound."

Stevens briefly recounted the day's meetings, then wrote a final, uneasy diary line for the day: "Never ending security threats..." The three dots of the ellipsis tailed off toward the edge of the page.

———

At 9:02 p.m., an unexpected vehicle drove down the gravel road outside the Compound: a Toyota pickup truck with SSC police insignia. The pickup parked outside the main C1 gate, but the men inside remained in their seats, never engaging with the Libyan guards or anyone else from the Compound. The SSC vehicle pulled away forty minutes after it arrived.

It's possible that the vehicle's brief presence came in response to the Americans' request for around-the-clock SSC protection during the ambassador's visit. Another possibility was more nefarious: Its movements were somehow connected to the mysterious photographer who'd arrived that morning in a vehicle with similar markings. Perhaps it had nothing to do with either. Or perhaps it was a signal. Almost the moment the SSC pickup pulled away from the Compound, shots and an explosion rang out.

Several dozen men, chanting in Arabic and firing AK-47s into the air, swarmed through the pedestrian entrance at the Compound's main gate. Eventually their numbers swelled to more than sixty. Some were bearded, some were clean-shaven. Some wore black T-shirts and camouflage pants, some wore jeans and white or brightly colored shirts. Some wore tactical military-style vests. Some wore flowing "man jammies." Some carried walkie-talkies. Some were young and lean, others were portly and middle-aged. A few hid their faces with scarves, but most didn't. The attackers didn't wear insignia, and none of the Americans saw where they'd assembled or knew exactly when they'd arrived outside the gate. One thing was certain: They displayed a common desire to terrorize Americans at the Special Mission Compound. Or worse.

Who opened the gate wasn't clear, but responsibility for the entrance rested with the Blue Mountain Libya guards. By some accounts the armed invaders threatened the unarmed guards, who immediately acquiesced. A US government review raised the possibility that the "poorly skilled" local guards left the pedestrian gate open "after initially seeing the attackers and fleeing the vicinity." No evidence has shown that the Blue Mountain guards were in league with the attackers, but maybe they were incompetent. As the report noted, "They had left the gate unlatched before."

Further complicating matters, the camera monitor in the guard booth at the front gate was broken, and new surveillance cameras shipped to the Compound had yet to be installed.

When the attackers rushed in, the three armed 17 February militiamen and the five unarmed Blue Mountain Libya guards fled to points south and east inside the Compound. Relying on the Libyan guards to sound the alarm, alert the DS agents, and serve as a first line of defense had been a mistake, as they did none of those things before abandoning their posts. They scurried through the darkness in the direction of the Cantina and the TOC, where they knew they'd find the better trained and better armed DS agents. Some of the Libyans employed at the Compound apparently kept going, all the way to the back gate that led out to the Fourth Ring Road.

With the main gate open and the guards gone, the attackers met no resistance. They surged unchecked onto the manicured grounds. Almost immediately upon storming the Compound, the attackers had the property under their complete control without a single shot being fired in their direction.

From that point forward, their actions suggested a blend of tactical planning, perhaps based on reconnaissance, and opportunistic rampage. The attackers grabbed five-gallon fuel cans that were stored alongside new, uninstalled generators next to the 17 February barracks, just inside the main gate. They sloshed diesel fuel around the barracks building and on two vehicles parked nearby, then set them ablaze. As orange flames and acrid black smoke shot into the night sky, the invaders rushed toward the heart of the Compound: Villa C.

Inside his room in the villa, Sean Smith heard the uproar as it began. "FUCK," he typed to one of his gaming friends. "GUNFIRE."

Alec Henderson, the DS agent doing paperwork in the TOC, heard shots, too, along with an explosion. The DS agents were used to hearing gunfire and fireworks when the sun went down, but these sounded much closer than usual. Henderson stood from his desk and walked to the TOC window but saw only the sandbags stacked outside. As he returned to his desk, Henderson glanced at a large video monitor that simultaneously displayed a checkerboard of black-and-white images from roughly a dozen surveillance cameras scattered around the Compound. His focus narrowed to a square on the monitor that showed the feed from a camera pointed at the main driveway.

In a matter of seconds, the screen showed sixteen to twenty armed attackers rushing into the Compound through the front gate. At least two carried banners the size of twin bedsheets, one black and one white, both with Arabic writing.

Tearing himself away from the monitor, Henderson flipped the switch on the alarm system, which blared its warning siren from speakers through-out the Compound. A recorded voice repeatedly warned: "Duck and cover! Get away from the windows!" Henderson pressed the talk button on the public address mic and shouted: "Attention on Compound, attention on Compound! This is not a drill!" He released the button and the recorded voice and alarm resumed, sounding like a British police siren with its endlessly alternating "hi-lo" cadence.

Henderson grabbed his iPhone and called the nearby CIA Annex and the US Embassy in Trip-oli. "Boss," he told John Martinec, the chief DS agent in Tripoli, "we're getting hit!"

As Henderson worked to alert the Compound and secure help, gunshots rang out from multiple locations as the terrorists gained control of the property. Following protocol, he returned to work and established himself as the emergency commu-nications officer, using his cell phone and radios to remain in contact with the Annex, Tripoli, and his fellow DS agents on the Compound.

———

The sudden explosion of gunfire and chanting from the men rushing into the Compound roused the four DS agents at Villa C. The Tripoli DS agent who was watching a movie ran outside to join Scott Wickland, David Ubben, and the other Tripoli agent on the patio. Ubben ran about fifty yards to the other side of the Compound with the Tripoli agents, toward the Cantina and the TOC, to collect their M4 assault rifles, armor, and other gear from their rooms.

As Stevens's "body man," Wickland had primary responsibility for the ambassador's safety. He ran inside Château Christophe and retrieved his kit, which included a combat shotgun along with his assault rifle, body armor, and radio.

Wickland quickly rounded up Stevens and Sean Smith in the semi-darkened villa. Shouts and chants and pops of gunfire echoed outside. Wickland instructed the ambassador and the communications expert to don their body armor as he locked all three of them behind the gate in the villa's safe-haven area. The DS agent gave Stevens his cell phone and radioed Alec Henderson in the TOC, to let him know their location and that they were secure for the moment.

With his rifle, shotgun, and pistol ready, Wickland found a protected place inside the safe haven from which he could watch the gate without being seen by anyone on the other side. The defensive position gave him a clear line of fire to anyone attempting to breach the safe haven.

Using Wickland's cell phone and his own, Stevens feverishly called the embassy in Tripoli and his local contacts for help. Stevens twice dialed the number for his top deputy in Tripoli, Gregory Hicks, but Hicks didn't answer.

———

Around 9:45 p.m. at the US Embassy in Tripoli, chief DS agent John Martinec burst into the villa where Hicks was watching one of his favorite television shows.

"Greg! Greg!" Martinec yelled. "The consulate's under attack!" By calling the Compound a consulate, Martinec was using common diplomatic shorthand; the Benghazi Special Mission was never officially a consulate. After delivering the message, Martinec rushed back to the embassy's Tactical Operations Center.

Hicks reached for his phone and found two missed calls, one from Stevens's cell phone number and one from a number he didn't recognize. He hit reply on the second number and Stevens answered: "Greg, we're under attack!"

As he spoke with Stevens, Hicks moved toward the embassy's TOC. Cell phone service was spotty in Tripoli, and Stevens's call cut out as Hicks began to reply: "OK…" He repeatedly tried both numbers from the missed calls on his phone but couldn't get through.

When he reached the embassy TOC, Hicks found John Martinec on the phone with Alec Henderson, his counterpart in Benghazi, who remained holed up in the TOC at the Benghazi Compound.

Henderson reported that all seven Americans on the Compound were accounted for, and that the ambassador and Sean Smith were inside the safe haven with Scott Wickland. Martinec spread the word.

Hicks showed another DS agent the unfamiliar number on his phone, the one he'd used to reach Stevens. The agent told Hicks that the number came from a cell phone belonging to the ambassador's body man, Scott Wickland.

Martinec ended his call with Henderson and briefed Hicks, telling him that at least twenty armed attackers had breached the Benghazi Compound. Hicks phoned Bob, the CIA chief in Benghazi, who told him that the Annex was aware and preparing to send help. The Annex's small team of operators was jocking up, each one ready, willing, and confident they could repel the attack and save the trapped Americans.

When he left Villa C, Ubben ran to his bedroom in the TOC to grab his kit. One of the Tripoli DS agents also rushed to the TOC, mistakenly believing that the ambassador was inside. When the agent learned that Stevens was in the villa, he sprinted several yards across a brick patio and into the Cantina, to reach his bedroom so he could arm and armor himself. There he ran into his fellow Tripoli-based DS agent, and together they decided to return to Villa C to help Chris Stevens, Sean Smith, and Scott Wickland.

A brick driveway, roughly five yards wide, separated the Cantina from Villa C. When the two Tripoli DS agents cautiously stepped outside the Cantina, they bumped into one of the local Blue Mountain guards who'd fled when the attack began. Staying together, the three men approached the driveway that they knew they'd have to cross to reach Villa C.

Armed intruders crowded the darkened driveway not far from where they intended to cross. Trying to reach Villa C would have exposed their whereabouts and made them easy targets in a firefight. The Tripoli DS agents and the Blue Mountain guard retreated inside the Cantina and barricaded themselves in a back room.

———

After gathering his guns and gear, David Ubben remained with his fellow DS agent Alec Henderson inside the securely locked TOC, working the phones and radios while watching the video monitors to see the ongoing attack around them. In addition to the US Embassy in Tripoli and the nearby CIA Annex, they called the headquarters of the 17 February militia and the Diplomatic Security Command Center in Washington, where the local time was approaching 4:00 p.m.

———

Within minutes of the attack, the seven Americans at the Special Mission Compound were thrown onto the defensive and separated into three locations: Two Benghazi-based DS agents, Alec Henderson and David Ubben, were locked inside the TOC; two DS agents from Tripoli were barricaded inside the Cantina with a local guard; and Ambassador Chris Stevens, communications expert Sean Smith, and DS agent Scott Wickland were left to fend for themselves in the villa's safe haven.

The armed invaders had gained the upper hand

with a surprise assault. Now they roamed freely through the dimly lit Compound, firing their weapons and chanting as they approached the buildings in packs, destroying what lay in their paths, some stealing what they could carry, all trying to find the Americans.

━━━

Immediately after Alec Henderson's initial call for help, the two-way radios scattered throughout the Annex snapped to life: "All GRS, meet in the CP."

The radio call came from the GRS Team Leader, calmly but firmly ordering the operators to muster in the Command Post, another name for the Sensitive Compartmented Information Facility in Building C. All of the operators were on the Annex property except for Oz, who was still at dinner with the case officer.

Tanto and D.B., unwinding with *Wrath of the Titans*, switched off the movie, rose from the couch, and began to gather themselves. Tanto, relaxing in cargo shorts, didn't think the radio call sounded especially urgent. He figured they were being hauled in for a routine dressing down, having somehow pissed off their bosses. It had happened before, such as the time Tanto hung a photo in the Command Post of actor Robert Downey Jr. from the movie *Tropic Thunder*, captioned with a line from the movie, "Never go full retard."

"Hey Tanto," D.B. asked, "what'd you do now?"

Tanto wondered the same thing, but he wasn't worried. He figured he'd take his licks and return to the movie.

Less than twenty seconds after the first call, the radio sounded again: "We need GRS in the room. NOW!" The tone was altogether different.

Tanto and D.B. caught each other's eyes. "Shit, something's really happening," Tanto said as he moved toward the door. Unaware that American lives were in danger, Tanto grew excited by the prospect of a sudden night move: "We're gonna get to do something fun tonight."

Tanto glanced at his wrist. No matter what anyone else would say later about the attack beginning at 9:42 p.m., Tanto was certain his watch read 9:32 p.m. He and D.B. grabbed their kits, including lightweight machine guns in addition to their pistols and assault rifles. They jocked up and moved toward Building C.

The operators hustled, swiftly but not frantically, to avoid panicking Annex workers who hadn't trained to be calm and collected in battle. The GRS Team Leader met them outside on the driveway, about halfway to Building C.

"The consulate is being overrun," he told Tanto and D.B.

In the distance, they heard explosions and gunfire from the direction of the Compound. Tanto heard someone shouting in Arabic on a megaphone. He couldn't make out much, but he could hear the distant amplified chant: *"Allahu Akbar! Allahu Akbar!"*

━━

Still naked in his room, Jack set aside his laptop when he heard the first muster call. He hadn't begun typing his nightly e-mail to his wife, but he figured he'd do so after a short interruption. At the first call, Jack began to dress, pulling on his jeans without underwear.

His roommate, Tig, in nightclothes, slid on flip-flops.

"Hang out here," Tig said from the other side of the hanging blanket that divided their room. "I'll see what's going on." Tig stepped outside. As he did, he heard the second muster call and ran across the driveway to Building C.

"Hey, State is under attack!" the Team Leader told Tig, who immediately turned and ran back to Building D. He found Jack shirtless outside.

"The consulate's getting attacked," Tig said. Both doubled their pace, pulling on civilian clothes then jocking up with a full array of weapons, armor, chest rigs containing ammunition, helmets, night-vision goggles, and other equipment. They also carried personal medical kits, with clotting agents, sterile Kerlix gauze dressings, and tourniquets already unwrapped so they could be applied with one hand if the other was injured, blown off, or holding a gun. That was among the tips that Rone had reinforced during his medical training exercise.

As the operators prepared to move out, each grabbed his individual go-bag, stuffed with items including a compass, a GPS unit, extra ammunition, a flashlight, batteries, and in some cases their diplomatic passports.

Jack popped in his contact lenses, but he did so too quickly and they weren't oriented correctly. He left Building D with blurry vision.

━━━

From the TOC at the US Embassy in Tripoli, Deputy Chief of Mission Gregory Hicks called the Operations Center at the State Department in Washington to report the attack and let officials there know what response was planned. Then he made a flurry of calls to Libyan officials. Hicks called the chief of staff to Libyan President Mohamed Magariaf to inform him of the attack and ask for immediate help. He made a similar request to the chief of staff of the Libyan prime minister. Then Hicks called the director of the Americas Desk at the Libyan Ministry of Foreign Affairs, Abdurrahman al-Gannas. Less than three weeks earlier, al-Gannas had held Chris Stevens's hand in Tripoli as they shared the honors at the Consular Section ribbon-cutting ceremony. Now Hicks wanted al-Gannas to repay Stevens's friendship by helping to save his life.

During a phone call between Hicks and Bob the Annex chief, they agreed to mobilize a response team consisting of American operators based at the embassy in Tripoli. One team member would be former Navy SEAL Glen "Bub" Doherty, who'd be joining his friends Rone, Jack, and Tanto. Hicks and other Tripoli embassy staffers went to work chartering a small Libyan commercial jet to fly the reinforcements to Benghazi.

Meanwhile, the embassy's defense attaché called leaders of Libya's Air Force and other Libyan armed forces, seeking help. The defense attaché also regularly updated officials in Washington and the US military's Africa Command, known as AFRICOM. Embassy staffers called officials at Benina International Airport to ask for logistical support and cooperation, in anticipation of the arrival of the operators from Tripoli and an eventual evacuation of all the Americans from Benghazi.

David McFarland, the embassy's political section chief, had just returned to Tripoli after ten days in Benghazi as the Special Mission's acting Principal Officer. McFarland called his militia contacts and trusted Libyans who worked various jobs at the Compound, to urge them to repulse the attack with overwhelming force.

Calls also went out from the American diplomats to leaders of the 17 February Martyrs Brigade militia, officials at the United Nations, and diplomats in friendly nations' embassies in Libya. Hicks then called Washington with another update.

———

At 10:05 p.m. Benghazi time, or 4:05 p.m. in Washington, the State Department Operations Center issued an alert to the White House Situation Room, the FBI, and the Office of the Director of National Intelligence, among other key government and intelligence agencies. "US Diplomatic Mission in Benghazi Under Attack," it said. "[A]pproximately twenty armed people fired shots; explosions have been heard as well. Ambassador Stevens, who is currently in Benghazi... [is] in the Compound safe haven."

▬

Within five minutes of Alec Henderson's first mayday call from the Compound, Tanto, D.B., Rone, Tig, and Jack were jocked up and assembled outside Building C. They talked among themselves, asking each other if anyone knew how many Americans were on the Compound and what kind of weapons were there. The answer: seven Americans with light weapons. From the gunfire and explosions they continued to hear, and from the reports of perhaps several dozen attackers, the operators knew that they'd be dealing with what Tanto called "a substantial force."

Tig told the GRS Team Leader they might want to drive up a narrow, rutted dirt pathway immediately west of the Annex, which the operators called "Smuggler's Alley," because it would lead them directly to the Fourth Ring Road and the Compound's back gate. But the Team Leader said he'd heard from the DS agents that they thought the Compound's back gate had been breached, so the operators should pick another route.

The GRS Team Leader told the operators they wouldn't be going in alone. He said they'd be linking up with a large group of 17 February fighters, who'd be fulfilling their militia's promise to serve as a Quick Reaction Force. The T.L. told them that the attackers seemed to be armed with AK-47s and rocket-propelled grenades, and that the Americans at the Compound were separated into several groups. The T.L. instructed the five operators to stay ready and wait for his signal to leave.

They tossed their gear into a dark-blue BMW sedan and a boxy, black Mercedes SUV. Both were armored, with bullet-resistant windows and tires called "run-flats," designed to live up to the name if hit by bullets, spikes, or shrapnel. Both vehicles were tuned like racecars but dusty and worn outside, so they wouldn't attract additional notice as they moved toward the Compound. The operators staged the vehicles outside Building C, pointing toward the gate, with the BMW in front.

Rone got behind the wheel of the BMW, Jack rode shotgun, and Tig slid into the backseat, armed with a grenade launcher in addition to a lightweight machine gun with two bandoliers of ammunition. Tanto and D.B. jumped into the front seat of the Mercedes, with Tanto behind the wheel. Along with his usual weapons Tanto brought a light machine gun with a bandolier of ammunition. He knew that there were other, similar bandoliers already in the car, in case he needed more ammo. The GRS Team Leader remained outside near Building C, talking on a cell phone.

Several of the operators demanded to know

what they were waiting for. The Team Leader pulled away from his phone: "We need to come up with a plan," he said, referring to how they'd coordinate with the 17 February militia. Also standing outside the vehicles talking on phones were Bob the Annex chief and his second-in-command, a CIA officer who'd earned the operators' esteem by treating them with respect.

Inside the vehicles, the five GRS operators triple-checked their gunsights, tightened their armor, and tried to figure out why they hadn't already left. They likely could have reached the Compound on foot in the time they'd been waiting. Most sat quietly, but Tanto tried to keep the atmosphere light by complaining that he had nowhere to put the coffee cup he'd brought with him. "Spend $250,000 on a damn Mercedes and there's no cup holder? What kind of bullshit is that?"

As minutes passed and they grew tense listening to the conversations outside the cars, the operators got the distinct impression that the rescue plan being discussed somehow didn't include them.

Standing outside the Mercedes, Tig called out, "Hey, we gotta go now! We're losing the initiative!"

"No, stand down, you need to wait," Bob the base chief yelled back.

"We need to come up with a plan," the Team Leader repeated.

"It's too fucking late to come up with a plan,"

Tig yelled. "We need to get in the fucking area and *then* come up with a plan."

Tanto got out of the Mercedes and approached the Team Leader and Bob. He asked them to request US military air support, specifically an unmanned ISR drone, named for its ability to provide intelligence, surveillance, and reconnaissance. Tanto also asked them to call in a heavily armed AC-130 Spectre gunship, a four-engine, fixed-wing plane designed for lethal ground assaults. In the meantime, Tanto told the bosses, he and the other operators were overdue to move out.

The CIA chief looked at Tanto, then at the Team Leader, then back to Tanto. Tanto felt as though the chief was looking right through him. "No," Bob said, "hold up. We're going to have the local militia handle it."

Tanto couldn't believe his ears. He turned to the Team Leader: "Hey, we need to go."

"No," the T.L. said, "we need to wait. The chief is trying to coordinate with 17 Feb and let them handle it."

"What do you mean, 'Let them handle it?'" Tanto demanded. He had little confidence in the 17 February militia, whose members he and several other operators considered as liable to turn on them as to serve alongside them. Tanto especially wouldn't trust the militia on its word when the objective was to save American lives. "We need to go. We're not letting 17 Feb handle it."

Tanto's memory flashed back to the airport standoff months earlier. He believed that Bob was repeating the go-slow, stand-down, let-the-friendly-militia-handle-it approach he'd taken when hostile militiamen held up Rone and another GRS operator. That incident was resolved peacefully, without injuries and without exposing the CIA presence in Benghazi, when Rone and his companion demonstrated that they wouldn't be robbed without a fight. This time, Tanto thought, Bob was taking the same passive tactic even though the fight had already begun and the Americans were losing, possibly dying.

"I've been through this before," Tanto told the T.L., "when the chief didn't let us go when our own guys were in trouble. Go ask Tyrone. He's right over there. He was one of the guys out there when the chief said to have 17 Feb handle it and held us back."

"Tanto, I know," the T.L. said. "I'm working on it."

Tanto returned to the Mercedes SUV and told D.B.: "This is a bunch of fucking bullshit." D.B. was incredulous. His head slumped forward in frustration. Yet both knew that it wasn't over. Plans were still forming and changing, with input and decisions flying between Benghazi, Tripoli, and Washington. They didn't know whom Bob was speaking with, but they hoped that the "wait" order would be reversed quickly and they'd be given a green light.

Tanto got on the radio and relayed his conversation to Rone, Jack, and Tig in the BMW. Rone looked over through the car window, his expression trapped between anger and disgust. Tanto held his palms up and shrugged.

Rone got on the radio and called out: "We gotta go, gotta go, gotta go!"

His vision still blurred from his misaligned contact lenses, Jack stared out the window of the BMW, wondering whether whoever was attacking the Compound might try a simultaneous assault on the Annex. He experienced the familiar yin and yang of the moment: disbelief that this was happening, contrasted by a sense that he had expected it all along. As he considered the situation, Jack remembered that he'd left his laptop on. The e-mail that he'd intended to send his wife remained unwritten.

From the driver's seat in the Mercedes, Tanto noticed a civilian named Henry, an owlish, balding, olive-skinned man with glasses, walking across the Annex driveway. Tanto bounded out of the SUV. Henry was a US citizen in his sixties working as an interpreter at the Annex. Some translators in hostile areas are designated combat interpreters because they've had specialized weapons training. Henry wasn't among them. He was an office worker who reviewed and translated documents from Arabic and occasionally went out on operations no more dangerous than dinner with locals. Tanto stopped Henry in his tracks.

"I've been through this before, and we need you to come with us," Tanto said. "If we're linking up with 17 Feb, none of us speaks the language well enough to communicate. We need you in here."

"Tanto," Henry replied, "I'm not weapons qualified."

"It doesn't matter," Tanto said. He pulled out a pistol and handed it to Henry. "Here's your weapon. Go get your helmet and your armor. We need you."

Without hesitating, Henry said: "Roger. I'll be right back."

Barely two minutes later, Henry was seated in the back of the Mercedes, his armor and helmet secured, Tanto's gun in his hand, and a look of pure fright on his weathered face. Tanto thought he resembled a Middle Eastern version of the comic Bob Newhart. He handed Henry an extra magazine of ammunition.

When Jack saw Henry jocked up and ready, he felt a flush of admiration. *Here's a guy*, Jack thought, *who's an administrative guy, and somebody gave him body armor and a helmet and a pistol. He volunteered to come basically on a suicide mission. For us, it's our job to do stuff like that. His job is to sit behind a desk and interpret Arabic into English. But he's doing what he thinks is right.*

From their idling vehicles, the operators could vaguely see the orange flames rising from the Compound. With their doors flung open, they could hear chanting in the distance. Tanto grabbed his radio, so everyone in the Annex would hear his message. He hoped it also would reach someone on the same frequency at the Compound. Tanto repeated his earlier request as a demand: "Get us an ISR [drone] and a Spectre gunship!"

━━━

Tanto didn't know it, but one part of his demand was already being fulfilled. Within the first half hour of the attack, at 9:59 p.m., the US military's Africa Command ordered a drone surveillance aircraft to reposition itself over the Special Mission Compound. It would take more than an hour to reach Benghazi, but once there the drone could monitor events and beam live images to Washington.

But a request for close air support wouldn't be so easy to fulfill. A Pentagon spokesman would say later that none of America's punishing AC-130 gunships were anywhere within range of Benghazi on the night of September 11, 2012.

━━━

As minutes ticked by and the operators waited for clearance to leave, the air in the vehicles grew thick with tension. The operators imagined bloody scenes of what was happening to their countrymen less than a mile away. And the longer they sat idle, the more likely the same fate awaited them.

As the hour neared 10:00 p.m., with the operators' radios tuned to the same frequency as those at the Compound, they heard the voice of one of the DS agents in the Compound TOC, Alec Henderson or David Ubben.

"We're being attacked!" one yelled, his voice tight with stress. "There's approximately twenty to thirty armed men, with AKs firing. We're being attacked! We need help! We need help now!"

Adrenaline surged through the operators' veins, but again they were told to wait. They were used to following orders, and they knew that insubordination could mean their jobs or worse. But a shared thought took hold in both vehicles: If they weren't given permission to move out soon, they'd take matters into their own hands.

FIVE

Overrun

BEHIND THE LOCKED STEEL GATE INSIDE THE VILLA'S safe haven, Ambassador Chris Stevens and communications expert Sean Smith cowered in the dark with DS agent Scott Wickland.

Wickland heard the intruders breaking through the villa's reinforced wooden front doors, apparently by blowing them open with a rocket-propelled grenade. Staying out of sight, the DS agent peered through the openings between the bars of the security gate. Wickland watched from his protected position as their enemies burst into the building carrying AK-47s.

They plundered the living room, destroying furniture as they swarmed through the villa. Several reached the safe-haven gate and banged on the bars. They tried to look inside but the area beyond the gate was dark, and they couldn't see Wickland or the two men he was determined to protect. The attackers attempted to break in, but the bolts and locks held.

Still unseen, Wickland aimed his assault rifle at the intruders when they reached the gate, ready to shoot if they tried to blast or force it open. Until they made that move, Wickland resolved, he'd hold his concealed position and his fire, to avoid revealing his location and the presence of the ambassador and the information officer. Wickland warned Stevens and Smith to brace themselves for an assault.

But instead of trying to blow open the gate and enter the safe haven, the attackers moved back. They hauled in the jerry cans of diesel fuel that they'd found near the Compound's new generator and had already used to torch the vehicles and the 17 February barracks. Wickland couldn't know whether the attackers believed that the American ambassador was locked inside the villa's safe haven, but it stands to reason that they knew the barred gate separated them from Americans that they had hoped to reach. The attackers' intent was evident: They meant to use the Americans' own fuel to smoke them out or roast them alive.

The attackers doused diesel on the overstuffed chairs, pillows, and couches, drenched the Persian rugs, and splashed the viscous fuel around the living room. As the intruders left, they set the villa ablaze. Outside, they spread more diesel to set fires against the building's exterior concrete walls.

Unable to see deep into the living room from his hiding place, at first Wickland couldn't tell what was happening. Then the light from the villa's lamps and chandeliers dimmed. The DS agent realized that he, Stevens, and Smith had a new enemy. The villa was on fire and rapidly filling with toxic smoke.

The Villa C safe haven was supposed to provide the ambassador and other Americans short-term protection against physical attack until host-country rescuers or American fighters could drive away the invaders or protesters. It wasn't designed to keep them safe indefinitely, and it wasn't built to safeguard them from fire or chemical agents. In that sense, the Benghazi safe haven was analogous to a shark cage used by ocean divers. The longer it remained in use, the greater the likelihood that killers would batter their way in or the air would run out. Time favored the enemy.

Visibility in the villa squeezed down to zero. Breathable air became scarce. The smoke of burning diesel fuel is a lethal black cloud containing dozens of poisons, including benzene, arsenic, and formaldehyde. The trapped Americans felt their breathing become labored. Each time they inhaled, the smoke tortured their lungs with soot, nitrogen dioxide, sulfur dioxide, and razor-like particles of hot ash. The smell of burning diesel can be overpowering by itself, a scrambled sulfur-and-egg mixture sometimes described as the scent of Satan cooking breakfast. Brief exposure triggers painful coughing, nausea, eye pain, and headaches. Loss of consciousness and organ damage come next. Extended contact causes death.

As the smoke intensified, the three Americans

dropped to the floor of the safe haven. Crawling on his hands and knees, Wickland led Stevens and Smith into a bathroom that he knew had a barred exterior window. He rolled wet towels in an attempt to seal the gap between the bottom of the door and the tile floor, but smoke continued to seep inside. Wickland rose to his feet and opened the window in the hope of improving ventilation, but it had the opposite effect. Smoke from outside the villa poured into the bathroom, making it even harder for the besieged men to breathe.

The villa had neither emergency sprinklers nor a foam fire-suppression system. If the Americans hoped to survive, they'd have to get outside among their enemies, either on their own or with help.

Wickland, Stevens, and Smith pressed their bodies against the floor, gulping at the little breathable air remaining. The smoke grew so thick that Wickland lost sight of the ambassador and the computer expert in the small bathroom. Starved for oxygen, confined to a smoke-filled room, unable to see his companions, Wickland realized that remaining in place meant death by suffocation.

The bars on the bathroom window were set in concrete, so Wickland yelled to Stevens and Smith to follow him to a nearby bedroom. There, Wickland knew, an emergency latch might allow him to open the metal window bars from inside. Still unable to see through the foul black smoke, the DS agent crawled out of the bathroom into the safe-haven hallway. He scuttled toward the bedroom. Wickland yelled and banged on the floor as he went, using sound to guide Stevens and Smith, who he believed were following close behind.

As Wickland moved toward the bedroom, he could hear explosions and gunfire from outside. Bullets and tracers screamed through the overrun Compound. The American DS agents and their paid Libyan militia guards had still mounted no resistance.

Thinking that Stevens and Smith had followed him from the bathroom, Wickland reached the window at the far end of the bedroom and unlatched the security grill. The vertical window, its lower edge about two feet off the floor, was about five feet tall and three feet wide. His strength waning, Wickland climbed through the window and crumpled onto a small outdoor patio that was partly enclosed by a four-foot-high wall of white sandbags.

Through a haze of oxygen deprivation, on the verge of passing out, Wickland grasped that he was alone. He'd somehow become separated from Stevens and Smith, while they were either in the smoke-filled bathroom or somewhere in the safe-haven hallway between there and the bedroom. Maybe they had taken a wrong turn, or maybe they had never followed him into the hallway to begin with. Either way, Wickland understood the horrifying reality: The two men he was sworn to protect, one of them the diplomatic representative of the United States, were trapped somewhere inside the burning safe haven. To add to his misery, Wickland heard gunfire and believed that someone was shooting at him from the other side of the sandbags.

The exhausted DS agent struggled to his feet. Wickland hauled himself back through the villa window, returning to the smoke-filled safe haven to search for Chris Stevens and Sean Smith.

———

At the Annex, each passing minute increased the GRS operators' anger. Rising with it was concern that the invaders had established defenses against a counterattack and tightened their grip on the Compound.

The attackers had used one of the oldest and most potent weapons of warfare: surprise. Without a quick and overwhelming counterpunch, the aggressors would have time to solidify their tactical gains and increase their chances of achieving their presumed objective: killing or capturing any Americans they could find, above all the ambassador. Chris Stevens's presence in Benghazi was widely known, especially after the local councilmen had alerted the media to the El Fadeel Hotel event the previous night. Killing or kidnapping an American ambassador on the anniversary of the September 11 attacks would be a major coup for any extreme Islamist group or militia. Reducing an American diplomatic outpost to a charred ruin would be a bonus.

Inside the Mercedes SUV, Tanto couldn't contain his fury. "You know how hard it's going to be?" he asked D.B. rhetorically. "You know how hard it's going to be to fight back on that objective? We're losing the initiative!"

If he had been alone with D.B., Tanto would have raged even hotter, unleashing a stream of creative, emphatic curses that ran through his mind. But with Henry the translator already looking green around the gills in the backseat, Tanto didn't want to spook the older man into a panic. The operators divided the world into two categories: shooters and non-shooters. Henry was a non-shooter.

Yet even as he seethed about being held in check, Tanto felt an inner calm. He considered it a gift, and he felt certain from years of military and contracting experience that the more chaotic things became, the more confident he'd grow. To distract himself from the delays, Tanto tried to focus on their assets. Their Quick Reaction Force team would be six shooters strong: five contract GRS operators—everyone but Oz, who was still at dinner—and the GRS Team Leader. Tanto and the other operators knew that they'd be outnumbered. But they weren't just any guys with guns. The operators were disciplined and experienced, abundantly armed and as expertly trained as any force their size on the planet. They had the protection of body armor and the advantage of night-vision goggles. All in all, Tanto liked the odds of the Annex team against what he expected would be a disorderly force of raw, chanting, gun-toting radicals.

That is, unless the continued passage of time gave the enemy an insurmountable edge.

If the Compound attackers had any military experience whatsoever, the GRS operators knew, they'd be preparing for a counterstrike. The more time the attackers had to dig in, the more likely they'd secure the Compound perimeter and organize defensive positions, at least until they achieved their objectives.

"They've got ahold of everything by now," Tanto groused. "The longer we're waiting, the bad guys are going to be entrenched. They're going to have their bearings."

In the passenger seat of the BMW, Jack sat blinking and rubbing his eyes, still trying to adjust his contacts. Even with blurred vision, he wished the delay would end and they could get to work. Ringing in his ears was the voice of the DS agent at the Compound reporting the attack and asking for help. Jack twisted toward the backseat, where Tig heard the same voice in his head.

"Why the fuck aren't we moving?" Tig asked, even as he knew the answer. It was plain to all the GRS operators that their superiors were still working the phones to get a firm commitment and a strategy from leaders of the 17 February militia. Tanto echoed Tig's lament on the radio: "Why the fuck aren't we moving?"

En masse, they decided that the time for asking permission had ended. The operators climbed out of their idling vehicles and assembled in a huddle outside Building C, near the Team Leader, Bob the CIA Annex chief, and his second-in-command. Jack caught Rone's attention and they exchanged incredulous, wide-eyed looks. To Jack, the meaning was clear: This delay is nuts. Worse, it's dangerous, for the guys at the Compound and also for us. *The situation is beyond serious, people need our help, and we're the only ones available*, Jack thought. *We need to go*.

Their radios again crackled with beseeching calls from the DS agents at the Compound TOC. "Armed men!"

"Taking fire!"

"Taking heavy fire!"

"They've overrun the Compound!"

"We're all locked up!"

"We need help!"

Yet the CIA base bosses and the Team Leader, all talking animatedly on their cell phones, still wouldn't give the operators the go-ahead. From overhearing the Annex staffers' side of the ongoing phone calls, the GRS contract operators became convinced that the agency wanted the 17 February militia to repel the attack entirely on its own, with no direct American involvement other than the DS agents already trapped inside the Compound.

Several GRS operators considered that wishful thinking at best, negligent leadership at worst. They suspected that they knew a motive for such idle hopes: If the operators' Quick Reaction Force remained at the Annex, the CIA wouldn't be forced to reveal or explain its presence in Benghazi. On the other hand, if American clandestine operators and contract security employees went into combat against radical Islamists, the battle would be guaranteed to attract global attention and massive scrutiny. Especially on September 11. During his previous trips to Benghazi, Tig had experienced multiple instances where Bob the base chief had told the operators to "stand down," even when Americans were potentially in danger, apparently to avoid the risk of exposing the CIA presence.

Another factor might also have contributed to the delay: The CIA chief seemed genuinely concerned that the Annex might come under fire. If all the GRS operators were at the Compound, the Americans left behind at the Annex would have little chance against a large force of attackers. The contract operators, routinely treated like excess baggage by many of the CIA case officers, were suddenly the most popular Americans in Benghazi.

▬▬▬

Another radio call came from the Compound. The warbling voice of a DS agent was so tightly controlled it sounded constricted. Several GRS operators sensed fear edging toward panic:

"If you guys do not get here, we're going to die!"

That was all it took. Roughly twenty minutes, possibly more, had elapsed since the operators had first mustered at Building C. They were long past ready to go. If a cavalry wanted to do any good, it needed to move out. With or without approval.

"We need to go," Tanto told the Team Leader. It wasn't a question. The four other operators felt the same. Tanto told the T.L.: "Get in the fucking car."

The Team Leader ended his phone call and got in.

They still lacked clearance or a firm idea what support they might get from the 17 February militia. And with the DS agents holed up, the operators had no inside intelligence on what they were about to face. But Rone, Jack, and Tig mounted up in the BMW at the head of the two-vehicle convoy. The GRS Team Leader got into the backseat of the Mercedes SUV, alongside Henry and behind Tanto and D.B.

Tanto put his hand on the gearshift and hailed Rone on the radio. "Is you up?" he asked, using slang to ask if the BMW team was ready.

Rone leaned out of the half-open driver's-side door. He glanced back at the BMW with a we-got-this smile. Rone stuck out his muscular arm, balled his hand into a fist, and flashed a thumbs-up. Tanto returned the thumbs-up.

Rone shifted the BMW into gear and Tanto did the same in the Mercedes.

As Tanto drove around the grassy triangular roundabout at the center of the Annex, heading for the gate, he tried to spot the little family of turtles that lived there. He wasn't sure why, but it was a small comfort, like saying goodbye to a family pet when leaving home for work.

During the delay, Rone had called Oz at dinner and told him to return to the Annex immediately.

"There's something going on over at the consulate," Rone said without elaborating. "Be very careful and don't go anywhere near there. There's a lot of activity going on."

Oz and the CIA case officer had already eaten dessert and thanked their hosts, but the case officer lingered over goodbye.

"We need to go," Oz told her in a low growl. He didn't mention Rone's call, not wanting to tip their hosts to what was happening. She continued making small talk. In a steelier tone he repeated himself: "We need to go. Right now."

She shot him a look.

Oz's patience ran out. "Get in the car. We're leaving."

Oz called a final goodbye to their hosts as he hustled the case officer into their vehicle, a small black Toyota SUV with dark-tinted windows. He explained what he knew as he turned on his two-way radio and drove toward the Annex. The case officer started firing questions, making suggestions, and giving Oz driving directions.

"You need to be quiet, sit back, and keep your eyes open," Oz told her. "You're in our world now. Let me do what I know how to do." She complied.

Oz already had in mind a circuitous route that would return them to the Annex while avoiding the diplomatic Compound. His route also would steer clear of potential roadblocks in an area where he knew that a black al-Qaeda-inspired flag regularly flew from an apartment building. He blended the Toyota into traffic, driving with a Goldilocks touch: neither too hot nor too cold, neither too fast nor too slow. The case officer wore a headscarf, but Oz was every inch the blond, blue-eyed, beef-fed Westerner. The last thing he wanted was to get stopped at a hostile checkpoint or an impromptu roadblock and try to explain why two Americans were out driving near 10:00 p.m. on a night when the American Compound was under attack.

Over the radio Oz could hear plaintive calls from the Compound. He wasn't sure whether the DS agent on the mic said they were "under fire" or buildings were "on fire." Either way, he knew it was bad. He focused his mind on the fight ahead.

Oz drove along the Third Ring Road to the Mediterranean coast, then turned onto the main coastal road heading toward the outskirts of Benghazi. He navigated back roads to cut through fallow farm fields; that brought them back onto the street they called Racetrack Road, southeast of the Annex. About twenty minutes after they left their hosts' home, Oz and the case officer turned onto Annex Road and pulled through the gate. The BMW and the Mercedes were already gone.

The situation at the Compound kept getting worse. After reentering the villa's safe-haven area through the bedroom window, DS agent Scott Wickland searched the smoke-filled hallway but still couldn't find Chris Stevens or Sean Smith. Wickland knew that the two men couldn't survive long in such conditions, but neither would he if he didn't get fresh air.

Fighting for breath, nearly overcome by the heat, Wickland returned to the bedroom and climbed out the window through the open grate. Out on the patio, he regained his bearings and caught his breath. He went back inside, only to be forced out again by the heat and smoke. Still Wickland saw no sign of the ambassador or the communications officer.

While Wickland continued his rescue effort, attackers swarmed the Cantina, where the two Tripoli-based DS agents were barricaded in a back room with a Blue Mountain guard. Another group of invaders approached the TOC, where Alec Henderson and Dave Ubben were locked inside the secure communications room.

As they watched the large video monitor, Henderson and Ubben saw multiple attackers trying to break through the building's reinforced wooden door to reach them. Ubben held his M4 assault rifle and Henderson gripped a shotgun, preparing for close-quarters combat. The intruders approached the TOC in ones, twos, and threes, testing the door and its steel drop bar with flying kicks. One crouched in a football stance some twenty-five feet away and rushed forward at full speed. He plowed his full body weight into the door but it held.

The intruders looted and sacked the Cantina, and tried unsuccessfully to break through the barricade. Back outside, with Ubben and Henderson watching them on the security monitors, the attackers hauled jerry cans to cars parked near the TOC. But the cans were almost empty, foiling the plan to set more vehicles ablaze.

Back at the villa, Wickland made several more unsuccessful attempts to find Stevens and Smith. Spent and unable to return inside for another try, Wickland knew that remaining on the patio would expose him to gunfire. If he blacked out, as he feared he would, he'd be easy prey. A few feet from the patio, a ladder leaning against the side of the villa led to the roof. Wickland climbed it and leapt over a nearly four-foot parapet around the edge of the villa's flat roof.

Wickland radioed his fellow DS agents Alec Henderson and David Ubben in the TOC for help, but his throat and lungs were so ravaged by smoke inhalation he could barely choke out the words. Finally his colleagues understood the awful message: Wickland couldn't find Ambassador Stevens or Sean Smith, and Villa C was in flames. After making the call, Wickland collapsed on the rooftop.

Until that moment, in the relative safety of the TOC, Henderson and Ubben had only a vague idea what was happening at the ambassador's residence some fifty yards away. The monitors in the TOC showed smoke but not fire at Villa C, and Henderson and Ubben had no line of sight from their location to the ruin that had been Château Christophe.

Before Wickland's call from the roof, all that the

DS agents in the TOC knew was that Wickland had ushered Ambassador Chris Stevens and communications specialist Sean Smith into the locked safe haven. To the best of their knowledge, the three men had remained there, waiting for help. Henderson and Ubben had no reason to presume otherwise. As a result, the DS agents' early radio and telephone calls to the Annex, Tripoli, Washington, and elsewhere didn't inform potential rescuers that the three Americans at Villa C had been separated in an inferno of fire and diesel smoke, and that they were in mortal peril. Whether that information would have shortened the delay in the operators' departure from the Annex can't be known.

Henderson and Ubben immediately spread word that Stevens and Smith were missing, and that Wickland was hurt and exhausted on the roof. With the surveillance monitor showing the attackers starting to peel away, Ubben decided to leave the TOC to see if he could help Wickland and find the missing Americans.

As the operators drove toward the Annex's front gate, D.B. turned his head to the backseat of the Mercedes and peppered the Team Leader with questions. They had moved out without a clear understanding of the arrangement, if any, with the 17 February militia. D.B. knew that the militia had a large base nearby, and depending on their route, the operators' vehicles might pass it on the way to the Compound. He didn't want any surprises or misunderstandings.

"How many guys are we linking up with from 17 February?" D.B. asked. "Do they know that we're coming? Do they know what they're looking for?"

The Team Leader wasn't sure, but he understood the potential hazards. He got on the radio to warn Rone and the men in the BMW: "Be advised, as we may be coming into friendly fire. We don't know if 17 Feb knows we're coming."

"Roger that," Rone said. "We're gonna take the back route."

They reached the front gate of the Annex, a guard raised the steel traffic bar, and Rone turned left onto the dark street they called "Annex Road." With Tanto following about fifty yards behind in the Mercedes, Rone drove a short distance and turned right onto an unnamed road. He soon reached an intersection and turned right again, onto Racetrack Road, driving past the dirt oval horse track as he headed west toward Gunfighter Road. There, he turned right a third time and headed north in the direction of the Compound.

Rone's intent was to minimize their time spent on the busy Fourth Ring Road. If they approached via the Fourth Ring, attackers at the Compound might see them coming from a long way off. Rone's route would take a minute or two longer, but the operators felt certain it was worth it, if they hoped to maintain any surprise for their counterattack. Rone had used the same back route, in reverse, when he and Tig drove past the then-quiet Compound after checking the location of the ambassador's scheduled meeting the next morning. The whole world had changed in the two hours since then.

Rone drove the BMW at just-above-normal speeds, with Tanto keeping pace at a distance in the Mercedes, so each could respond to the other in case of an attack. They bypassed several other cars without drawing unwanted attention. Rone and Tanto worried that if they raced at high speed toward the Compound, any 17 February militiamen they encountered might mistake them for enemy extremists looking to join in the attack. Or, overaggressive police from the already-suspect Libyan SSC might try to pull them over in the hope of extorting a bribe. Little talk passed among the seven men in the two luxury-vehicles-turned-troop-carriers as the Compound drew closer.

Jack considered Rone the best driver among them, so he felt comfortable with his old friend at the wheel of the lead car. Yet he worried that they'd be ambushed along the way. His eyes still weren't focusing properly, but he kept his head on a swivel, scanning back and forth, left and right, for hostile fighters or anything that looked out of place. Tig did the same in the backseat.

Jack mentally ticked off a list of possible hazards: roadside bombs, rocket-propelled grenades, snipers. Jack's conflicting emotions ran on a loop in his mind: *Fuck them. How dare they attack us?* On the other hand: *I'll probably never see my wife and kids again.* But that's the job: *We don't have a choice. There are Americans that need our help, and we would want somebody to do the same for us. We'll never be able to live with ourselves if we don't make the effort.* Finally he came full circle on his enemy: *Fuck them.*

Shortly after the two Quick Reaction Force vehicles left the Annex, a DS agent from the Compound came onto the radio again. This time he made no effort to disguise the panic in his voice. By then Scott Wickland had told his fellow DS agents Alec Henderson and David Ubben that Villa C was on fire and the ambassador and Sean Smith were missing. It wasn't clear whether the new radio call came from Wickland on the villa roof or Henderson and Ubben in the Compound TOC.

Jack heard the voice say: "We need help. They're lighting the building on fire . . . filling with smoke."

In the BMW, the three operators said nothing to one another about the agent's plea. They didn't need to. The operators knew that their job was to remain focused on the tasks and the dangers ahead. In Jack's decade-long career as a Navy SEAL, he typically had time to plan an operation meticulously, taking into account every imaginable obstacle. This was the opposite. They had to be ready for anything.

■■■

Traffic was light on Gunfighter Road, or as the locals called it, Shari' al-Andalus. Then the operators approached an intersection where they'd have to cross the Fourth Ring Road. Cars were stopped and pedestrians milled around. Rone and Tanto slowed the vehicles and passed cautiously through the intersection.

A few hundred yards ahead, at the pitch-dark corner of an east-west gravel road that led from Gunfighter to the front gate of the Special Mission Compound, Jack saw a group of Arab men with weapons, standing around several vehicles. Some of the men wore black ski masks. Jack spotted a Technical—a pickup truck with what he thought was a mounted heavy machine gun, called a "Dushka." From the backseat, Tig thought it might be an anti-aircraft gun. If Tig was right, it would be useless in this fight because it only pointed skyward. If Jack was right, a Dushka could blow them clear off the road.

From that distance, seeing the world through the green fog of night-vision goggles, the operators didn't know whether the Arab men were a platoon of friendly 17 February militiamen or part of the attack force, intent on blocking the road to the Compound. Either way, the operators had no choice. They'd keep moving forward.

Rone turned off the BMW's headlights and slowed to a crawl before the intersection. He stopped the car next to an eight-foot cement-block wall. Tanto pulled the Mercedes in behind. The Arab men made no hostile moves toward them, so the operators began to hope they were in fact 17 February allies.

As they parked, the operators heard an anxious DS agent in the Compound broadcast another beseeching radio message: "You need to hurry up. The buildings are on fire." Then he repeated the earlier, desperate plea: "If you don't get here soon, we're all going to die!"

Rone warned the other operators in the BMW to get out slowly, so they wouldn't spook potentially friendly militiamen into thinking they were bad guys.

From the back of the Mercedes, the GRS Team Leader said he believed the intersection was supposed to be their meeting point with 17 February militiamen. When the Arab men remained at ease, the operators prepared to leave their vehicles. Tanto turned to the translator. "Henry, get this stuff coordinated and find out who the commander is. We need to get moving. We're way behind."

Henry and the GRS Team Leader warily approached the men in the intersection, hunched forward, weapons in hand but angled downward. Rone, Jack, Tig, Tanto, and D.B. remained on alert by the vehicles, weapons ready.

Suddenly gunshots rang out close by, and everyone snapped to attention. The sound crackled and echoed off the roadside walls and buildings, making it difficult to tell their origin. The shots came in sporadic and random bursts, one, two, three at a time.

As they tucked close to the walls or inside the vehicles, it occurred to several operators that if anyone got panicky about taking fire, a shootout could easily erupt among the men assembled at the intersection. A gunfight on Gunfighter Road. The operators weren't worried about each other, but they still weren't sure what to make of the Arab men with whom they apparently were supposed to join forces. Jack imagined the worst possibility: a deadly friendly-fire incident.

When he first heard the shots, Jack thought someone was firing directly at them from farther north up Gunfighter Road. Then he realized that the shots were coming from the direction of the Compound, some four hundred yards away to the east. Someone was shooting toward the intersection where the Arab men stood. Rounds from that direction couldn't reach the operators, who remained just south of the intersection, protected by the wall and out of the line of fire.

In the darkness and the confusion, with rounds flying and cars passing and people moving in all directions, Jack wondered if some of the shots came from snipers in the three- and four-story buildings near the intersection. Crouching inside the BMW, the passenger door flung open, he held his assault rifle down between his legs, ready to raise it and return fire.

Henry and the Team Leader were relieved to learn the Arab men at the intersection were, in fact, 17 February militiamen, and that their commander spoke passable English. The commander confirmed that he and his men would help the Americans to regain control of the Compound. Or at least try.

Still, Tanto didn't like the scene. He'd already

expressed his doubts about the 17 February Martyrs Brigade to his fellow operators, suspecting that the militia was neither adequately trained nor wholly genuine in its claimed friendship with the Americans. Watching the militiamen in action, he judged them undisciplined and disorganized, as they spread out and stood around in no apparent order or military bearing. Several seemed mainly interested in controlling traffic between Gunfighter Road and the Fourth Ring Road. Yet occasionally cars still cruised by, their occupants staring at the armor-wearing, gun-toting, goggle-eyed, helmet-topped Americans in the street.

Incredulous, Tanto turned to D.B.: "We were waiting for *these* guys?"

The only militiaman who impressed Tanto was a black African fighter in a ski mask. As sporadic incoming gunfire continued, the militiaman dropped prone onto the ground and fired a Kalashnikov light machine gun, called a PKM, answering the incoming gunfire by firing east toward the Compound. As far as Tanto was concerned, the masked man's comrades didn't seem to know what to do.

Tig heard the militia commander say that he and his men had tried to drive down the road to the Compound but had turned back when they came under fire. The Team Leader, Rone, and the commander discussed a new approach.

As the plan took shape, Tanto and D.B. moved cautiously from their car toward the intersection. They looked down the gravel road. "It's a fucking fatal funnel," Tanto said, imagining how exposed they'd be to enemy fire if they tried walking or driving on the road toward the Compound. They could see swirling black smoke and orange firelight rising from their destination. The sky above buildings close to the Compound seemed to glow amber. Tanto briefly tilted his head back farther and saw pinpoints of starlight, radiating an eerie green in his night-vision goggles. When they wore the goggles, the operators had no peripheral vision and little depth perception, making it seem as though they were looking at the world through narrow cardboard tubes with green cellophane on the ends.

Several minutes after they arrived in the intersection, as strategy talks continued, D.B. turned to Tanto.

"Hey Tanto, let's get high."

"Roger that. I'll try."

D.B. was thinking like the Marine sniper he'd trained to be. He'd noticed a four- or five-story building on the other side of the eight-foot wall where they'd parked for cover. If they could reach an upper floor, they might be able to establish a vantage point to see who was firing at them and what was happening inside the Compound. They might even be able to pick off the enemy shooters.

First, though, they'd have to get over that eight-foot wall. A thought crossed Tanto's mind: *Jesus Christ, I'm getting too old for this.* He'd left the Annex still in his cargo shorts, and he knew that he'd be scraping skin the whole way over the wall.

Tanto approached the Team Leader and the 17 February commander.

"Me and D.B. are going on foot," Tanto said. "We can't wait any longer."

The Team Leader gave them the go-ahead, and Tanto went to Ronc. "Hey buddy, we're going. I'll maintain contact, let you know when I think it's clear to go down that road."

Tanto slung his assault rifle over his left shoulder, grabbed his light machine gun, and draped a bandolier of ammunition across his chest. He threw his go-bag over his right shoulder. He filled his pockets with magazines. As he finished jocking up, Tanto caught sight of two young 17 February militiamen with AK-47s, watching him.

"Hey, you two, come with us." The militiamen nodded their heads in agreement. Tanto and D.B. led them toward the wall.

Locked inside the Compound TOC, DS agent Alec Henderson continued to communicate with the Annex, the embassy in Tripoli, and the State Department in Washington. He spread word that Scott Wickland was suffering from severe smoke inhalation on the roof of Villa C, and that Chris Stevens and Sean Smith remained missing. He described the fires and the attackers roaming the Compound.

DS agent David Ubben knew that they needed only one agent in the TOC to maintain communications. From what he and Henderson could see on the monitor, it looked as though the attackers had moved away from the TOC and the Cantina after unsuccessfully trying to reach the Americans inside both. If Ubben could get to the two Tripoli DS agents still barricaded in the Cantina with a local guard, maybe they could team up and find the lost men. He described his plan to the agents in the Cantina via radio.

In full combat gear, weapon in hand, Ubben cracked open the door to the TOC and threw a smoke grenade into the brick walkway separating the TOC from the Cantina. Henderson provided cover as Ubben prepared to leave. Using the white smoke to conceal his movements, Ubben ran across the walkway and inside the looted Cantina. Making his way through the ransacked building, Ubben found the room where the two Tripoli DS agents were waiting with the Blue Mountain guard. They removed the barricade that had kept out the attackers, and the two Tripoli DS agents joined Ubben in the effort to reach Villa C. They told the local guard to stay hidden in the Cantina.

Unsure where the attackers might be, going on foot seemed like a death wish. Outside the TOC was an armored vehicle that the attackers had failed to burn when they ran out of diesel. After retrieving the keys from inside the TOC, Ubben and the two Tripoli-based agents leapt in and drove the short way to the villa. They ran to the patio where Wickland had come through the open bedroom window. The three DS agents climbed the ladder up to the roof and found Wickland vomiting from severe smoke inhalation and on the brink of unconsciousness.

Desperate to find Stevens and Smith, Ubben and the two Tripoli-based agents scrambled back down. Noxious diesel smoke still filled the safe haven. Visibility remained poor. Two of the agents set up a defensive perimeter to guard the window, while the third went inside, crawling across the floor to search for the ambassador and the communications expert. He could only remain inside briefly before the lack of air drove him back to the window.

Ubben and the two other DS agents rotated between the grim, strenuous search duty and manning the defensive perimeter. Each time one man came out of the villa breathless and empty-handed, a new man went in.

SIX

Gunfighter Road

———

Upon driving into the Annex, Oz headed directly for Building C. There he found Bob the base chief and several other agency staffers standing outside, talking on their cell phones. Oz's dinner companion rushed from the Toyota and went inside Building C to find out what was happening. Other Annex staffers roamed the walled property, moving at will from building to building. Some grabbed personal belongings from their living quarters. To Oz, several Annex residents seemed caught up in the commotion, unsure where to go or what to do.

This is gonna be like herding cats, Oz thought.

His body armor and kit were in his room, but there wasn't yet time for that. Still in the brown pants and long-sleeved collared shirt he'd worn to dinner, Oz strode directly to Bob and swamped him with questions. "What's the latest? Did the guys take enough weapons? Where, exactly, is everyone who's still here?"

Bob hurriedly brought Oz up to speed then returned to his phone calls. Oz didn't object, understanding that Bob needed to help coordinate the response, deal with the 17 February militia, and update Washington and Tripoli on the ongoing attack.

As he looked around the Annex, an uneasy feeling settled in Oz's stomach. From the way people were milling around, it seemed as though it hadn't occurred to them that the Compound might not be the only target for violent anti-American extremists. Defenses needed to be organized and hardened immediately at the Annex. That job fell to him as the only GRS operator not en route to the Compound.

Even as Oz swept into action, he tamped down a gnawing sense of frustration and disappointment that had begun during the drive back from dinner. Years earlier, his wife had given him a T-shirt with a question on the front: "Do you know the difference between you and me?" The answer was on the back: "You're running away from fire and I'm running toward it." Oz wore the shirt proudly and lived by its message. Now, though, as the only operator not on the Compound rescue squad, he felt sidelined. *I want to be taking the fight to them, instead of sitting here waiting for them to come to us,* he thought. *I don't want to be blocking and tackling. I want to be running the football to the end zone.*

Oz knew he couldn't dwell on those thoughts, so he occupied his mind and devoted his energy to devising an improvised defensive plan using the limited assets and personnel at hand. Although all the CIA case officers at the Annex had some training and familiarity with weapons, Oz considered most of them ill-equipped for combat. In other words, non-shooters. He took a mental roll call and concluded that his core team consisted of six fighters with varying degrees of military experience and training, three Americans and three Libyans.

The Americans were himself, the head of Annex security, and a case officer who'd had combat experience in Afghanistan. The three Libyans were the Annex guards, all of them friends or family members of the property's landlord, who insisted that they be hired when the Americans rented the Annex. Although Oz would rely on the five men, he considered protecting everyone at the Annex to be his responsibility alone.

Oz directed the remaining Americans at the Annex to congregate in Building C. There, the reinforced Sensitive Compartmented Information Facility could serve as their last refuge if the Annex were overrun. He posted an Annex support staffer outside Building C with an assault rifle and told him to make sure no more than one person went to another building at a time, and only if absolutely necessary. That way Oz wouldn't have to round up more than one straggler in the event of an emergency. Oz knew that cell phone service was spotty inside Building C, so he told the staffer to allow anyone making official calls to loiter outside as long as they stayed close.

When Bob the Annex chief took a brief pause between phone calls, Oz asked him to help enforce the rule about keeping everyone congregated in or around Building C. "My biggest concern is accountability," Oz told him. "I need to know where everybody's at, at all times." Bob agreed, and with the base chief's blessing the gun-wielding staffer took his place as the door monitor.

Oz hurried across the driveway to Building B, ducking into his bedroom to collect his kit. Without changing clothes, he pulled on his body armor, his helmet, and his night-vision goggles. Oz grabbed his assault rifle and his go-bag, which contained a dozen extra magazines, two tourniquets, and other medical gear. Determined not to run out of ammo, he swept up a half-dozen spare mags and shoved them in his rear and side pockets as he ran back outside.

Carrying his own assault rifle, the case officer with military experience in Afghanistan spotted Oz and asked how he could help. Oz directed him to a ladder at the northeast corner of Building C. The ladder led to a flat cement roof with a three-and-a-half-foot-high cinder-block parapet that could be used as cover. In the months previous, the operators had designed an Annex defense plan under which they'd use the Building C rooftop as their primary fighting position. On the roof were sealed green metal cans with thousands of rounds of ammunition, including linked rounds for a belt-fed machine gun, magazines for assault rifles, and grenades that resembled oversize salt shakers, to be used with a grenade launcher. The plan called for the weapons to be brought up when the fight began, to keep them from getting gummed up with sand and dust.

Oz climbed to the roof with the military-trained case officer for a look around. To the northwest, in the direction of the Compound, he saw bright flashes from tracer rounds streaking across the night sky. Nothing seemed out of the ordinary in the immediate vicinity of the Annex. He scanned the surrounding area through his night-vision goggles but couldn't see anyone trying to sneak up on them from the desolate area to the north and east they called Zombieland. Oz told the case officer to remain atop the roof on sentry duty and let him know by radio if he heard or saw anything unusual. Oz climbed down and continued his rounds.

He positioned the Annex security leader at the front gate, giving him leeway to move back and forth between there and Building C, some sixty yards away. Oz felt confident in the man's judgment and knew that he'd make the right decisions about where to be. The priority, they both knew, was to protect the people in Building C. If attackers breached the Annex walls and came gunning for them, they needed shooters inside the building, a position of relative strength if invaders tried to enter through doors, one or two at a time.

With the case officer and the security leader in place, Oz went to work arranging his outer line of defense: the three Libyan guards. Months earlier, the operators had built several steel platforms close to the Annex walls to use as fighting positions if they came under attack. The floors of the rusty, orange brown platforms were high enough to enable the operators or other Annex defenders to shoot over the walls. The platforms, which the operators called "towers," were large enough for two fighters to move and crouch comfortably without knocking each other off.

Oz positioned one of the Libyan guards on a tower near the front gate. He put one on a tower to the rear left of Building C. Oz placed the third on the tower at the southeast corner of the property. Oz moved from one to the next, to be sure the guards had enough ammo and were prepared to fight. At the very least, he hoped they'd hold their positions and warn him about an attack.

As Oz walked around inside the Annex, he heard the radio traffic between his operator teammates and the DS agents inside the Compound. He was too busy to focus on everything they said, but he could tell that it didn't sound good. After positioning the men on the towers, Oz returned to Building C, still hoping that the local Libyan guards were brave and loyal enough not to flee at the first sign of trouble. He had the same thought about the 17 February militiamen who were supposed to support his friends at the Compound.

As Oz organized the Annex defenses, a supervisor of the three Libyan guards came to the front gate asking to speak with Bob. Annex staff members were familiar with the man, so Oz allowed him inside carrying his pistol. The guard supervisor told Oz that he'd come to the Annex to urge the CIA base chief to evacuate immediately.

"You guys got to go," the supervisor told Oz. "It's not safe for you here."

Oz took him to Building C to see Bob. Oz returned to his duties while the guard supervisor and the base chief spoke outside, but Oz already knew the outcome. Six operators and a translator from the Annex were en route to a burning, over-run US diplomatic Compound where an ambassador and six other Americans were in mortal danger. If some or all of those fourteen Americans made it out alive, they'd need a place to take refuge. The men and women at the Annex weren't going anywhere.

━━━

Near the southeast corner of the intersection of Gunfighter Road and the gravel street leading to the Compound, Tanto, D.B., and the two young 17 February militiamen approached the wall they intended to climb. With any luck, it would lead them to a tall building they could use as a sniper roost and reconnaissance tower. Tanto remained apprehensive about the 17 February fighters, but he sensed that these two were trustworthy.

As the sniper/observation team moved out, Rone, Jack, and Tig left the BMW and headed toward the intersection. Cement-block walls surrounded most of the homes and other properties in the area, so the operators used the walls as cover. They moved cautiously north up Gunfighter in the "low ready" position, rifle butts at their shoulders, barrels pointed safely downward. Index fingers stayed close to the triggers but not on them. Thumbs caressed the safety switches, ready to make the weapons live.

Rone approached the driver's side of the Technical truck with the mounted gun, taking cover behind the engine block. Jack stationed himself on the southeast corner of the intersection. Ambient light from homes and the occasional flickering streetlight made his night-vision goggles unnecessary for the moment. Jack poked his head around the corner to peer toward the front gate of the Compound, four hundred yards down the gravel street. He got his first look at some of the attackers who'd stormed the Compound and now were shooting in his direction. He saw eight or nine Arab men, at least some with weapons visible.

Sometimes the attackers fired at the operators and the 17 February militiamen from behind the concrete Jersey barriers outside the Compound gate. Other times they milled around in the open. They were too far away for Jack to identify them. All he could see were shadowy figures moving near the gate.

Suddenly Jack heard loud gunfire coming from close by. One of the militiamen fired several large-caliber rounds from the Technical in the direction of the Compound. The operators could feel the shock waves of the shots reverberating in their chests.

Rone moved around the truck and Jack leaned

around the corner to join in the shooting. After firing several rounds, they ducked back behind cover. Three 17 February militiamen who occupied the northeast corner of Gunfighter Road and the gravel street returned the attackers' fire, as well. The attackers answered with pops of sporadic gunfire.

As Tig moved to join in, a 17 February militiaman on the west side of Gunfighter Road fired two rocket-propelled grenades toward the men outside the Compound gate. The grenade-firing militiaman was positioned about twenty yards behind Tig, who heard the alarming sound of shells whizzing over his head. The grenades didn't faze the attackers, who kept firing.

Tig answered with added firepower. He'd brought a grenade launcher of his own, and he fired three high-explosive, dual-purpose cartridges, capable of killing anyone within a five-yard radius and wounding anyone within fifteen yards. Each round launched with a resounding *fwump*, followed by a momentary silence punctuated by a powerful *coc-coom* explosion. The launcher had a range of about 350 yards, but Tig purposely lobbed the grenades short, to put the explosives well in front of the attackers and to avoid hitting the Compound gate. He worried that a direct hit on the gate would slow the operators, exposing them to fire, when it came time for them to move through it to reach the Compound.

The operators couldn't see if Tig's grenades injured or killed the men outside the Compound, but there was no doubt that the powerful rounds cleared them out. The gunfire from the attackers toward Gunfighter Road stopped. When the operators looked down the street after Tig's third shot, no one stood between them and the main gate. It was time for the operators to move in.

First, Tig rushed back toward the car, to get his assault rifle, a belt-fed machine gun, and two two-hundred-round drums of ammunition. With more than enough to carry, he left his go-bag in the BMW. As Tig collected his gear, he heard a DS agent repeat his radio plea: "We're going to die if you don't get here!" the agent said, choking out the words and struggling to breathe.

After the firefight, the GRS Team Leader and Henry the translator resumed talking with the 17 February commander. The discussions focused on coordination of the combined forces and the possibility that the militia would provide heavy weapons for a counterassault, a prospect that seemed to be going nowhere.

Tig listened as the Team Leader and Henry the translator discussed their conversation with the militia commander. The commander had told them that he didn't want to move his troops toward the Compound gate. Instead, he told the T.L., he'd make a phone call to the attackers to negotiate for the release of the trapped Americans. Tig wondered how the militia commander knew whom to call and how he was on good enough terms with someone connected to the attackers to think he could work out a deal.

One positive development of the talks was that the 17 February militiamen finally appeared ready to set up roadblocks at all intersections leading to the Compound, to prevent the attackers from calling in reinforcements and overwhelming the fourteen Americans—seven from the Compound and seven from the Annex's Quick Reaction Force—who'd be there.

With no sign that the militia would move beyond the perimeter of the battle, Tig, Rone, and Jack were done waiting. "Fuck it," Tig said. "We're going."

Rone called Tanto by radio: "Hey guys, we're going to start moving on foot. What are you seeing, Tanto?"

Tanto, D.B., and the two militiamen had yet to reach high ground, so Tanto radioed back: "I think you're fine. I'm not hearing much fire coming down that road anymore. The consulate is definitely on fire, it's in blazes. Just do your thing. Shoot, move, and communicate, and you'll be good."

"Roger that."

Tig radioed the Annex to let Bob and the others there know that they were moving out.

———

Leaning forward, guns up, Rone, Jack, and Tig rounded the corner onto the potholed, two-lane gravel street leading to the Compound. They hugged the wall on the south side, ducking in and out of cutouts that led to entranceways or marked the separation between properties. Alternating the lead position, watching each other's backs, and exposing themselves as little as possible, Rone, Tig, and Jack bobbed in and out of two construction sites, moving steadily through the dark toward the Compound. Their muscles tensed as they scanned from side to side. With each step, they expected to encounter the enemy.

Jack's contact lenses had finally cleared enough for him to see straight, but in the confusion of the firefight he momentarily lost his bearings. He called to Tig: "Is the gate on the left or the right?" Tig told him it was on the right, and Jack reoriented himself. Tig had his own vision problems, caused by the weather. The temperature had reached 84 degrees Fahrenheit during the day, and the night was only a dozen or so degrees cooler. As Tig's body overheated from exertion, his goggles fogged so much he found them useless and lifted them to his helmet.

About 150 yards down the street, the three operators came across an unarmed man in his forties talking on a cell phone. Wearing long pants and a polo shirt, the man seemed to have wandered out of one of the homes to see what was happening, as though a parade was passing by.

"Get down! Get down!" the operators shouted.

The man pointed to his phone and kept talking. The operators concluded that he might be a threat to himself, but not to them. Shaking their heads and shooting him dirty looks, they kept moving.

Jack and Tig heard voices speaking Arabic in

clipped, urgent tones. They glanced to their left and saw movement on the opposite side of the street, fifteen or twenty yards behind them.

Fuck, Jack thought. *Who the hell are THESE guys?*

With a quick look, he realized that the three men posed no danger. To the contrary, they were the operators' self-appointed backup. The men were the militiamen who'd returned fire at attackers from the northeast corner of the intersection. Now they were shadowing the operators' movements on the opposite side of the street. Jack and Tig noticed that the militiamen learned from the Americans as they went, slipping in and out of construction sites and entranceways as they sought cover moving east.

Jack didn't know how useful the trio would be, but at least they were there. After all the uncertainty, at least five members of the 17 February Martyrs Brigade had fulfilled their promise to support the American Quick Reaction Force: three on the gravel road and two searching for a sniper location with Tanto and D.B.

Ahead the three operators saw a large mound of dirt outside a construction site, about one hundred yards from the Compound gate. Jack and Tig looked to the peak, more than fifteen feet high, and had the same thought: vantage point.

Having a sniper in position from the street as they moved into the Compound would provide them with cover fire and a tactical advantage. They hoped that the dirt pile was firm, but as soon as

Jack and Tig began to climb, they felt like they were scaling a sand dune. Their legs sank to their knees as they trudged higher. Each man carried forty or more pounds of weapons, ammo, body armor, and equipment, and the weight seemed to grow with every step.

"Son of a bitch," Tig said, his breaths growing labored.

Jack felt winded, too, and he assumed that he was worse off than his partner. He knew that Tig's workouts included long runs around the Annex, so Jack blamed himself for focusing on his upper body strength and neglecting his lower limbs.

"Man," Jack said halfway up, sweating buckets and huffing for breath. "I need to do more legs."

But Tig felt equally smoked. His long runs had left his leg muscles sore.

"Man," he panted, "I should be running a lot *less*!"

Both coughed out a laugh.

As they reached the top, Jack and Tig discovered that they weren't high enough to see inside the Compound walls. They'd climbed the mound for nothing. Doubling their frustration, as they slid down, the ammo drum on Tig's belt-fed machine gun fell off. They had no time to reattach it, so Tig went "Rambo-style." He broke off more than a hundred rounds from the lost drum and split them in two, leaving half dangling from the gun and draping the other half over his shoulder.

Tig knew that their goal was to save lives in the Compound, but that wasn't foremost on his mind as he moved closer to their destination. His first thought was survival. With each footfall, his eyes darting left and right, he clutched his machine gun tighter. The former Marine replayed a single existential thought: *Is somebody going to engage us?*

━━━

While Tig and Jack scaled the dirt mound, Rone had kept moving forward toward the gate. He hunched down behind one of the concrete traffic barriers to the right of the Compound entrance, waiting for his partners. Rone radioed Tanto and D.B. to say they'd reached the gate and were getting ready to move in.

First to join Rone were the three militiamen, who took cover positions nearby at the barriers. Before them stood a concrete archway some twenty feet wide and fifteen feet high, painted a friendly shade of pale yellow. Deep inside the archway were the Compound's heavy gates, their wrought-iron balusters backed by solid steel plates, to prevent anyone from ramming them open, climbing over, or shooting through. Normally closed except when vehicles entered or exited, the gates were thrown wide open. Someone had taken the time to latch the bottom of the gates to fixed anchors in the driveway, to keep them from swinging closed. Also open was the adjacent steel pedestrian gate.

When Jack reached the Jersey barriers, he noticed that one of the militiamen crouching nearby had not only an AK-47 but also a rocket-propelled grenade launcher strapped across his back. Jack momentarily worried that the man might be a threat to Rone, so Jack watched him, gun up, ready to shoot if the militiaman aimed his gun in Rone's direction. The militiaman showed no sign of being a threat, so Jack concluded that he must be one of the good guys. Jack scuttled forward, dropped in, and kneeled to the man's left. Six inches separated their shoulders as they looked toward the gate.

A few yards away, Tig continued to struggle with the ammunition for his belt-fed machine gun. He fought to get his second drum out of an improvised canvas pouch. Tig wanted the drum clipped securely in place on the weapon, so he wouldn't run out of rounds when the shooting started. He radioed the Annex: "We're moving onto the Compound."

Rone took Tig's radio call as a signal. Without warning his companions, he sprang to his feet and

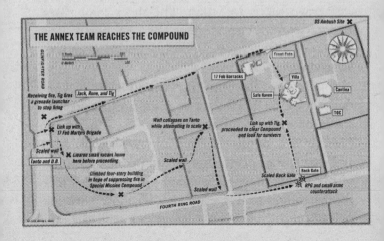

quick-stepped around the concrete barrier. Rone rounded a corner of low hedges and ran headlong through the gate into the Compound, his assault rifle pointing the way forward.

Jack had expected that they'd make eye contact or otherwise communicate before moving. But when he saw Rone move, his training kicked into gear. A bedrock rule among SEALs and other Special Operations fighters is that no one goes in alone, ever, regardless of whether they're entering a room or an open space. Rone had been trained the same way, so Jack knew that when he led the charge, Rone felt confident that Jack and Tig would have his back.

Jack popped up, stepped around the barrier, and sprinted into the Compound.

Tig was wrestling with his weapon when Rone and Jack moved. He was on his feet seconds later, but that brief gap was just enough time for someone to begin shooting at him from farther east down the gravel road. The shots came from an intersection with a street the operators called Adidas Road because a sporting goods store was located there.

Tig dropped flat onto the ground behind a barrier as a round zipped above his head. He pressed the talk button on his radio: "Hey base, I'm taking fire, but I'm not hit!" Pinned down, Tig looked up and saw flashes of gunfire passing over him. One of the 17 February militiamen jumped to his feet about ten feet to Tig's left. He let loose with his AK-47 on full automatic, firing in bursts at a rate of six hundred rounds per minute. His magazine spent, the militiaman dropped down to reload. Tig pulled his night-vision goggles over his eyes and stepped into the fight. He brought up his fully loaded machine gun, resting it atop the barrier.

As Tig prepared to fire, an unarmed man rushed toward him, hands raised, from the darkened street.

"Friendly! Friendly! 17 February!"

Still ready to blast away, Tig caught the eye of the militiaman reloading his AK-47.

"Friendly!" the unarmed man yelled again. "17 February!"

Tig and the armed militiaman exchanged quizzical looks that Tig translated into universal soldier language: *Who the fuck is this nut?*

Tig exhaled. Whoever had been firing at them from up the street had run off, or was dead or wounded from the AK-47 barrage. Either way, the incoming gunfire had stopped. Tig pointed two fingers at his eyes, pantomiming to the armed militiaman to keep watch on the new arrival. The militiaman nodded.

Tig rose. His machine gun up and ready, he sprinted into the Compound to catch up with Rone and Jack.

D.B. took the lead as the sniper/observation team approached the eight-foot wall near the corner of Gunfighter Road and the gravel road leading to the Compound. He climbed over, then dropped to one knee, to provide cover for the two 17 February militiamen and finally Tanto as they joined him on the other side.

Ahead was the tall building they hoped to use as their perch. But before they moved that way, they wanted to be sure no one was waiting to ambush them. Next door to their chosen building was a cinder-block house under construction. Tanto provided cover while D.B. and the two militiamen made sure it was empty.

When the trio returned, the squad moved toward the tall building. But as they got closer, Tanto and D.B. realized that even if they reached the top, they'd be too far from the Compound to see much. They changed plans and kept going, one taking a knee as the others reached cover, then moving again, using the property walls as shields as they hopscotched steadily from one lot to the next. Each time they reached a corner they couldn't see beyond, Tanto or D.B. used a tactical technique called "slicing the pie" or "pieing the corner." The lead man approached the corner close to the wall. A few feet from the corner, he took small, sideways steps away from the wall with his gun up and ready. With each outward step he cleared a "slice" of the dark area on the far side of the corner, allowing him incrementally to determine that no one was there, without exposing himself all at once.

As Tanto held one corner, he heard the radio call from Rone asking whether it looked safe for the operators to move up the gravel road. After telling Rone that he couldn't see but didn't hear any gunfire, Tanto moved ahead to the next corner.

They made their way from one lot to the next, studying the shadows and the unlit passageways to see if anyone was hiding. Like their fellow operators on the street, they expected gunfire in their direction at every moment. The two operators and their militiamen shadows tried to remain quiet and unobserved, not knowing whether a large force of attackers was waiting to engage them at the next lot or on the far side of the Compound. Yet as they balanced moving fast against remaining safe, they found themselves cheating toward speed because they knew Americans were in danger inside the Compound.

As they led their team down the block, Tanto and D.B. realized that most of the buildings were single-story homes that wouldn't do them any good as sniper/observation towers. But through their goggles they saw a building under construction a hundred yards ahead that might work.

"Let's get on top of that and see what we can see," D.B. said.

They moved into the tall, unlit building with care, clearing each floor and the stairwells as they went. Their breathing grew heavier. Sweat soaked the operators' shirts under their body armor. The machine gun in Tanto's arms and the assault rifle slung over his back seemed to be gaining weight. He went up the stairs first, climbing carefully toward the unfinished fourth floor.

At the top, Tanto stepped out and saw a bird's-eye view at once spectacular and horrifying. Flames engulfed the 17 February barracks near the Compound's front gate. The main villa was ablaze, with orange sparks rising into the inky Mediterranean sky. Black smoke curled and swirled from the buildings, cloaking the silvery stars above. Under different circumstances Tanto might have called it strangely beautiful. He shifted his attention from the view to his radio. Realizing that he hadn't heard any recent calls from the Compound, Tanto wondered if the Americans there were still alive.

The fourth-floor view was arresting but frustrating. A row of trees obscured any movement on the Compound grounds, making it impossible for them to establish a sniper or reconnaissance position. D.B. reached the top floor and stood alongside Tanto.

"This is worthless," he said.

They headed back down, rejoined the 17 February militiamen, and kept moving. The four-man squad jackrabbited across an open field of dirt and weeds, climbed over a wall, then repeated the process with another barren field and another wall. Their travels took them to yet another wall, this one running perpendicular to the wall that enclosed the west side of the Compound. D.B. threw over the go-bag containing his medical kit, extra ammunition, and his GPS unit, intending to climb after it.

Tig's low voice came over the radio: "We're moving onto the Compound."

"Roger that," Tanto replied in a whisper. "We still haven't gotten there. We're trying to meet you there."

D.B. and Tanto climbed the wall perpendicular to the Compound. When they reached the top, they realized that they still couldn't see inside the grounds. That meant there was no point for them to drop over to the other side. A better plan, they agreed, would be to work their way around to the south side of the Compound and see if they could enter through the rear B1 gate, which opened out to the Fourth Ring Road. The burning villa was toward the front of the Compound. By approaching from the rear, Tanto, D.B., and the militiamen conceivably could ambush any attackers driven to the back gate by Rone, Jack, and Tig.

As Tanto started to climb down, part of the wall collapsed beneath him. He slammed to the ground, scraping and badly bruising his left leg. Blood oozed from cuts and scrapes on his left arm.

D.B. jumped down from the wall. He and one of the 17 February militiamen rushed over.

"Damn," D.B. said. "You OK?"

"Yeah," Tanto said. His leg hurt but nothing was broken. "I'm fine. We gotta go."

D.B. looked back at the wall. "Oh shit, my bag."

They'd already suffered too many delays, first at the Annex and now as they tried to reach the Compound. The radios were silent. That couldn't mean good news. Climbing over a half-crumpled wall to search for D.B.'s bag in the dark would cost more time, time that might mean lives.

"Dude," Tanto said, "fuck it. I got extra mags." D.B. knew he was right.

They rushed toward the Fourth Ring Road. As they ran side by side, huffing and puffing, D.B. caught Tanto's eye and smiled. "This sucks," D.B. said. Too winded to answer, Tanto returned the grin.

After clearing another wall, they found themselves near a grocery store about fifty yards from the Compound's back gate. A dozen or so bystanders stood outside the store, looking toward the fires inside the Compound. Tanto told their two 17 February companions to watch the crowd as he and D.B. went to the gate.

As they moved away from the store, Tanto and D.B. came face-to-face with a 17 February commander talking on a telephone in Arabic. It wasn't clear how the militia leader had arrived at their location, but Tanto thought the two militiamen they'd brought with them must have called him on their radios.

"Hey dude," Tanto said, pointing toward the grocery store onlookers. "Are those your guys? Are they friendly?"

"No, they aren't," the commander said in English.

"So, make sure they don't shoot at us," Tanto said. "If they do, kill them."

The militia commander nodded as he continued talking on the phone.

As Tanto headed toward the gate, he mumbled under his breath to D.B.: "Man, I wish I could understand Arabic better. I got the gut feeling he's talking to the bad guys, telling them that we're coming in."

━━━

More than forty minutes had elapsed since DS agent Alec Henderson pressed the duck-and-cover alarm at the sight and sounds of armed attackers pouring onto the Compound.

During that time, an alert about the ongoing attack had gone out from the State Department's Diplomatic Security Command Center, informing the White House Situation Room, the Office of the Director of National Intelligence, and the FBI, according to an official Defense Department timeline. In response to that alert, at 10:32 p.m. Benghazi time, or 4:32 p.m. in Washington, the National Military Command Center at the Pentagon notified the Office of the Secretary of Defense. Word quickly reached Defense Secretary Leon Panetta and General Martin Dempsey, chairman of the Joint Chiefs of Staff.

Panetta and Dempsey had a previously scheduled meeting with President Obama within the half hour, at 5:00 p.m. Washington time, or 11:00 p.m. Benghazi time. There, Panetta testified later, they discussed potential responses. Panetta told a congressional committee that Obama ordered the Defense Department to respond with "all available DOD assets." Panetta testified that he didn't speak directly with the president again on September 11.

Meanwhile, according to a letter the White House sent to Republicans on the Senate Armed Services Committee, at Obama's request Secretary of State Hillary Clinton called Libyan President Mohamed Magariaf "to coordinate additional support to protect Americans in Libya and access to Libyan territory." Magariaf pledged "full cooperation," the letter said.

As military options remained under discussion, the unarmed US surveillance drone neared Libyan airspace over Benghazi, to provide live video images of the burning Compound. But at 10:30 p.m. Benghazi time, the drone remained more than a half hour away. As the GRS operators moved inside the Compound walls, they did so blind.

As the attack continued, Panetta later testified to Congress, two Marine security platoons stationed in Spain were ordered to prepare for deployment, one to Benghazi and the other to Tripoli. A Special Operations force in the midst of a training exercise in central Europe was ordered to prepare to deploy to a staging base in southern Europe. A US-based Special Operations team was told to get ready to travel to the same staging base.

But in the end, none of them was sent to Benghazi.

Panetta said consideration also was given to sending armed aircraft, along with refueling tankers and other support. But, he added, it would have taken at least nine hours for them to get there. Panetta described it as "a problem of distance and time." Embassy officials in Tripoli took part in those discussions. Gregory Hicks, the embassy's deputy chief, testified to Congress that the embassy's defense attaché talked with officials at AFRICOM and the Joint Chiefs of Staff. Hicks said he asked the defense attaché: "Is anything coming? Will they be sending us any help? Is there something out there?" Hicks testified that he was told that the nearest help was at the US air base in Aviano, Italy, where Air Force fighter planes were two to three hours away. But no tankers were available for them to refuel, so hours longer would pass before any fighters could take off.

"And I said, 'Thank you very much,'" Hicks testified, "and we went on with our work." In the end, no American warplanes were sent to Benghazi.

The nearest and most likely help from American ground forces remained the seven-man, Tripoli-based GRS team, which included two active-duty Delta Force operators, former SEAL Glen "Bub" Doherty, and a linguist who'd act as translator.

As minutes passed and the Compound burned, talk of response options and available assets continued in Washington, Tripoli, at AFRICOM headquarters in Stuttgart, Germany, and elsewhere. Later in the night, a global conference call would include representatives from AFRICOM, the European Command, the Central Command, the Special Operations Command, the Transportation Command, and the Army, Navy, Air Force, and Marines.

———

None of those discussions mattered to the operators already on the ground in Benghazi. The members of the Annex's GRS security team had long since concluded that they couldn't wait for outside help. They couldn't wait for drones or gunships or Marines stationed in Spain. They couldn't wait for Special Ops teams in central Europe or the United States, or even their fellow GRS operators and Special Ops soldiers en route from Tripoli. They couldn't wait for action by the presidents of the United States or Libya, or the secretaries of State or Defense. They couldn't wait for the United Nations, the United States Army, Air Force, Marines, or Navy, the Libyan Air Force, or anyone else.

The Special Mission Compound in Benghazi was overrun. Buildings and cars were on fire. Armed enemies of the United States roamed freely inside the walls. Ambassador J. Christopher Stevens and communications expert Sean Smith were missing inside a burning villa. Five other Americans also were in danger.

The operators' only option was to act. At the Annex, Oz prepared to withstand and repel a possible second wave. At the Compound, Tanto and D.B. headed toward the back gate. Rone, Jack, and Tig rushed through the front gate.

None had any idea what would happen next.

SEVEN

Man Down

JACK TORE THROUGH THE COMPOUND GATE BEHIND Rone. As he passed under the entrance archway, he saw the back of Rone's orange plaid shirt some twenty-five yards ahead of him. Rone sprinted toward the flaming, smoke-spewing villa, and Jack followed in his wake.

As Jack came onto the Compound's manicured grounds, he cut sharply to his right, a move that took him off the brick driveway and onto a thick swath of well-tended grass. From there, the Compound wall would serve to partially cover his back, in case their enemies followed him through the gate. His rifle at his shoulder, his finger near the trigger, Jack dropped to a knee. He scanned back and forth, right and left, covering Rone.

To Jack's right, past a row of low hedges and several palm trees, he saw the burning 17 February barracks building. His every sense hyper-aware, Jack heard scattered gunshots ring out from somewhere inside the Compound. Jack didn't see any shooters in the darkness and he couldn't tell from which direction the shots originated. He knew that he was vulnerable and exposed, but he wouldn't move until Rone was clear.

When Jack saw Rone reach the villa, he sprang to his feet and ran to join him near the building's charred front entrance. Two DS agents who'd been searching for the ambassador and Sean Smith were already there. They stood to the right of the blown-open front doors, on the patio area near the low window that the DS agents had used in their repeated forays into the safe-haven area in attempts to find the missing men. The operators and the DS agents gathered in a loose circle by the four-foot pile of sandbags stacked along the patio's edge. At their feet were clods of dirt and shards of pottery, remnants of a smashed two-foot clay planter.

One of the DS agents who met Jack and Rone was Scott Wickland. Suffering from smoke inhalation, his lungs scarred by diesel fumes, Wickland had climbed down from the villa roof to rejoin the rescue effort. Jack barely recognized him. Wickland looked like a chimney sweep, his boyish face and light-brown hair coated in black soot. Red vines of broken blood vessels covered his heavy-lidded eyes. Wickland's shoulders slumped. His feet were bare. His clothes were blackened rags. The other DS agent, standing alongside Wickland, was big David Ubben, drooping from fatigue, his T-shirt smudged with ash, his meaty face slack. Only days earlier, the four men had sat outside the villa discussing their worries about the under-staffed Compound security team; now their worst fears had been realized.

For a few seconds no one said anything, as the two former SEALs and the two DS agents looked at one another in disbelief. Ubben and Wickland shook their heads and looked at the ground. They'd trained for this and had known that it was possible. They'd responded to the best of their abilities. But now it was real and awful, and it wasn't nearly over.

From the corner of his eye Jack glanced toward the open front doors. The villa's entrance foyer was dark, but through the smoky haze he could see red-hot coals from the wood of incinerated furniture, smoldering on the ruined marble tile floors. It reminded Jack of looking inside a wood-fired pizza oven. He could feel the intense heat pulsing from within.

His voice hoarse from smoke, Ubben broke the silence: "There's still guys in the building."

Immediately Rone and Jack went to the window at the far end of the patio. Wickland, Ubben, and the two DS agents from Tripoli had already gone through it multiple times, and now the window hung crooked in its frame, attached to the building from only one top corner. Jack didn't know where the Tripoli-based agents had gone, but he got the impression that Wickland and Ubben were on the verge of collapse. He could tell that they were deeply relieved to see him and Rone take over the search for Chris Stevens and Sean Smith.

As they rushed to the window, Rone and Jack shared a brief, can-this-possibly-get-worse look. Jack believed that it would take a miracle to pull anyone out alive, and they'd need to be vigilant if they wanted to get out themselves.

Jack climbed through the window into the bedroom in the villa's safe-haven area. The moment his feet hit the floor he felt the most intense blast of heat he'd ever experienced. The only comparison he could think of was opening an oven door on Thanksgiving after a turkey had been roasting all day. His nose and eyes recoiled from the noxious vapors and caustic diesel smoke. Sharp fumes from burning textiles and plastic added to the stench. Jack felt his contact lenses dry out instantly. He wondered if they might melt against his eyeballs.

Rone and Jack took deep breaths and held them for as long as possible. They bulled their way past furniture and mattresses strewn around the bedroom from the DS agents' previous searches. They went as far as they could, as fast as they could, inside the bedroom. But with no clean air, that wasn't far. They rushed back to the window for fresh breaths. With each trip inside, they tried to reach deeper, to push themselves farther on a single chestful of air, even as they knew they were tempting fate. *Go too far, or take a wrong turn, or lose your way in the dark*, Jack told himself, *and you'll be a missing man, too.*

Coughing and feeling light-headed, Jack and Rone began to alternate their searches of the safe haven, taking turns going inside the villa through the window. Time after time they emerged alone. Frustrated that they couldn't explore the far reaches of the safe haven, they tried going in through the front doors. Depending on which way they went, the operators might be able to sneak in a few tolerable breaths inside and search a minute or two longer. But inevitably the furnace pushed them back outside.

In much of the villa, visibility was a few feet or less. Rone and Jack lit the flashlights mounted on their weapons, but the white beams barely penetrated the smoky blackness. They moved or lifted whatever furniture they came upon, in the hope of finding their missing countrymen underneath. Anyone still inside was likely to be on the ground, they reasoned, so they focused their searches close to the floor. The heat was slightly less intense down low, but their feet still baked in their boots.

Jack felt a wave of gloom. *There's no way in hell that they could possibly be alive*, he thought. *There's no way to survive this for more than a few minutes.*

Yet he and Rone continued looking.

After more than a dozen attempts each, Jack and Rone grew discouraged that they still hadn't been able to reach some parts of the back half of the villa. Each time they'd tried, they'd been forced out by the smoke and heat. From outside on the patio, they ran around to the rear of the building to see if they could get in another way. They heard pops of gunfire in the distance, but the attackers had fallen back from the area around the villa and were nowhere in sight. Still, Jack and Rone moved on high alert, guns up, elbows tucked close to their torsos, heads swiveling, eyes scanning for targets.

They found an open back door and stepped inside. But it was just as dark, hot, and smoky, and they couldn't explore far before they were forced back to the door for breaths. After several attempts with the same dispiriting results, they abandoned that approach and moved outside. Jack ran around to the front of the villa, expecting Rone to follow. But in the darkness the two operators became separated.

Jack continued alone toward the patio area near the bedroom window.

━━━

Tig had approached the villa by running up the same brick driveway and across the same grass field as Rone and Jack. He reached the building while his fellow operators were inside searching. No one was on the patio when he arrived, so Tig positioned himself behind the sandbags to create a perimeter defense while he waited. When he'd first entered the Compound, Tig saw a Libyan man in camouflage pants and a T-shirt walking away from the burning 17 February barracks. The man was unarmed, and he seemed to belong there, so Tig didn't shoot him. Otherwise, Tig found the Compound quiet except for the crackling of burning buildings.

As he stood near the sandbag fighting position toward the front of the villa, Tig heard loud noises and crashing sounds from inside. He heard someone kick in a door. Tig wasn't sure who was inside, but he concluded that the racket must be coming from Jack, Rone, DS agents, or militiamen overturning furniture and clearing rooms. As Tig waited for them to emerge, he was startled by the sight of a gray Land Cruiser speeding around a corner in front of the villa.

Here come the bad guys, Tig thought.

He raised his belt-fed machine gun and followed the SUV's movements with the weapon's barrel. Tig prepared to unload as the vehicle drove past him toward the front of the villa. At the last second before he opened fire, Tig recognized David Ubben's face through the windshield. Also in the vehicle was one of the Tripoli-based DS agents.

Tig took his finger off the trigger, lowered the machine gun, and exhaled.

———

When Jack returned to the front of the villa, he found several 17 February militiamen going in and out through the main entrance, trying to help with the search. Jack went to the patio and poked his head inside the bedroom window, intending to try again. Immediately he saw two DS agents, Dave Ubben and the taller of the two agents from Tripoli, coming toward the window through the smoke wearing gas masks. Jack's first thought was to wonder where they'd gotten the gear and how he could get similar masks for himself and his fellow operators.

As the agents grew closer, Jack's smoke strained

eyes focused. The two DS agents stood on either side of a limp man, dragging him toward the window. The man faced upward, wearing dark jeans and a gray T-shirt. Dave Ubben and the Tripoli agent each had the man by an arm, holding his torso and bald head off the ground. His legs and rear dragged along the ashy floor. Jack leaned through the window and reached out with both arms. When the agents approached, Jack slid his hands under the man's arms and locked them in front of his chest. Jack pulled the unresponsive man up and through the window, then gently laid him on a concrete pad protected behind the sandbags. Jack didn't recognize the man. He couldn't tell whether he was American or Libyan.

Jack dropped to his knees to the right of the man's head. He knew from his SEAL training that even before trying to establish an airway, he needed to make sure the man wasn't in danger of bleeding to death. Jack lifted the man's T-shirt and checked his torso for chest or stomach trauma. He found no signs of injury. No blood appeared to be seeping through his pants. Jack pulled up the man's shirt all the way to his neck. He turned the man onto one side, to look and feel around his back for blood or trauma that might reveal internal bleeding. Finding none, Jack eased the man down onto his back. The man flopped limply each time Jack moved his body or limbs.

Jack leaned down and put his ear to the man's nose and mouth. He listened and felt for breath but found none. He searched fruitlessly for a pulse.

Jack's hands were on the man's bare chest, and he noticed that the skin felt deathly cold to the touch. He looked at the man's face and saw a dark ring around his lips, from inhaling diesel smoke. Jack considered trying CPR, but he felt certain it would do no good. The DS agents stood over Jack as he worked, watching and hoping.

Jack looked up at Dave Ubben. "No," Jack said. "He's gone."

Ubben shook his head and turned away. Jack saw tears in his eyes.

Soon Jack would learn that the man he'd just declared dead was Sean Smith, a thirty-four-year-old State Department communications expert, a married father of two young children, a star video-game player known to his online friends as Vile Rat. Only hours earlier, Smith had written an online message complaining about the Libyan "police" photographing the Compound that morning. Smith had begun that message with what now seemed like an anxious prophecy: "assuming we don't die tonight."

Jack didn't know Smith well. They'd met several days earlier when they were introduced during a dinner at the Annex kitchen. Jack felt miserable about Smith's death, but there was no time to mourn him. Jack and the other DS agent lifted Smith's body and carried it to a spot near the villa's front doors.

While Jack was trying to help Smith, he heard one of the DS agents say they weren't finished searching the villa: "The ambo's still missing."

Jack resumed searching, as did the DS agents and several of the 17 February militia members who'd come onto the Compound as the attackers fell back. At one point Jack counted more than ten searchers, but the inside of the villa still burned hot. They focused as much as possible on the safe-haven area, but no one could find Ambassador Chris Stevens.

━━━

After getting separated from Jack in the dark on their way back to the front entrance, Rone ran into Tig outside the villa. Together, they saw Jack bent over Sean Smith's body. "Is that one of ours?" Tig asked. Rone didn't know.

Word spread that Stevens remained lost and the villa hadn't yet been declared clear. Tig and Rone turned on the flashlights on their assault rifles and went through the front doors side by side.

Tig had been in the villa months earlier, so he had a mental picture of the floor plan that he thought would be helpful to the search. They went in low, crouching to stay beneath the smoke, but on their first trip the heat was so overpowering they lasted only about thirty seconds and reached no more than fifteen feet inside. Even with their lights, they could barely see beyond the end of their rifle barrels. It reminded Tig of turning on a car's headlights in a thick fog.

"Holy shit," Tig said outside, sweat dripping from every pore. "This is gonna be rough."

They took deep breaths and went back in, lasting

about a minute on their second trip. On the third attempt, Tig went farther than he had earlier, reaching a pile of furniture outside the steel gate to the safe haven. The gate looked as though it remained locked, and Tig couldn't get through the furniture to reach it.

Tig called for the ambassador at the top of his lungs.

From behind him, outside the villa, came an answer, "Yeah, I'm here."

Tig recognized the voice as belonging to the Team Leader, who'd joined them by driving the Mercedes SUV with Henry the translator from the Gunfighter Road intersection into the Compound.

Coughing from the smoke, Tig called back: "No, not you! Chris Stevens!" Tig got no reply from inside the safe haven.

Calling out the ambassador's name filled Tig's lungs with smoke. He and Rone went back out to the front steps. After a few deep breaths, they gave it a fourth try. Again they went to the deepest part of the open living space, but again they found no sign of Stevens. Tig circled back around toward the front doors. He couldn't see more than a foot in either direction, but he thought that Rone was next to him the whole time.

"I'm lost!" Rone called from somewhere across the smoke-filled room. "I can't find my way out!"

Tig turned toward his friend. "Come to my voice!"

"I'm lost!" Rone called.

"Follow my voice!"

Each breath filling their lungs with smoke, they continued the call-and-response exchange several times. From the direction of Rone's calls, Tig realized that Rone was disoriented and moving toward the kitchen. From his previous searches, Tig knew that that part of the villa remained engulfed in flames. He yelled to Rone to keep talking, then rushed toward Rone's voice. When he caught sight of Rone through the smoke, Tig reached out and grabbed him.

Both were coughing madly, their lungs desperate for fresh air, as Tig led Rone to the front doors and safely outside.

As the two operators caught their breath, bent over with hands on knees, their rifles dangling, Tig and Rone heard a radio call from Tanto and D.B. saying that they were ready to move into the Compound through the back gate. DS agents and militiamen continued to search the villa, so Tig and Rone moved to cover the incoming operators.

Rone and Tig went to a dirt pathway that bisected the Compound, stretching from the north wall to the south wall. Along much of the path, toward the rear half of the Compound, an orchard and a vineyard provided abundant potential hiding places for their enemies. Tig and Rone took positions on either side of the path.

Rone was still thinking about the deadly serious game of Marco Polo they'd played inside the villa. "Hey dude, thanks," Rone said. "You just saved my life. I thought I was gonna die in there."

Tig knew that Rone would have done the same for him. "Hopefully we'll all get out of this alive," Tig said.

Standing a dozen feet apart across the dirt pathway, Tig and Rone watched the darkened areas of trees and vines to make sure Tanto and D.B. weren't walking into an ambush. A man walked slowly out of the orchard, and the operators trained their sights on him. But Tig recognized the man as a Blue Mountain guard who'd apparently hidden among the trees, waiting for the Americans to arrive.

———

Before moving to the Compound's back gate, Tanto and D.B. took cover behind concrete Jersey barriers on the Fourth Ring Road, anticipating that some of the attackers might flee that way when Rone and Tig moved toward the rear of the property. But after several minutes no one came through, so Tanto radioed Tig.

"We're starting to come in," Tanto said. "Don't shoot at us."

"Roger that."

Tanto and D.B. tested the back gate but found it locked. D.B. moved down the property wall to the southwest corner, to see if he could locate another way in. Finding no other entrance and no easy way over the wall topped with razor wire, D.B. decided to climb over the gate. Tanto thought he had a better idea, so he ran back to the 17 February commander outside the grocery store to ask for help.

"Hey, get one of your trucks in here to push this gate open," Tanto said. "We're thinking we're going to need to jump it, but if you got one of those trucks we can ram it open."

"No sir. No," the militia commander said, politely but firmly.

"Get a fucking truck over here and ram it open," Tanto demanded.

"No, I don't think we can do that," the commander said. "We don't have a truck."

Tanto noticed that the militia had failed to block traffic on the Fourth Ring Road, so cars kept driving past, with drivers honking horns as rubbernecking passengers tried to see the burning buildings inside the Compound.

"Well, then let's commandeer one of these fucking vehicles," Tanto said, pointing to the cars and trucks cruising by.

"No sir, we don't want to do that."

So much for a helpful, friendly militia. Tanto fought to keep his cool. D.B. had heard enough. He climbed over the gate and checked a small guard shack inside the Compound to be sure it was empty. Tanto stood by the gate, expecting D.B. to open it from the inside. But after clearing the guard shack, D.B. ran to meet up with Tig and Rone.

Loaded down with weapons and gear, already sore and bleeding from the collapsed wall, Tanto continued waiting outside the property with the two young militiamen he'd grown to trust. Also nearby were a couple dozen militiamen with a commander he'd begun to hate.

He yelled to his partner: "D.B., open the fucking gate for me!" He laughed at the absurdity of the situation, throwing back his head and looking to the dark sky for help. *I'm out here by myself with all these militia guys*, Tanto thought. *Nobody is shooting at me—not yet. D.B., come back and OPEN THE FUCKING GATE!* Tanto tried several times to raise D.B. on the radio, but he couldn't get through.

D.B. had, in fact, heard Tanto. He'd yelled "No!" in response, though Tanto didn't hear him. With an unsecured guard shack and a darkened vineyard before him, D.B. wasn't about to turn his back to potential threats and unlock the gate.

Finally Tanto loaded his weapons onto his shoulders, caught his breath, and climbed over the gate. Before he could catch up with his fellow operators, Tanto heard the voice of one of his two young 17 February militiamen companions.

"Sir, sir! Gate!" he said.

Tanto returned to the rear wall and opened the gate from the inside. He called out to the militia commander, assuming that he'd bring in his troops, as well: "As soon as you come through, close this gate and lock it."

"OK," the commander said. "Yes sir!"

Tanto and the militiamen ran toward Tig, Rone, and D.B. Along the way, Tanto noticed that the operators had stopped watching the unlit orchard, where he suspected that some of the attackers might be lying in wait. Tanto dropped down on the side of the dirt path that cut through the

Compound and trained his weapon on the trees.
From his prone position, Tanto got his first good
look at the main villa, still afire, its exterior walls
blackened near the windows where flames had shot
out. Farther away, he saw flames and smoke above
the burning 17 February barracks. As he held that
position, sweating and bleeding, Tanto took the
opportunity to catch his breath and regroup.

Tig came on the radio and told Tanto that he
needed to move to the other side of the pathway,
to cover the opposite side of the orchard.

"You sonofabitch!" Tanto told Tig. "You turn
your ass around and protect that side. I just want
to lay here. I'm tired, motherfucker!" Tanto's complaints momentarily lightened the mood, raising
smiles from Tig and D.B. Even as he grumbled,
Tanto moved to watch the other stand of trees.

Jack remained near the villa to continue the
search, but none of the other operators was in one
place for long. Frequently they roamed back and
forth between the villa, the other buildings on the
Compound, and the orchard and vineyard area.
They didn't know where the attackers had gone,
but they expected them back at any minute.

Rone moved from the orchard toward the Tactical Operations Center and the Cantina. Tanto
joined Tig, D.B., and the militiamen on the dirt
pathway, and from there they spread out through
the orchard. They didn't have time to clear it completely, but they satisfied themselves that it was safe

enough for them to head back toward the front of the Compound, to the villa and the other buildings.

A handful of 17 February militiamen had joined them on their march through the orchard, mirroring their actions and trying to be useful. One 17 February member whom Tanto didn't see was the commander who'd promised to lock the back gate. He'd apparently remained safely in the rear.

As Tig approached the dirt path at the end of one row of trees, he watched one of the militiamen whip around a corner and pop off roughly twenty rounds from his AK-47 into the darkness. Tig prepared to join in the shooting, but he never saw a target. He suspected that the young militiaman was either jumpy or simply wanted to say that he'd been in a firefight.

Tanto, D.B., and Tig moved toward the Cantina and the TOC. Rone rejoined their crew, and they split into pairs. Rone and D.B. headed to clear the Cantina. They found no one inside the ransacked building, which was strewn with broken furniture and ruined food ripped from shelves and refrigerators.

Meanwhile, Tig and Tanto went to clear the TOC. It wasn't immediately clear whether DS agent Alec Henderson was still locked inside, so Tig and Tanto tried to reach him on their radios. That didn't work, so they stood outside and called through the TOC door.

"Is anybody inside?" Tanto asked. He stood near a video camera. "Can you see us? We're friendlies, and we need to come in."

Tanto received no answer, so he and Tig flanked the building's main window while several 17 February militiamen tried to kick in the reinforced wooden door. The door held fast, so Tig tried kicking it in himself. Still it wouldn't budge. Tig got back on the radio: "If you guys are in there, open up. Or else I'm going to shoot your fucking door open." He took a knee and aimed his weapon at the door.

Henderson immediately came on the radio: "Yes, I'm in here! I'm in here!"

The DS agent explained that he thought that the attackers who'd tried earlier to break into the TOC had returned. "Get in front of the camera so I can see you," he said. Tig stood beneath the lens by the entrance door and waved. Henderson lowered his shotgun, unlocked the door, and removed the steel drop bar that had kept it secure. Tig and Tanto burst into the TOC in a hard entry, to make sure no attackers were inside.

"No, no!" Henderson yelled as he lurched outside, disoriented. "Nobody got in here!"

Tig stepped back out and walked to a carport about fifteen yards away, to provide perimeter security. He set up his belt-fed machine gun on the hood of a gray Land Cruiser and took a quick breather.

Rone and D.B. joined Tanto at the TOC, and together they cleared the rest of the building. Then Henderson went back inside to gather and destroy classified documents and data, computer equipment, and other sensitive materials.

No enemy attackers seemed to remain on or near the Compound. Members of the 17 February militia continued to filter onto the property, roaming freely from one end to the other. Some wore black T-shirts, some wore white T-shirts, some wore jeans, some wore desert camouflage, and some wore woodland army-green camouflage. Some wore beards, some were clean-shaven, and some wore balaclavas covering their faces. Some were armed, some were not. None of them wore insignia to declare their allegiance. In almost every way, they were physically indistinguishable from the attackers who'd swarmed the Compound. The only difference worth noting was that, unlike the attackers, none of them carried banners with Arabic writing.

As the operators and DS agents ruefully joked: "What's the difference between how Libyans look when they're coming to help you versus when they're coming to kill you? Not much."

To the operators, some of the militiamen seemed genuinely willing to fight, search for the ambassador, and hunt for attackers who might be hiding in the dark corners of the Compound. The operators continued to view the 17 February members with varying degrees of trust, but all adopted a Benghazi modification of the Golden Rule: If they don't pose a threat, we won't shoot them.

After clearing the Cantina and the TOC, Rone returned to the villa. He helped Jack and the Team

Leader with the frustrating effort to get deep enough inside to see if the ambassador might yet be located.

Tanto and D.B. helped Alec Henderson collect and destroy classified material from the TOC, while Tig remained posted outside at the carport. Henry the translator, who'd come onto the Compound in the Mercedes SUV driven by the Team Leader, remained out of sight, hunched low inside the vehicle.

The time was somewhere around 11:00 p.m. Sean Smith was confirmed dead, apparently from smoke inhalation. Ambassador Chris Stevens was missing. The main villa and the militia barracks still burned. But the attackers apparently had left, perhaps retreating to nearby streets and homes to regroup. The Americans had regained at least temporary control of the Special Mission Compound. The sound of gunfire had all but ceased.

To the uninitiated, it might have been tempting to imagine that the lull in the action meant that the fighting was over. The operators harbored no such illusions. To a man, they believed that their night and their enemies were just getting started.

EIGHT

Counterattack

AFTER CLEARING THE TOC AND THE CANTINA, THE operators, DS agents, and their 17 February reinforcements returned to the villa. It was difficult to say how many of the militiamen had found their way inside the Compound, but the operators estimated the number to be as high as forty to fifty.

All the Americans were at the villa except Tig, who mistakenly believed that his colleagues were still destroying classified material at the TOC. They left without alerting him, so he spent about five minutes alone at the carport, providing solo security for an empty building.

"Where are you?" the Team Leader called to Tig over the radio.

"I'm over by the TOC," Tig answered.

"We're not over there anymore, man."

"Oh. Fuck." Tig sprinted to the villa, where he found clusters of 17 February militiamen standing around while the operators and DS agents alternated searching for the ambassador. Based on radio reports from apparently friendly militiamen, a consensus began to form that the attackers were likely to return, and the Americans couldn't remain at the Compound much longer.

Tig overheard a discussion during which the DS agents told the GRS Team Leader that they lacked adequate weapons to defend themselves on the drive to the Annex. Tig gave Ubben his belt-fed machine gun and his remaining drum of ammunition. Tig kept his assault rifle for his own protection.

———

After clearing out sensitive materials from the TOC, DS agent Alec Henderson joined the villa search. He pulled off his shirt, dipped it in the swimming pool, and wrapped it around his head in an attempt to withstand the heat and smoke. As Henderson passed through the front doors on one trip, part of the living room ceiling collapsed. He rushed out, unhurt.

Dave Ubben wasn't so lucky. On a separate search trip through the villa, Ubben suffered a jagged cut on his forearm while moving through the window into the darkened bedroom. Blood dripped down his arm and onto his clothes. Rone put his paramedic skills to use dressing the wound, and Ubben continued searching.

Having entered the Compound after their fellow operators and via a different gate, Tanto and D.B. were still catching up with all that had happened. D.B. heard the bad news first.

"Hey," he told Tanto. "We lost one."

"We lost one? Who?" Tanto said.

"I don't know him, the computer guy. And we can't find the ambassador."

Having worked together for a decade, in Iraq, Afghanistan, and now Libya, Tanto and D.B. could read each other's moods and signals. Tanto knew that the former Marine sniper typically was cool and composed, even under the most difficult circumstances. But now Tanto saw anger in his friend's eyes. Tanto felt the same way, not only toward the attackers who'd killed Smith but also about their delayed departure from the Annex. The time they'd spent idling in the Mercedes and BMW had come back to haunt them. They'd worried that the wait would have consequences. Now, Tanto feared, the cost was high: one dead, one missing.

For D.B., the losses cut especially deep. The devotee of Joseph Campbell's writings had arranged his life around a straightforward code that called upon him to fulfill his promises and obligations to the people who counted on him. His greatest fear was letting down someone who relied on him. Sean Smith had relied on all of them, and now he was dead. Chris Stevens had relied on them, too, and he was missing.

Tanto tried to ease his friend's angst.

"Hey, relax dude," Tanto said. "We got a long night ahead of us."

When D.B. didn't immediately respond, Tanto pushed him harder. "Hey sergeant, relax!"

"Yeah, I got it," D.B. said, shooting him a look. "Dude, I'm good."

━━━

After giving Ubben his machine gun, Tig rejoined the search crew. Visibility had barely improved and breathing continued to be difficult. Tig tried to open a window around the corner from the bedroom window they'd been using for access, but the release was stuck or melted shut.

His lungs felt like he'd inhaled broken glass, so Tig went back outside. He radioed the Annex: "We cannot locate the ambassador. He is already gone or we just can't find him inside the house." He returned inside the villa. Jack, Rone, D.B., and Tanto also searched repeatedly for Stevens, but their efforts proved futile.

During one search, Tanto ran into Scott Wickland. The DS agent primarily responsible for the ambassador's safety had found flip-flops for his bare feet, but he seemed exhausted and his face remained covered with soot.

"Get out of here, dude," Tanto told him. "You don't need to be in here. Get yourself together and get ready to go."

Wickland shook his head and continued searching.

━━━

As they searched, the Americans and the militiamen at the Compound received confirmation via radio and cell phone that the attackers appeared to be regrouping and adding reinforcements for a renewed assault. Outside the villa, operators heard the Team Leader talking with the DS agents about leaving the Compound immediately and driving to the Annex. They didn't want to go without Stevens, but they understood that they were sitting ducks if they stayed too long.

Jack watched as one of the DS agents from Tripoli drove the Land Cruiser to within twenty feet of the villa's front doors and opened the rear hatch, in preparation to load up and leave.

With Chris Stevens still missing despite the searches, the operators began to wonder whether the attackers had kidnapped the ambassador by entering the villa's safe-haven area through the same window that Wickland had used to escape. If so, the abduction would have taken place after Scott Wickland had lost sight of Chris Stevens and Sean Smith. Only a short time elapsed between when Wickland climbed to the roof and Ubben and the two other DS agents resumed the search, which had continued since then without pause. But the operators couldn't rule out abduction. The attackers had moved with apparent, if rough, military tactics into the Compound. Perhaps they'd planned all along to snatch Stevens, and the fires they'd set gave them cover and just enough time.

Standing near the window leading to the safe haven, Rone and Jack noticed a square support column with a bloody handprint about five feet above the ground. It looked as though an injured person had tried to grab hold of the concrete column as he was being carried away.

"I wonder if that's the ambassador's handprint," Rone told Jack.

The more the operators discussed it, the more a kidnapping seemed plausible. When Wickland last saw them, Chris Stevens and Sean Smith were together. Why had they been able to find Smith but not Stevens? Why had the attackers left almost as quickly as they'd come? Had they already achieved their objective?

Another possibility some of the searchers considered was that Stevens had somehow escaped on his own through the window when Wickland was on the roof, and was hiding in the unlit orchard. But that seemed like wishful thinking.

━━━

A short time later, outside the villa, Dave Ubben asked Jack to help him retrieve laptops and more classified material from the TOC before the DS agents left. Jack saw Tanto nearby and called him over to help. The three-man team moved tactically, crouched down, guns raised. They believed that the attackers were on their way back to the Compound, and they still harbored concerns that some friendly militiamen might yet turn unfriendly. Although Tanto had previously cleared the TOC with Rone and D.B., he and Jack knew that they needed to consider it under "negative control."

When they reached the TOC building, Tanto told Jack: "You guys go ahead. I'll stand by outside and make sure nobody comes in." Dripping with sweat, his arm throbbing, Tanto took a knee about ten feet from the TOC entrance, covering them. Again he found himself thinking how bright the stars looked in the black sky.

Tanto focused his attention on the northeast corner of the Compound, a darkened area where an empty gardener's shack was built against the wall. With no light in that area, and a large expanse of dirt around it, Tanto worried that an attack could come from that corner without anyone noticing. He kept watch in that direction.

Jack led the way into the TOC building. He and Dave Ubben moved quickly to the room where Alec Henderson had established the command and communications center when the attack began. They made a two-man tactical entry, with Jack taking the lead and Ubben following immediately behind him. When they were sure it was empty, both men let their weapons hang.

Wasting no time, they grabbed every laptop in the well-lit, ten-by-fifteen-foot room. Hard drives needed to be taken, too, but they were held in place by half-inch-thick black wires. Disconnecting them would take too long, so Ubben held the wires taut while Jack cut them with a serrated paramilitary knife. They added the hard drives to the laptop pile. As they worked, Jack steered clear of a large window opposite the entry door. The lights were on in the TOC, which meant that they were illuminated, easy targets if someone wanted to take a potshot through the window.

After one last look around, Ubben told Jack: "We've got everything we need."

Their guns still hanging by their sides, the two men scooped up the laptop computers and hard drives, and headed for the door. Before stepping outside, Jack caught Tanto's eye. They exchanged nods.

"We're good," Tanto called, still on his knee, gun up, scanning for trouble.

As they returned to the villa, Tanto noticed that the back gate remained open. His mind flashed to the 17 February commander he'd told to lock it behind them. *God dang it*, Tanto thought. *That cockbag motherfucker didn't shut the back gate.* The gate was perhaps a hundred yards away, so Tanto knew that he couldn't do anything but stew about it.

Tanto took the point, moving on high alert with his rifle at the low ready position. Jack and Ubben looked like they'd just robbed a Best Buy. They hustled back toward the villa, half crouching as they ran in the dark. Jack felt defenseless with his gun down and his arms filled with computer equipment, so he kept especially close behind Tanto.

They went directly to the rear of the DS agents' gray Land Cruiser. The open rear hatch was already half-filled with weapons, but Jack and Ubben dumped the computer equipment atop the long guns and ammo anyway. The armored Land Cruiser, which had bullet-resistant windows and run-flat tires, faced toward the Compound's front gate. Someone had staged the operators' Mercedes next to the Land Cruiser, about fifteen feet apart, pointed in the opposite direction.

The Compound before September 11, 2012. At the top right is the main gate; at the top left is the building converted into a barracks for 17 February militia guards. (State Department photo)

The pool outside the diplomatic Compound's main villa. (State Department photo)

A sandbag fighting position outside the main villa on the Compound, before September 11, 2012. (State Department photo)

A sandbag fighting position on the Compound, before September 11, 2012. (State Department photo)

The vineyard on the diplomatic Compound. (State Department photo)

A view of the front of the villa before September 11, 2012. (State Department photo)

Interior views of the villa before September 11, 2012. (State Department photos)

The main gate to the CIA Annex in Benghazi. (AP photo/ Mohammad Hannon)

Satellite image of the Annex. (Map data: © 2014 DigitalGlobe)

Inside the walls of the Annex, showing the operators' "prison gym" under construction. (John Tiegen)

Ambassador J. Christopher Stevens and Abdurrahman al-Gannas of the Libyan Ministry of Foreign Affairs cut a ceremonial ribbon on August 26, 2012, marking the reopening of a visa-granting Consular Section at the US Embassy in Tripoli. (State Department photo)

State Department computer specialist Sean Smith. (State Department photo)

Ambassador Christopher Stevens. (State Department photo)

Damage at the Compound from an explosive device on June 6, 2012. (State Department photo)

The interior of a vehicle damaged when militants attacked the British ambassador in Benghazi on June 11, 2012. (State Department photo)

Image of an intruder at the US diplomatic Compound taken by security cameras on September 11, 2012. (FBI photo)

Images of intruders at
the US diplomatic
Compound taken by
security cameras on
September 11, 2012.
(FBI photos)

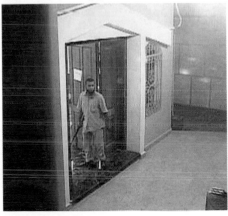

FBI "Seeking Information" poster. (FBI photos)

Buildings and cars at the US diplomatic Compound in Benghazi set afire the night of September 11, 2012. (REUTERS/ Esam Al-Fetori)

(STR/AFP/ Getty Images)

(STR/AFP/ Getty Images)

Buildings and cars at the US diplomatic Compound in Benghazi set afire the night of September 11, 2012. (REUTERS/ Esam Al-Fetori)

A view inside a Compound building after the attack. (FBI photo)

Images of the Compound in the aftermath of the attack. (GIANLUIGI GUERCIA/ AFP/Getty Images)

Images of the Compound in the aftermath of the attack. (GIANLUIGI GUERCIA/ AFP/Getty Images)

(REUTERS/ Esam Al Fetori)

(FBI photo)

Images of the Compound in the aftermath of the attack. (GIANLUIGI GUERCIA/ AFP/Getty Images)

Mark "Oz" Geist

Kris "Tanto" Paronto

John "Tig" Tiegen

Tyrone "Rone" Woods

Jack Silva

Dave "D.B."
Benton

Glen "Bub" Doherty

Libyan civilians remove an unresponsive Ambassador Christopher Stevens from the villa at the US diplomatic Compound early on September 12, 2012. (AFP/AFP/Getty Images)

President Obama and Secretary of State Hillary Clinton embrace during a September 14, 2012, ceremony at Andrews Air Force Base marking the arrival of the remains of the Americans killed in Benghazi. (JEWEL SAMAD/AFP/Getty Images)

On the grass and the brick driveway outside the villa, everyone who wasn't searching for the ambassador was buzzing with concern about their enemies massing for a renewed attack. A shared sentiment took hold that the Americans and their militia allies needed to abandon the Compound immediately. Jack overheard one of the DS agents say that he'd received a phone call warning that "large groups of bad guys are coming." Jack didn't know the source of the call, but he had no reason to doubt it.

The operators also learned that the 17 February militiamen who were supposed to block the roadways leading to the Compound either couldn't or wouldn't be able to hold off a second assault. The GRS Team Leader called the 17 February commander by cell phone, asking him to fortify their positions so the Land Cruiser and the Mercedes could travel safely back to the Annex. Accounts of the response differ, but several operators said the militia commander admitted that his men were falling back. In that case, the attackers would have a clear path to return and finish what they'd started. Also, there would be nothing to stop them if they decided to move from the Compound to the lightly defended Annex.

The pings and pops of gunfire began to pick up from beyond the Compound walls. Tanto heard a crack, then another, from the Fourth Ring Road. The open back gate infuriated him more. He also heard shots coming from the east side of the Compound, near the gardener's shack he'd been watching. Several bullets hit the side of the Land Cruiser, making a sound like coins being flicked against a tin can.

Even as they prepared to leave, and even though their hopes of finding Stevens had fallen, Jack, Rone, and D.B. continued to search the villa for the ambassador. Tanto took up a defensive position on the ground outside. After a short while he began patrolling the grounds, watching several dozen 17 February militiamen who milled around the Compound. Most were young and wiry, but Tanto became intrigued by a short, heavyset man who looked to be in his fifties. The man carried a shiny, nickel-plated AK-47 and dressed as though he'd just left an office job, with dark-blue pants and a tan button-down dress shirt. Tanto couldn't tell if the man was a battle tourist or a fighter. Tanto kept watching the gates and the walls through his night-vision goggles, checking the dark corners to see if anyone was climbing over.

━━━

A call came over the radio from the Team Leader for everyone to muster at the vehicles for immediate departure. No one wanted to leave with Chris Stevens unaccounted for. But they'd searched repeatedly with no success, so it seemed likely to several of the operators that he was in enemy hands. If Stevens somehow did remain inside the villa, perhaps deep within part of the safe haven they couldn't reach through the flames, Sean Smith's death by apparent smoke inhalation convinced the operators that the ambassador was surely dead, too. In that case, the work would no longer be a rescue mission, but a recovery effort. With a force of attackers approaching from beyond the walls, they couldn't justify retrieving a body if it meant more American casualties. The T.L. made the call to leave, and all the operators were in agreement.

Rone and Jack carried Sean Smith's body to the back of the Mercedes SUV and placed it inside the cargo area as gently as they could. Tanto came over to see Smith and pay his respects. He'd spoken with Smith only once, and he wanted to be sure that this was the man he'd met. Tanto gently turned Smith's head to see if he recognized him. It was hard to tell, as Smith's face was still blackened by soot. Tanto laid his head down and shut the cargo door.

Rone slid into the Mercedes's driver's seat. The Team Leader and Henry the translator continued talking with the 17 February militiamen.

The five DS agents crowded into the Land Cruiser, ready to go. Although still worn out from his ordeal and suffering from smoke inhalation, Scott Wickland took the wheel. An agent from Tripoli rode shotgun. Dave Ubben and Alec Henderson squeezed in back with the other Tripoli agent.

Before heading toward the Mercedes, the Team Leader and several other operators warned Wickland to turn left, not right, when he drove out of the Compound. Going to the right, which would have taken him to the east, might have seemed the more natural route, because the Annex was located southeast of the Compound. Also, that was the route the DS agents normally traveled to the Annex. But the Team Leader had heard by phone that the attackers were massing in that area, and a right turn would put the Land Cruiser directly into their path. By turning to the left, the DS agents would be retracing the route the operators had used, in reverse, which would steer them through areas that might still be protected by the 17 February militia.

From the Land Cruiser's back seat, Dave Ubben opened the door and called to Jack, who was outside near the Mercedes: "Hey, we don't have a radio. Do you guys have one?"

Jack went to Rone, who had somehow acquired a second radio. Jack carried it to Ubben so they could remain in contact. As he walked back to the Mercedes, Jack heard a whooshing sound, followed a split second later by an explosion.

———

Several minutes earlier, Tig had decided to make a few final search runs inside the villa. He called the T.L. on his radio: "I'm going in one more time."

"No," the Team Leader replied. Eager to get everyone evacuated, he told Tig: "Stand by. Stand by."

Tig complied, but only briefly. The operators and DS agents were hanging around the vehicles, so he figured he'd attempt one last search before they left. He considered it most likely that Stevens was still somewhere inside. Tig had been thinking about the aftermath of the 1993 Battle of Mogadishu in Somalia, memorialized in *Black*

Hawk Down, particularly the part when locals had dragged the bodies of American soldiers through the streets. *They're going to be doing the exact same thing to the ambassador*, Tig told himself. *That's something I don't want to see. We gotta find him.*

Tig stripped off his heavy Rhodesian assault vest and left his assault rifle outside the villa window. He'd broken his night-vision goggles when he banged them on the window frame during a previous search, so he left them and his helmet outside, too. Carrying only his flashlight and pistol, wearing his thin body armor over his shirt, Tig took several extra-large breaths, held the last one, and went inside through the bedroom window.

The rooms remained hot and smoky, so Tig crawled or slid on his belly. He moved through the bedroom and checked both sides of the bed. Finding nothing, he crept toward the safe-haven hallway, hoping to go deeper into the villa, to other rooms none of the searchers had yet reached.

Tig was halfway out of the bedroom doorway when he heard the explosion.

Tanto was walking between the Land Cruiser and the Mercedes when he heard it: *Kajoom!* He felt the concussive pressure of the explosion, but wasn't sure where it had come from. He spun toward the front gate and saw 17 February militiamen taking cover. As Tanto ran toward the front of the villa, he came upon two militiamen, one with his left hand bloody and badly mangled.

"What happened?" Tanto yelled.

"Grenade!" the injured man's friend told him.

At first, Tanto mistakenly thought the man had tried to throw a grenade but held it too long. Moments later, when a second explosion hit, Tanto realized that the Compound was under attack from rocket-propelled grenades, fired from the direction of the open back gate. Gunfire sputtered toward the Americans and their militia supporters from the area of the Fourth Ring Road.

Counterattack, Tanto thought. *They're going to start coming in. They're going to try to take this thing back over.*

Scanning to see where the attackers might enter the Compound, Tanto caught sight of D.B. running to join him near the front of the villa. Bullets flew around them in the dark, sounding like whips cracking again and again.

"Are those motherfuckers shooting at us?" Tanto asked D.B. "Really?"

They were exposed on the front lawn, so Tanto and D.B. ran to take cover at the Land Cruiser. Tanto saw muzzle flashes coming from the back gate. He placed his weapon across the hood of the armored SUV and began firing. Tanto wasn't wearing earplugs, so the reports from his rifle blew out his left eardrum.

After the first grenade, the Team Leader had radioed the DS agents in the Land Cruiser: "Get the fuck out of here! Go! Go! Go!"

Tanto had arrived at the SUV before Scott Wickland could shift into gear. The DS agents stared at Tanto through the windshield, their faces twisted in anxious grimaces. Tanto called out, "Sorry!" He lifted his gun and stepped back from the Land Cruiser. Tanto gave them a traffic cop wave to send the DS agents on their way.

With the operators and several militiamen providing waves of cover fire, Wickland hit the gas and drove toward the Compound's open front gate. When he passed under the entrance arch and reached the gravel road, Wickland either disregarded or forgot the operators' repeated warnings about which way to go. The disoriented DS agent turned the Land Cruiser to the right, directly into the path of the returning attackers.

"Those dumb motherfuckers!" Tanto said aloud. "Are you kidding me?"

Around the same time as the second Compound attack began, at approximately 11:10 p.m. Benghazi time, the unarmed US drone arrived over the city. It immediately began sending live video back to Washington and Tripoli, so policymakers could watch grainy overhead images of the battle as it happened.

After the Land Cruiser pulled away, Tanto stepped to the other side of the brick driveway, moving across the firing line, for a better angle to engage the attackers. He took a knee and continued shooting. Whenever he saw a muzzle flash he returned fire. Tanto knew that he was exposed, but he felt enveloped by a blanket of protection he attributed to his faith.

D.B. took cover by the villa when the Land Cruiser sped off. He and the Team Leader weren't so sanguine. "Tanto! Get over here!" the T.L. shouted over the radio. D.B. echoed him: "Get behind cover!"

Tanto stayed put. He believed that if he hadn't been shot yet, a spiritual power must be watching over him. Tanto's other motive was his training on how to respond to an ambush. Tanto intended to aggressively engage their attackers, to demonstrate superior firepower and prevent the enemy from feeling emboldened. *Throw everything at them. Put them back on their heels*, he told himself.

Tanto heard gunfire originating from his right. He looked over to see a 17 February militiaman, none other than the older man with the civilian clothes and the nickel-plated AK-47, supporting his position from about ten feet away. The younger militiamen were nowhere to be found. But this short, stout, fifty-something man was on one knee, firing alongside Tanto toward the back gate. Tanto couldn't help but smile.

It was still just the two of them, and despite his trust in angels on his shoulders, Tanto felt out-numbered. He grabbed his radio with his non-shooting hand and pressed the talk button with his thumb: "Hey, I could use some help. It'd be nice if someone could join me over here."

"Roger that," D.B. answered, running over to assist the former Ranger and the senior militiaman, as they poured bullets toward the back gate. Knowing that Tanto had been spending rounds freely, D.B. slid him an extra magazine across the driveway.

———

After the first RPG, Jack heard a sustained volley of gunfire, as rounds snapped past his head. Most of the militiamen and operators who'd been standing around the SUVs ran toward the villa for cover. When Jack reached the villa wall, to his right he saw a line of militiamen, laying fire toward the back gate.

Jack's training taught him to always establish 360-degree security, with coverage from the front, back, sides, and all angles. He saw the line of militiamen taking cover against the villa and realized that an attacker with an automatic weapon could run down an alleyway on the left side of the villa and mow them down like ducks in a row. It was a textbook example of soldiers leaving themselves vulnerable to attack from an unprotected flank.

Jack ran to the building's corner on the left flank, took a knee, and scanned down the alley and to the east to ensure that no one came from either direction. He noticed that Henry the translator was taking cover behind him, against the villa wall. Jack caught Henry's eye and they exchanged tired smiles. Henry had held up admirably under fire, but now his eyes looked to be the size of baseballs. Jack wanted to place Henry back with the Team Leader, so the translator could talk to the 17 February commander about what was happening.

The T.L. was thinking the same thing. As he struggled to communicate with the militia commander, he asked Tanto and D.B. to find the translator. A minute later, D.B. came around the corner where Jack was keeping watch over Henry.

"Hey, follow me," D.B. told Henry. "I'm gonna stick you with the Team Lead. Hang on to him. Wherever he goes, you go. He needs you."

———

When the first RPG hit, Tig leapt up from the hallway entrance inside the villa and rushed back to the bedroom window. The second rocket-propelled grenade exploded as he stepped through onto the patio. Using the sandbags as cover, Tig threw on his Rhodesian vest and helmet, and grabbed his rifle. As he jocked up, he heard the zips and snaps of rounds coming in his direction. Tig looked toward the front of the villa and saw a 17 February militiaman in jeans, a T-shirt, and a protective vest similar to his. The lone young militiaman returned fire toward the back gate with an AK-47.

As Tig looked around, he saw the ladder that led to the roof. He climbed to the top, leapt over the concrete parapet, and scanned the roof to make sure he was alone. Although the fire raged below, the poured-concrete roof seemed in no immediate danger of collapse. The more imminent threat came from bullets flying in Tig's direction. He radioed the Team Leader to report his location. *If I get shot*, Tig thought, *I want somebody to know that I'm up here.*

Tig looked for flashes of gunfire coming from the northeast corner of the Compound, but didn't see any. Staying low, Tig moved across the roof to the corner facing the rear gate, which led out to the Fourth Ring Road. Gunfire kept coming from that direction, and he wanted to suppress it.

Tig popped up with his assault rifle ready. Framed by the open back gate was the silhouette of a man. He stood in the road, about five yards back from the gate, with a rocket-propelled grenade launcher on his shoulder. His head was tilted a few degrees off center, in the firing position. The RPG pointed directly toward the villa.

As quickly as Tig could, he squeezed the trigger on the semi-automatic assault rifle and let loose with ten to fifteen rounds.

The man with the RPG dropped backward onto the street. His arms flopped down and the launcher skittered off to the side. One of Tig's rounds apparently struck the grenade as it launched, sending it spinning harmlessly off to one side. The moment was captured on film by a security camera inside the Compound.

The steady gunfire that had been coming from the back gate stopped almost immediately, as though the sight of the fallen grenade shooter stunned the other attackers into silence.

When the shooting by the attackers stopped, a radio call went out telling the operators to join Tig on the villa roof. Rone had already begun

providing medical care to several injured militiamen. He finished quickly and rose up the ladder.

Before Tanto went to the roof, a 17 February
militiaman approached him outside the front of
the villa.

"Sir," he said. "I found this."

The militiaman handed Tanto a BlackBerry
smartphone covered in soot. Tanto wiped the
screen with his thumb and saw what looked like
a US phone number. He thanked the militiaman
and put the device in his pocket. He climbed the
ladder, as did D.B.

Jack felt spent as he moved to join his teammates
up the ladder, his body armor weighing him down
like a man trying to climb from the bottom of an
empty well. He'd known that feeling before, and
it reminded him of his SEAL training days. Even
more, it reminded Jack how he'd felt when he first
tried to pass the screening test to win admission to
the SEAL training program. As Jack climbed the
ladder to the villa roof, the SEAL screener's question remained seared in his memory: "If I light
a fire under your ass, can you get over the bar?"
Now fire literally was under his ass.

Jack gathered his strength, pulled himself to the
roof, and spread out with his fellow operators. All
took fighting positions, establishing a defensive
perimeter from their elevated vantage point.

━━━

Before heading to the villa roof, D.B. had told the
Team Leader that time was their enemy. Not only

were they in danger at the Compound, but the Annex grew more insecure the longer it remained without the full complement of operators. "We need to round up all the Americans we can and evacuate," D.B. told the T.L.

Within minutes of the operators assembling on the roof, their radios rang out again with a call from the Team Leader: "Consolidate now. We're getting the hell out of here." They climbed back down, with Tig covering the others as the last man down.

Rone got behind the wheel of the Mercedes. Jack rode shotgun. Tanto got in the backseat. D.B. and Tig climbed into the rear cargo area with Sean Smith's body. They positioned themselves to watch through the rear window to make sure no one was following them. The Team Leader and Henry remained outside talking with a 17 February militia leader.

Jack opened the Mercedes door.

"Get the fuck in the car," he told the T.L. "We've got to get out of here."

The Team Leader looked over to him. Without a word, he and Henry got in the backseat, alongside Tanto. The barrels of their guns still hot, seven men and the body of an eighth were crammed together in the armored Mercedes SUV.

Tanto gazed through the side window at the faces of several stunned-looking militiamen who he felt certain had just experienced their first firefight. Beyond them, Tanto saw the villa and the barracks still on fire. The light cast by the flames across the thick lawn made Tanto think of a flawless soccer field, ready for a night game.

It was about 11:30 p.m., or roughly two hours since the attack began. As they sat in the Mercedes, none of the operators knew how many of the attackers their bullets had hit in the dark. The Compound wasn't littered with bodies, as some armchair warriors would later suggest, but the operators knew that in their defense of their countrymen and themselves, they had inflicted damage on at least some of their enemies.

Rone did a three-point turn, steering the SUV in the opposite direction, toward the front gate. Squeezed shoulder to shoulder and thigh to thigh, the sweaty, weary men collected their thoughts. Jack braced himself and gripped his gun between his knees, knowing that they might be heading directly into an ambush.

Rone drove the packed Mercedes forward. The moment they reached the gate, the United States Special Mission Compound in Benghazi would effectively cease to exist.

NINE

Zombieland

―――――

WHEN SCOTT WICKLAND TURNED RIGHT OUT OF the Compound's front entrance with his four fellow DS agents, gunshots struck the armored Land Cruiser. They drove on, but more trouble lay directly ahead. Just as they'd been warned, Wickland and his passengers saw a menacing crowd looming farther east down the gravel road. Wickland threw the Land Cruiser into reverse and turned it in the opposite direction, heading west as he'd been advised, toward the intersection with Gunfighter Road where the operators had initially left their vehicles.

As they began driving west, the DS agents saw a man they believed to be a friendly 17 February militiaman waving at them to turn around. The confused DS agents interpreted the signal to be a warning that they were driving into an ambush. Wickland put his trust in the man and turned a second time, back east toward clumps of Arab men lining the gravel road in the dark.

One reason the operators had told Wickland not to turn right was the warning they'd received from genuinely friendly 17 February militia leaders. Attackers were massing to the east of the Compound, the militia leaders said, and their fighters couldn't hold their positions. Another reason was the operators' educated belief that radical Islamists from the Ansar al-Sharia militia had established a base on one of the residential properties a short distance east of the Compound. Days earlier, Tanto had spoken about the Ansar al-Sharia base with Henry, who'd translated documents that described how the fundamentalist, rabidly anti-American militia had furtively become a neighbor to the US Special Mission Compound.

The Benghazi DS agents also knew about the neighboring compound, which they considered to be one of several dozen nearby properties controlled by potentially hostile militias.

After the second turnaround, Wickland drove cautiously, holding steady at about 15 mph. As the Land Cruiser approached the armed men lining the street, none of the Libyans raised his weapon. Wickland continued heading east. Less than a quarter-mile from the main Compound gate, a man stepped into the street and waved his hands in an attempt to direct the Land Cruiser into a driveway. It wasn't clear whether this was the suspected Ansar al-Sharia base the operators and DS agents had heard about, but Wickland and his fellow agents suspected a trap. Several called out to keep moving, and Wickland tried to speed away.

Immediately the men along the roadway leveled their guns and opened fire. Bullets pounded against the sides of the Land Cruiser. Attackers rolled two grenades under the vehicle. The explosions rocked the SUV and blew out two tires. Spiderweb cracks spread across the bullet-resistant windows. But the armor held, the men inside remained unhurt, and the Land Cruiser kept gaining speed on its run-flat tires.

The attackers surged forward, some firing AK-47 rounds from as close as two feet as Wickland drove on. The windows didn't roll down, so the DS agents couldn't return fire without opening the doors, something they weren't about to do.

Dave Ubben grabbed the radio Jack had given him. He called to the operators and the Annex: "We're taking heavy fire! We're on our run-flats!"

Still wheezing from smoke inhalation, Wickland steered through the crowd and around a roadblock. He neared the end of the gravel road, where it reached a T-intersection with the street the operators called Adidas Road. The road's real name was Shari' al-Qayrawan, and it ran through the heart of a commercial district lined with retail shops. Wickland turned a hard right at the corner, avoided pedestrians in the street, and ran into a typical late-night Benghazi traffic jam.

Fearing that the attackers were close behind, Wickland steered the Land Cruiser over a curb and drove as fast as he could along the grass-and-dirt center median. When the street became less choked with traffic, he bounced the Land Cruiser down off the median and weaved through oncoming cars. After a short distance Wickland tugged the wheel and shifted the SUV rightward into the proper lane.

As they drove on toward the Annex, the rattled DS agents braced again for battle when they spotted two cars that appeared to be following them. The first turned off not long after it began tailing the SUV, but the second remained behind the Land Cruiser with its lights off. When the Land Cruiser neared the Annex, the second tail car peeled off into the area of warehouses at the edge of the barren area the operators called Zombieland.

<hr />

As he patrolled inside the Annex shortly after 11:00 p.m., Oz heard gunfire from perhaps a half mile away. That was his first notice that the DS agents were en route. Confirmation came in a radio call from the operators, who remained at the Compound: "State Department is leaving."

The Annex's exterior video cameras showed the damaged Land Cruiser racing down Annex Road. Alec Henderson radioed that they were coming in hot. The security officer at the front entrance opened the gate and lifted the steel arm bar to let them roll right in. He quickly dropped the arm and locked the gate behind them.

Oz heard the *flop-flop* sound of flattened tires as he came down the ladder from the roof of Building C. He rushed to see whether the DS agents were injured inside the bullet-ridden SUV. Wickland steered the Land Cruiser to a stop at a carport between Buildings B and C. Bob the base chief and several Annex officials wanted to rush out of Building C to greet the DS agents, but Oz convinced them to remain inside where he could protect them. Oz promised to send at least one agent inside for a debriefing.

The five DS agents stepped out of the SUV looking exactly as Oz expected from men who'd just been attacked by militants, repeatedly searched a burning building, and driven through gunfire and explosions. Oz thought Alec Henderson could use a tall glass of water, or something stronger, and a place to lie down. But Henderson went inside Building C to tell Bob and other Annex officials about what happened at the Compound during the previous two hours.

When Scott Wickland came out from behind the wheel, he looked like a performer in a blackface burlesque, with patches of ghostly white skin peeking out from swaths of soot. His damaged lungs weren't delivering enough oxygen, so Wickland went into Building C for rest and medical care. Oz took a quick look at Dave Ubben's injured forearm, but Ubben said he was fine.

"I need people up on the roofs," Oz told Ubben and the two DS agents from Tripoli. He wanted them in place quickly, as an added layer of defense in case the cars that tailed the SUV foretold an attack, or if the operators returned with enemies in tow. Oz sent Ubben to the roof of Building D, on the west side of the Annex property. He separated

the two Tripoli-based agents, sending one to
Building A, near the front gate, and the other to
Building B, on the east side. Oz returned to his
post on the Building C roof.

Oz had begun hearing more worrisome sounds,
ranging from tires screeching to periodic gunfire
from the direction of the Compound. He occasionally saw tracers cutting through the black sky,
some green, some red. The tracers' purpose was to
help shooters to see the trajectory of their rounds
and to correct their aim. Oz could only hope the
tracers came from the American side.

He radioed the operators to check their status
and was told they were mustering at the Mercedes
and preparing to leave. Knowing that his teammates would soon be on the way, Oz climbed
down the ladder to make one last check of Annex
defenses. Then he made sure the front gate would
be opened quickly, so Rone could pull inside without waiting.

———

As Rone drove the Mercedes under the archway to
exit the Compound, his fellow operators called out
in unison: "Left. Go left!"

"I got it, guys," Rone answered calmly.

Now that Jack knew the attackers had rocket-
propelled grenades, his concerns rose. The armor
beneath the Mercedes's metal skin could stop
AK-47 rounds, but RPGs were a deadlier story.
He felt certain that their enemies would be waiting for them in the street, to repeat the ambush

they'd sprung on the DS agents. He'd heard via radio that the Land Cruiser had made it to the Annex without casualties. Jack doubted they'd be so fortunate.

As they pulled out through the gate, Jack realized that he'd felt safer inside the destroyed Compound than he did locked in an SUV heading into uncertain territory beyond the walls. He gripped a handle on the dashboard in front of him, to brace for an explosion he felt certain would come. Not for the first time during the two hours since the attack began, Jack thought about his family. He told himself: *OK, probably not going to make it out of this one, but got to keep trying.*

To the operators' surprise, no one shot at the Mercedes when they turned left to drive west on the gravel road. Still, Tanto thought Rone's foot was too heavy on the gas. "Whoa, whoa," he said. "Slow down, man, we need to blend." Rone eased off and cautiously approached the Gunfighter Road intersection. He kept the headlights off on the dark street, to attract less attention.

When the operators reached the corner where they'd left the BMW roughly an hour earlier, they saw several bearded men wandering around, some holding rifles. The operators had no way to know whether the men were friendly 17 February members, or if those militiamen had been replaced by rivals from Ansar al-Sharia or another zealously anti-American militia.

The Arab men stared stone-faced at the packed SUV. A few covered their features with balaclavas.

Rone and the Team Leader gave the men small, confident waves. Jack made eye contact with an especially tall man in sandals and loose-fitting "man jammies." The man held an AK-47, but he made no move to raise it.

Tanto found himself looking out the window and memorizing details about the path that he and D.B. had taken on foot from this point to the Compound. So much had happened in so little time. Only two hours earlier they'd been watching *Wrath of the Titans.*

Tig stewed about the ambush that befell the DS agents, blaming the 17 February militia for not locking down the entire Western Fwayhat neighborhood. With friends like that, they didn't need enemies. When Rone turned left onto Gunfighter, Tig looked mournfully through the rear window at their abandoned BMW. When he'd grabbed his grenade launcher and gone to the corner to return fire, Tig had left his go-bag in the car. It contained his medical kit, extra magazines, and worst of all, his passport. He knew that it would be tempting danger to stop, so he kept silent as Rone drove past. *It's not worth getting into a gunfight over,* Tig told himself.

Several of the armed men in the street called for the Mercedes to stop. The passengers told Rone to keep going, but he was way ahead of them. No shots or cars pursued them from the intersection.

The operators continued south down Gunfighter across the Fourth Ring Road. They momentarily relaxed as they neared their destination without engaging enemy gunmen, then quickly returned to high alert. Rone made a few swift detours to make sure they weren't being followed. Tanto pulled down his night-vision goggles but saw no one moving in the open fields around the Annex. He noticed that the nearby 17 February base looked desolate, as it often did late at night. The Rancilio Café, a neighborhood coffee shop, seemed open, but Tanto saw no one inside. Gates were down and shutters were closed on local stores. With little traffic on the roads and no pedestrians in sight, Tanto thought it looked like a typical night when they returned from a move.

Rone felt confident enough to turn on the headlights as they cruised along darkened streets. He kept an easy pace with the light traffic around them. The idea was to disguise three uncomfortable facts: The Mercedes SUV had a dead body in the back, it was packed with heavily armed American operators, and it was seeking refuge in a covert CIA Annex.

———

When they were one minute away, Tanto radioed the Annex: "Coming in hot." Not wanting to give the misimpression that they were being followed, Tanto quickly amended his radio call: "Disregard. We're coming in lukewarm."

Rone parked near Building A and the operators got out. Sean Smith's body remained in the cargo area of the Mercedes. D.B. made sure someone found a bedsheet to cover him.

While the Team Leader spoke with Bob, Henry the translator got a well-deserved respite among the non-shooters inside Building C. Others inside the building kept busy destroying classified material in anticipation of evacuating. They also filled dozens of magazines with ammunition for the rooftop and tower security teams.

Rone went inside, too, to care for Scott Wickland. The other operators rushed to their assigned battle stations. Before heading to his post on Building B, Tanto told D.B. he wanted an update from inside Building C, to see how much external support and overhead firepower they might expect.

Jack moved toward the ladder leading to the roof of Building D. Looking across the grassy triangle where the turtle family lived, Jack saw the battle-scarred Land Cruiser and considered the DS agents lucky to be alive. At the very least, it was a battered tribute to the engineers who'd designed the SUV's protective armor.

As they climbed to the flat-topped roofs, none of the operators allowed himself to imagine that they were out of danger. Yet several experienced a brief wave of relief. Although everyone at the Annex felt a pall from the death of Sean Smith and the disappearance of Chris Stevens, Jack detected an uptick in morale now that all the other Americans were together inside the Annex and none had been injured or killed during their escape from the Compound.

As midnight approached and September 11, 2012, neared its end, Annex defenses settled into

place. The taller of the two Tripoli DS agents was on the roof of Building A, watching the south wall and the front gate. The view was obscured, so soon he'd move to join Tanto and D.B. as they readied themselves behind the parapet on the roof of Building B. The CIA case officer with battle experience in Afghanistan remained atop Building C, soon to be joined there by Rone. Atop Building D were Jack, Dave Ubben, and the second DS agent from Tripoli, a stocky African-American Army veteran. The T.L. remained inside Building C, with occasional trips outside to the building's patio.

The Annex security leader positioned himself near the front gate but moved elsewhere at times. The three Libyan guards were on the steel towers. One remained near the front gate, but the guard who'd been at the northwest tower moved to join his friend at the southeast corner of the property. Oz was on the move, bringing water and ammo where needed, and checking to see that everyone was in position. When that was done, Oz moved to the tower fighting position located to the northeast of Building C. Tig linked up with two of the local guards and spent some time with them on the tower at the Annex's southeast corner.

As the Annex's defenders steeled themselves for whatever lay ahead, midnight passed and September 11 ended. Minutes after the start of the new day, the State Department's Operations Center in

Washington sent an e-mail to the White House, Pentagon, FBI, and other government agencies. The e-mail, sent at 12:06 a.m. Benghazi time, September 12, 2012, had the subject line, "Update 2: Ansar al-Sharia Claims Responsibility For Benghazi Attack." The message said: "Embassy Tripoli reports the group claimed responsibility on Facebook and Twitter and has called for an attack on Embassy Tripoli."

When the e-mail was revealed, weeks later, it set off a firestorm about when the Obama administration knew that the Compound attack wasn't simply a disorganized, spontaneous protest over the anti-Muhammad *Innocence of Muslims* video on YouTube, as several administration officials initially suggested. But the issue became muddied further when an investigation by a fellow at the Washington Institute for Near East Policy found no evidence that the radical militia group had made any such statements on social media.

Around the same time the e-mail was sent, the gates of the embassy in Tripoli opened, and out rode the reinforcement security team for a private charter flight to Benghazi. The seven-member force consisted of former Navy SEAL Glen "Bub" Doherty; two Delta Force members; the top GRS Team Leader in Libya; two other GRS operators; and a linguist.

———

From his position on the southeast tower, Tig asked over the radio for someone to turn on the

exterior perimeter floodlights that pointed beyond
the Annex walls. The exterior lights soon shone,
but someone also turned on spotlights that illuminated inside the Annex property. Those lights
made it easier to move around in the dark, but they
silhouetted the rooftop and tower-based defenders, exposing their positions. Equally troubling,
the interior lights blinded them from looking out
beyond the Annex walls to where any attackers
might be hiding.

Jack got on the radio and asked that the interior
lights be switched off. Tig seconded the request.
When nothing happened, Jack considered shooting them out, just as he'd done as a Navy SEAL
on nighttime assaults of ships at sea. On one mission, Jack's SEAL team received intelligence that
one of Osama bin Laden's sons was hiding on a
vessel off the coast of Pakistan. They brought a fast
boat alongside the ship, hooked on ladders, and
climbed aboard. Their search turned up no trace
of any bin Laden. The only shots they fired that
night were to kill the lights.

Atop Building D, Jack stewed about the lights
but he hesitated to shoot, not wanting to draw
attention to the Annex with gunfire. As minutes passed that seemed like hours, Jack began to
reconsider. Just then, Tig's southwestern twang
came raging over the airwaves: "Someone turn off
the fucking lights!"

Sheepishly, an Annex security staffer called back:
"I'm on it. I'm on it." By the time Jack stopped
laughing, the interior lights had been switched off.

The operators on Building B got a kick out of Tig's outburst, too. From their perch on the east side of the Annex, Tanto and D.B. heard a voice somewhere in the distance, chanting and speaking in animated tones in Arabic over a megaphone. Tanto wondered if someone was riling up students at a nearby medical college to march on the Annex, as a cover for Ansar al-Sharia militiamen or other enemies of the United States who might sneak in among the students to attack. Other scenarios rocketed through Tanto's mind, all of them climaxing with gunfire. Waiting patiently wasn't Tanto's strong suit. *God dang those sons of bitches*, he thought. *If you're gonna attack us, attack us now.*

Tanto got on the radio and asked the Team Leader, "What's the status on that Spectre gunship? We really could use that now." He also asked about an unmanned drone, not knowing that one had already begun transmitting images from somewhere overhead. The T.L. told Tanto that he'd try to find out.

When they first took to the roofs, Tanto asked whether someone inside Building C would bring them food, drinks, and chairs while they waited. The female case officer who'd gone to dinner with Oz hustled over with Gatorade, water, and candy bars. She tripped as she stepped over the parapet and landed hard, face-first on the roof. Tanto thought she must have hurt herself badly, but she popped to her feet, said she was fine, and continued making deliveries. A male support officer followed with white plastic lawn chairs.

Soon after, with no sign of movement from beyond the walls, Tanto decided he could use a grenade launcher to bolster their defenses. He climbed down and searched the vehicles, with no luck. When he asked over the radio if anyone knew where he might locate one, no one replied. Tanto went to Building C to ask around, but again he struck out. As staffers shredded documents, destroyed sensitive materials, and performed other prescribed tasks to prepare to abandon the Annex, Tanto stuffed extra mags of ammo in his pocket and headed for the door.

On his way out, Tanto came across base chief Bob sitting on the floor in a main hallway, his back against the wall, his head in his hands. Tanto thought Bob looked as though he'd given up. Even if Bob was talking on the phone, Tanto thought, his body language sent a message of defeat. Tanto shook his head with disdain but kept quiet. A withering monologue spooled in his mind: *As a leader you sure as hell do not show that. Don't show that to the fricking people that you're in charge of. Maybe you're sitting there talking on the phone, but it doesn't look it. Find a way to look positive and look proactive. Find a way that everybody's morale stays up.* He suppressed a desire to punch the base chief in the face.

Standing over Bob, Tanto remembered the BlackBerry the militiaman gave him outside the villa. None of the DS agents had reported losing one, so Tanto thought that it might belong to Chris Stevens.

"Hey sir," Tanto said, holding it out to Bob. "Here's a phone we found over at the consulate. You might want to check it out." The base chief silently took the BlackBerry, and Tanto returned to Building B. Tanto never learned its owner.

━━━

Atop the roofs, the men talked, snacked on candy, and replenished their fluids. Most suffered from varying degrees of smoke inhalation. Tig felt as though he might cough up a lung. A few went inside buildings for quick bathroom breaks. They checked their gunsights and weapons. They determined their fields of fire, so each man knew which area to be watching for attackers.

As they waited, the Team Leader came on the radio to let the operators know that the surveillance drone was overhead. He had no word on a gunship. The T.L. asked the men on each building and tower to remove a strobe light from the ammunition cans, to help the drone identify their locations.

Tanto hoped that the strobes also would guide a gunship, so he flipped one on and placed it in the middle of the roof. But soon after, he abandoned his hope for armed air support. "I don't think we're getting a gunship," Tanto told D.B.

D.B. had reached the same conclusion. He let out a rueful laugh.

"Fuck it," Tanto said. "What are we going to do about it? We'll just do what we can."

Across the driveway, atop Building D, Jack heard the Team Leader's request differently. Jack understood the T.L. to mean that he wanted the operators to put infrared strobe lights on their helmets. Jack knew that the drone was unarmed, and he held out no hope for a gunship. Wearing a strobe wouldn't do him any good personally. Worse, if one of the attackers had somehow obtained a pair of night-vision goggles, the light would act like a bull's-eye on Jack's head. He ignored the order.

Being on the roof gave Jack time to look himself over. He noticed that his jeans were soaking wet. At first Jack thought he must have fallen in water without realizing it, but then he grasped that his jeans were drenched with sweat. While looking at his pants, Jack saw a large rip on the left leg. A pocket-size flap just below his crotch hung open to the light Mediterranean breeze. He had no idea how it happened. He was just glad the tear wasn't a couple of inches higher. When the first muster call came, he'd pulled on his jeans without wasting time for underwear.

As the exterior lights continued to illuminate the area outside the Annex, a man who lived in a compound on the south side of Annex Road came to the wall opposite the tower where Tig stood. He demanded in Arabic that the exterior lights be turned off. Tig found one of the local guards who spoke English and asked him to translate. The guard told Tig that the neighbor said they should "turn off these lights, because they're going to know where you are."

The comment disturbed Tig. *What does he mean*

"they"? Tig wondered. *How does he even know what's going on here?* He told the guard to tell the neighbor to ignore the lights and go back inside his house. The man huffed away. A few minutes later, a Toyota pickup truck and four cars sped out of the man's property, one after another. Tig walked to Building C to tell the Team Leader, but neither knew what it might portend, if anything. While talking with the T.L., Tig left his helmet and broken night-vision goggles on the Building C patio.

After caring for Scott Wickland in Building C, Rone made radio calls asking if anyone else was hurt and needed his help. He had no immediate takers, but he told Dave Ubben that he wanted another look at Ubben's injured arm. An Annex staffer noticed Rone prowling through the building, eager to climb to his rooftop fighting post.

Rone looked completely at home and in his element, the staffer told Jack later. He moved with confidence and wore a predator's grin. Rone's self-assurance buoyed the non-shooting staffers in Building C, who had finally acknowledged that their lives depended on the operators. The staffer told Jack: "He was like, 'Yeah, we're going to unleash hate on these guys.' He was ready to go to war, and he didn't care how many of them were coming."

As he watched Rone jock up, the staffer couldn't get over how much the muscular former SEAL with the sculpted beard resembled King Leonidas from the movie *300*. Jack understood completely.

━━━

While making his rounds, Oz climbed atop Building D and spent a few minutes talking with Jack, to learn as much as he could about what had happened at the Compound. Oz told Jack he felt frustrated that he wasn't among them and asked if they'd killed many attackers. Jack told him he didn't know. Oz made sure they had enough supplies and ammo, then climbed down.

While marking time on the roof, Jack and the DS agent from Tripoli talked about how unprepared the Compound had been for the assault. The agent told Jack that if the attackers hadn't begun chanting as they swarmed through the pedestrian gate, the outcome might have been worse, because the agents at the villa would have been caught even more by surprise.

The agent's comment made Jack think about the difference between what happened at the Compound and what they were prepared to withstand at the Annex. When the Compound came under fire, three DS agents were relaxing outside the villa, one was inside watching a movie, and the fifth was doing paperwork in the TOC. One of the four 17 February militiamen who'd been hired for Compound security was absent, and the Blue Mountain guards were unarmed. By contrast, the Annex's active defense team featured six heavily armed, highly skilled operators stationed on fortified rooftops and tower fighting positions, girding for battle. Supporting them were three DS agents, two experienced Annex staffers, and if they remained at their posts, three armed Libyan guards the operators hoped were ready to fight.

Another major difference was that the men at the Annex knew the enemy was coming. Any attackers who tried to get inside the walls would be met by a ferocious response. The Compound was a relatively soft target; the operators felt certain that the Annex wouldn't be.

———

When Oz climbed down after his talk with Jack, he stationed himself atop the tower platform near the northeast corner of the wall. That tower, known as Fighting Position Three, allowed Oz to overlook Zombieland and two large, open pens packed with several hundred filthy sheep. Now and then, two men Oz presumed to be shepherds walked around the area. Oz watched them closely but they didn't seem to be armed. He studied the sheep, too, concerned that attackers might try to use the animals as concealment and crawl among them toward the wall.

———

Sometime before 12:30 a.m., Tanto and D.B. saw a car arrive at a dimly lit parking area on Annex Road, about three hundred yards east of their position. The operators often used the lot as a drop-off point for vehicles they needed to have serviced, leaving them there for a British-owned company to collect by tow truck. Near the parking area was a house owned by a family that didn't welcome the Americans' presence on their street. The teenage boys who lived there walked around the neighborhood with their friends trying to look tough, like a street gang armed with sticks and knives. Sometimes they fired bottle rockets and threw M-80 fireworks from Zombieland over the east Annex wall.

Another car pulled into the parking area, then two more. At least two other cars arrived in the minutes that followed. Tanto and D.B. looked at each other, then slid their night-vision goggles down from their helmets. They focused hard on the parking area. Two Benghazi police cars stopped at the lot, but soon drove off. Tanto narrated the events on the radio, punctuating the sequence of comings and goings with a complaint: "Hey, the cops are leaving!" The other cars remained.

"Are we expecting any friendlies to come and set up a perimeter around us?" Tanto called to the Team Leader. "'Cause, you know, there's some cars starting to mass in that parking lot where we drop our cars off."

"Let me check," the T.L. answered. "I'm not aware of any."

With each new car in the lot, Tanto and D.B. grew more anxious.

"Man, I don't think we're expecting anybody," Tanto said. They tried to determine whether the men looked like 17 February militia members, but they had no way to know.

D.B. told Tanto that he saw men moving away from the cars, in the general direction of the Annex.

"Are they the locals that live there, or are they bad guys?" Tanto asked.

"I can't tell," D.B. said. "It looks like they're moving. But they're not moving normally. They're moving tactically." After a pause, D.B. added: "I think these guys are starting to move on us."

His adrenaline flowing, Tanto called out over the radio: "Be advised, we've got unknowns moving toward our compound from the drop-off parking lot."

Tanto looked out over an area of trees and brush and saw one man advancing. He continued peering into the dark and saw another. Soon Tanto counted a half dozen men approaching. Tanto wondered how many more of them he couldn't see in the dark. The men had nowhere to take cover, but Tanto and D.B. watched as they tried to conceal themselves by moving steadily from bush to bush, from one spindly tree to the next. Tanto thought the approaching men's movements resembled kids playing hide-and-seek. The operators' pulse rates rose.

Tanto repeated his radio call to the Team Leader. "Are we expecting any friendlies at all? We got guys moving on us now. If we have friendlies, I need to know."

"Tanto," the T.L. said, "I have got no word, no confirmation that there are any friendlies."

"Well, then are we cleared hot to shoot, if we need to shoot?"

"You make the call," the Team Leader said. "But right now we have no friendlies."

"Roger that," Tanto said.

The approaching men increased in number. Some wore white T-shirts. Illuminated by the exterior Annex lights and the moonlight from above, they glowed a fluorescent green in the operators' night-vision goggles. When the men among the trees came within a hundred yards of the Annex's east wall, Tanto counted nine of them. Still he wondered if others, perhaps wearing black shirts or hidden in the grove, remained invisible to him. He focused his mind on the fields of fire that he, D.B., and the DS agent on Building B had established, to ensure that they had cross-covered the area beyond the walls, so their gunfire would spread across interlocking sectors.

Tanto squeezed his left hand around an area near the barrel of his assault rifle that the operators called the "broom handle," to illuminate his laser sight for three-second intervals. He switched the beam to a setting that was invisible to the naked eye, but appeared as a bright dot on any object it hit when seen through night-vision goggles.

Tanto moved the beam from one approaching figure to the next, allowing a pause between sightings in case any of the men outside the walls had night-vision goggles, too. If so, they could use the goggles to reverse-target the laser-firing Americans on the rooftops. Each time he hit one with the beam, he'd ask D.B., "Is that the guy you're seeing?" When D.B. confirmed it, Tanto moved to another. That way, they knew that both had identified the same potential enemies. When the targeting began, the DS agent didn't have night-vision goggles, so he could only strain his eyes and hope to spot the oncoming men on his own.

As Tanto pointed out each possible target, he called on the radio to Oz, whose vantage point on the northeast corner tower gave him a similar view of the approaching men. Oz saw them coming, too, replying "Roger" each time he saw Tanto's laser hit one. Although the technology gave them an advantage, the operators knew that the area beyond the wall was rife with dead spots, dark areas where their goggles couldn't help them see.

As they prepared to engage, the operators kept thinking about the teenagers who lived in the nearby house. The Americans resolved that they wouldn't shoot until fired upon, or until some other action demonstrated that the figures outside the Annex were enemies, and not quasi-friendly militiamen or tough local teens armed with nothing more powerful than firecrackers.

Tanto kept watching men trying to conceal themselves in his assigned sector, but he didn't see weapons. Then D.B. spotted an armed man in his sector. He called out: "I got AKs." Tanto looked again and saw rifles, too.

From their stealthy movements to the weapons they carried, by all indications the men were enemy attackers approaching the Annex from the area east of the wall. But the Americans wanted even more confirmation before engaging. The possibility remained, no matter how small, that the men were 17 February militiamen coming to help. All Tanto could say on the radio was: "Guys, be advised. I believe we've got bad guys coming up on us. Stand by."

Then Tanto saw a man drop to one knee.

———

Before Tanto and D.B. noticed the arriving cars and the approaching men, Tanto had called to ask if anyone had a spare pair of night-vision goggles for the DS agent on Building B. A case officer at Building C produced a pair and gave them to Tig, to bring to Building B on his rounds. On his way to deliver the goggles, Tig stopped at Building A to grab two cases of water from a front hallway.

He climbed the ladder on the side of Building B and dropped off the goggles. By then, Tanto, D.B., and the DS agent were already occupied watching the men nearing the Annex wall.

His rifle hanging loose on its straps in front of him, Tig walked to the east side of Building C, toward the area the operators called their prison gym. He could see Oz in position at the northeast tower, some thirty yards ahead, so he lugged the water bottles that way. As Tig approached the workout area, something flew over the wall in his direction.

He couldn't see what it was, but sparks sputtered from one end. It had a lit fuse.

TEN

Hard Target

———

TIG WAS MID-STRIDE, APPROACHING THE OPERATORS' prison gym, when the bomb landed at the far edge of the workout area. He had protection from his heavy Rhodesian vest and his body armor, but Tig's head was bare. He'd accidentally left his helmet around the corner at Building C while talking with the Team Leader about the nosy neighbor. Tig froze, dropped the water he'd brought for Oz, and braced for impact.

His mind focused on a single thought: *This is gonna hurt.*

But when the white light flashed and the boom sounded, the twenty-five feet that separated Tig from the explosion was just enough to save him. He took stock and, to his surprise, found himself intact and without a scratch.

Tig couldn't be certain, but based on the sight and sound of the blast, and the absence of shrapnel, he believed that the improvised explosive device lobbed over the wall was a small "jelly" or "gelatina" bomb. An easy-to-produce favorite of radical Libyan militias, gelatina bombs were cheap, moldable explosives made from gelignite, a material similar to dynamite but more stable and abundant. Benghazi fishermen used gelatina bombs to ease their labors, tossing them into the Mediterranean, waiting for the geyser, then collecting the fish that rose to the surface. The attackers seemed to be using the bomb for a similar purpose, to stun or distract the Americans before swooping in for the kill.

The moment the blast went off, the men who'd been sneaking toward the east wall opened fire on the Annex.

Tig sprinted to reach Oz at the northeast tower. He climbed on, stood to Oz's left, and found his friend already engaging their enemies.

———

Before the blast, Oz stood on the steel platform looking forward to Tig's arrival with the water bottles. He heard the *whoosh* of something flying over the east wall, but wasn't immediately sure what it was. When the explosion hit and gunfire followed, Oz understood that the bomb was the attackers' signal to begin their assault, just as the Americans sometimes used stun grenades or "flash bangs" to initiate an action.

From the laser spotting he'd done via radio with Tanto, Oz already had a general idea where some of the attackers were located, spread out in the dark among the trees and brush. He focused on those areas when the shooting began, watching for muzzle flashes and snatches of white shirts in the moonlight. Whenever he spotted one, Oz fired in that direction.

As bullets passed overhead, Oz saw his enemies attempting to shoot out the lights illuminating the eastern exterior of the Annex.

———

The gelatina bomb apparently was the attackers' signal to commence firing, but it wasn't the only explosive they'd brought. Somewhere in the trees east of the wall, an attacker shouldered a rocket-propelled grenade and fired it toward the Annex. Tanto heard the signature sound of the launch, a sizzling gargle then a *whoosh*, followed a few seconds later by an explosion. The shooter evidently aimed too high, and the RPG flew over the Annex entirely, landing somewhere beyond the far west wall.

Yet Tanto's hearing was so bad from the gunfight at the Compound that he still wasn't entirely sure that an Annex firefight had just begun. Even after seeing the attacker take a knee, Tanto held a sliver of concern that the sounds he heard came from firecrackers.

"Dude," he asked D.B., "did somebody just shoot at us?"

"Man, I think so," D.B. answered. He radioed the Team Leader to ask if he knew whether 17 February militiamen were en route to the Annex, to be sure this wasn't a friendly-fire incident.

"We don't know," the T.L. said. "But if you're fired on, fire back."

"Fuck this," Tanto said. He began shooting.

D.B. did the same, targeting the armed men he'd identified earlier, even as he seethed about the Team Leader remaining safely inside Building C. D.B. didn't need anyone to tell him the rules of engagement, especially when that person wasn't holding a gun. Angering him further, D.B. interpreted the T.L.'s "fire back" comment as a smart-ass way of responding, when all D.B. wanted was to be sure that he didn't kill a good guy.

Tanto lined up the kneeling attacker with the infrared gunsight mounted on his assault rifle, but when he fired, he watched as the first few rounds splashed in the dirt as far as ten feet to the left of his target. Tanto didn't have time to adjust his sight, so he corrected his aim using a method that shooters call "Kentucky windage," fine-tuning where he shot by experience and feel. With his corrections made, Tanto watched as men that he and D.B. had targeted earlier began to flinch from being hit. Some of the injured attackers tried to conceal themselves or regroup. Some zigzagged as they limped back and forth through the trees and brush. The operators kept shooting, leaning their weapons on the rooftop parapet and aiming down at the attackers coming toward them from beyond the east wall.

While Tanto and D.B. engaged the shooters, the Tripoli-based DS agent did his job by covering the area to the south, beyond the Annex's front wall. No one approached from a large open area in that direction, but the operators were covering the east and northeast, so they were happy to know that the DS agent was watching their flank.

Tanto found himself entranced by the sight of tracers and rounds whizzing into the dark. The night-vision goggles even picked up the heat signature of bullets. It looked like a laser light show, and Tanto felt like a kid inside a video game. After the frustration of being on the defensive at the Compound, Tanto sensed that the tables had turned. The attackers were falling back in disarray, apparently having expected a repeat of what had happened at the Compound three hours earlier.

We're fucking kicking these dudes' asses, Tanto thought.

———

The exchange of gunfire continued. Rounds zipped above the operators' heads and pinged against the walls, gouging craters in the cinder block.

Standing alongside Oz on the tower, Tig turned sideways to the wall as he unloaded his assault rifle toward the attackers. During a volley of incoming rounds, Tig felt the wind get knocked from his lungs.

"Aw fuck, I think I got shot," he told Oz.

Tig doubled over in pain and let loose a stream of curses. He snaked his right hand inside his shirt, beneath his vest and armor, but didn't feel any blood or find any holes in his skin. He concluded that shrapnel must have punched him like a heavyweight, then bounced off his protective gear. Tig's side ached but he wasn't seriously injured, so he resumed shooting, answering muzzle flashes with rounds of his own. With his helmet back at Building C, Tig knew that he was lucky the shrapnel hadn't reached him eighteen inches higher.

As Oz continued to engage, an incoming round hit the top of the wall directly in front of him. Stone fragments flew into his face just below his night-vision goggles. A stream of blood flowed from the bridge of his nose. Stunned, Oz composed himself and realized that he wasn't shot or seriously hurt. He wiped away the blood and returned to the fight.

An enemy round hit an exterior floodlight to the right of their tower position, shredding the bulb in an explosion of glass.

As they repelled the assault, the operators and DS agents kept their rifles set on semi-automatic, to conserve rounds and keep their aim true. Fantasy soldiers, video-game players, and young militiamen might favor the wild spray of bullets from a fully automatic rifle, but the operators considered that a tactical error and a waste of good ammo.

As the firefight continued, the shooting wasn't constant. They shot in controlled bursts, one or two well-aimed rounds, then a pause, then one or two more. During a ten-minute period, several operators said, each shot anywhere from thirty to sixty rounds. They didn't know how many attackers they hit in the dark.

Tanto and Oz couldn't be sure how many men they faced overall. But from the silhouettes and white T-shirts they saw through their goggles, plus the number of flashes coming from different places, they estimated fifteen to twenty, possibly as many as thirty.

All the while, from their tower position Tig and Oz tried to keep track of the two shepherds and the sheep pens, to make sure no one was trying to sneak through the animals to approach the wall. The shepherds stayed out of the line of fire, but Oz thought they seemed oddly nonchalant about the bullets flying around them. He suspected that they were somehow connected to the men shooting at the Annex, but until they displayed a weapon Oz wouldn't engage.

Neither he nor Tig had worn earplugs, and soon Oz's ears throbbed from the thunderous noise created by the two of them firing side by side on the small tower. During a break in the action, Oz tore off hunks of Kerlix gauze from a roll in his medical kit, balled them up, and stuffed them in his ears. He asked Tig if he wanted some, but Tig thought Oz looked too funny to emulate and just funny enough to ridicule.

"Oh, so that was a little too loud for you?" Tig asked with mock concern.

━━━

Tanto saw some of the attackers turn and run toward the house where he knew the teenagers lived, near the parking area. He continued firing until they reached the house, then stopped. Although Tanto wouldn't have been surprised if the family that lived there supported the attackers, he didn't want to shoot anyone who wasn't clearly a threat to the Annex. As far as he knew, the family might have been innocent bystanders whose house was commandeered by militants. When the attackers reached the parking area, Tanto saw two cars speed away north around the corner from Annex Road.

After he stopped shooting, Tanto double-checked his decision with D.B.

"Hey dude," he asked, "should we keep firing?"

"Man, I don't know if there's still kids in that house," answered D.B.

Tanto was tempted to lay waste to the house, but he knew that D.B. was right. If they shot one bystander, no matter how much good they might accomplish this night, they'd be censured or worse.

With D.B. shooting from four feet away, by the time the firefight ended Tanto's left ear was ringing and almost useless. "You motherfucker," he told D.B., a smile softening his accusation. "I can't hear for shit now. Thanks, man."

"Hey," D.B. answered, smiling back. "Casualty of war. Guess you shoulda worn earplugs."

Tanto flipped him the bird.

Between the banter, both felt as though they'd turned a corner and begun taking control. If the attackers had expected this assault to follow the pattern set by the siege of the Compound, where they'd gained access to the Americans' sanctum without dodging bullets, the operators wanted them to know that the Annex wouldn't be such easy pickings.

About ten minutes after it started, the shooting from the attackers petered out entirely. When the firefight ended, Oz heard scuffling sounds and groans coming from the bushes where the attackers had tried to conceal themselves, perhaps one hundred yards from the wall. From atop Building B, D.B. heard moaning along with what he thought might be the sound of men trying to reload their weapons.

From radio calls among the various positions, the operators learned that other than the minor injuries to Oz and Tig, and a cathedral-full of bells ringing in their ears, everyone in the Annex was fine.

As they gulped water and Gatorade and tried to relax, letting the adrenaline reabsorb into their systems, the air around them reeked of the pungent scent of gunpowder.

To amuse his fellow operators, at around 12:45 a.m. Tanto called the Team Leader on the radio: "Well, I guess we're not going to get that Spectre gunship, are we?" The T.L. didn't answer, so Tanto filled in the blank: "Roger that. Just asking."

Reflecting on the freshly won firefight, Tanto wished that he'd been able to find the grenade launcher he'd searched for earlier. *A couple of those would have just killed all of them*, he told himself.

━━━

Because the attack came from the east side of the Annex, the men atop Buildings C and D were forced to remain on the sidelines during the fire-fight. They knew that they couldn't shoot toward the east wall because they'd be firing at the backs of Oz and Tig on the tower and Tanto, D.B., and the DS agent on Building B.

Frustrated that he couldn't participate in the fight, Jack kept close watch over the areas beyond the north and west walls. If the attackers wanted to open a second front, that might be their choice. Jack was particularly concerned with the narrow north-south pathway close to the Annex that the operators knew as "Smuggler's Alley," which ran between Annex Road and the Fourth Ring Road. During moves, he and Rone had driven on the dirt alley several times, to vary their routine in case someone was watching them. Jack knew that high walls on both sides made it almost a concealed corridor that attackers might use to approach the Annex from the back gate of the burning diplomatic Compound.

Jack scanned in the direction of the alley for signs of movement but saw none. Still, he knew his job was to remain vigilant no matter how bleary-eyed he might become. Occasionally Jack's mind wandered to his family and the hope that he'd live to see his third child born. In the stretches of silence punctuated by gunshots, Jack also wondered how the praying mantis in the olive tree next to his post had fared amid the fight.

Several times Jack looked toward the southwest corner of the Annex, to a shack that housed a gardener who kept the property lush. Tall and thin, a clean-shaven man in his forties, the gardener repeatedly wandered outside his shack as the bullets flew, smoking cigarettes and dropping onto his knees to pray. Jack found it almost comical. *Here we are in a fight for our lives*, Jack thought, *and he's just down there, hoping for the best, smoking a cigarette.*

During and after the firefight, Jack, Dave Ubben, and the DS agent on Building D imagined different scenarios for new or related attacks on their position. They worried especially about a four-story building under construction to the southeast. The building was a concrete shell that an enemy could use as a sniper position, with a direct view of the Annex rooftops. To the Annex defenders' surprise it apparently remained empty. They felt grateful that their enemies seemed to be poorly trained in battle tactics and techniques.

Jack also watched a residential compound to the immediate northwest, with a large house only twenty-five yards from the Annex wall. As the firefight raged, two unarmed men walked out the front door and stood outside smoking cigarettes, as though it was just another Tuesday night in Benghazi. Jack passed word of the men over the radio, so no one mistook them for hostile attackers. The call was part of Jack's straightforward battle mantra: *It's all about communicating. If you communicate well and shoot, you're ahead of the game.*

━━━

After the firefight ended, Tanto reached for his night-vision goggles. But a screw that attached them to his helmet had come loose, and the goggles fell and broke. *You've got to be shitting me*, Tanto thought. He called over the radio to see if anyone had a spare pair. When no one offered, Tanto climbed down to look for one.

On his way to Building C, eating a Snickers bar, Tanto decided to check on the three local men who'd been hired to serve as the Annex guard force. Tanto knew that Tig and Oz had placed them in fighting positions, so he figured he'd see if they needed ammunition or anything else. But when he reached the guards' assigned places, they were gone. When he looked outside the Annex, their cars were gone, too. "They split," Tanto told his fellow operators.

He went to the GRS Team Room in Building C, but couldn't find an extra pair of goggles. An Annex security team member sought him out. "I've got these," the security member said, holding out a pair. "I'm not going to need them." The gift provided more evidence that the operators had won the staffers' respect.

Tanto thanked him and attached the goggles to his helmet. He grabbed a handful of candy and rejoined D.B. and the DS agent on Building B. They sat in the white lawn chairs trying not to focus on how mentally exhausted they were. D.B. was comfortable with silence, but Tanto wasn't the type to sit quietly for long.

"Hey man," Tanto told D.B. "If they come at us with anything bigger than RPGs or AKs, or they come with a Technical mounted, bro, we're not going to be able to fight that off. We don't have the weaponry for that."

"Yeah, I know," D.B. told him.

"Well fuck, I hope they don't come with the Technical, 'cause if they do, me and you we're going to have to get down off this building and start getting out of this compound. We're going to have to move towards them. And we're going to have to attack them direct."

Again D.B. nodded and said, "Yeah, I know."

D.B.'s brief acknowledgment was exactly what Tanto had hoped to hear. When D.B. said he accepted the odds they might face together, Tanto considered it reaffirmation of the bond they'd developed over the previous decade, responding to each other's close calls in Iraq, Afghanistan, and now Libya. Tanto's comments also were his way of saying that if they had to leave the Annex with fewer than a dozen fighters to confront a large, heavily armed force, he'd feel confident with D.B. beside him. Knowing Tanto as he did, D.B. got the message.

━━━

The discussion of what weapons and tactics they might encounter beyond rocket-propelled grenades and AK-47s made Tanto think about his wife and children. The idea that he might not talk to them again gave him chills. Tanto tried to force the thought from his mind.

Tanto recalled a scene from the HBO television series *Band of Brothers* in which an officer tells a frightened soldier in a foxhole to start fighting.

He remembered a line about embracing death as a way to find the strength to fight. *I don't want to die*, Tanto thought. *None of us wants to die. But it's a possibility, and if you don't accept that, it's just going to be in the back of your head the whole time, and you're not going to be able to function. So you accept it, you realize that you're not going to be able to talk to your family possibly ever again.*

Tanto took comfort in knowing that he'd told his wife and children how much he loved them during their most recent phone call, less than twenty-four hours earlier. But again he tried to squeeze them out of his thoughts. He knew that it was a vicious cycle. The more Tanto focused on his family, the less he could focus on doing his job well, which was the very thing that would increase his chances of returning to them.

Tanto took off his helmet and poured water over his head, then shook it off like a dog emerging from a stream. He slid from the lawn chair to the rooftop, sitting with his elbows on his knees, his fingers intertwined in front of his face. Tanto checked his pockets for ammo and his knife, to be sure that he was ready for whatever came next. His assault rifle within reach, he made a point of trying to remember everything that had happened so far, down to the smallest detail. If he made it home, he wanted to be able to tell the story of what occurred this night in Benghazi. And if one of his fellow operators didn't make it home, Tanto wanted to be able to tell that man's family how brave he'd been and how much good he'd done.

Sitting on the roof, Tanto thought back to the amount of time they'd lost at the beginning of the battle, waiting for the OK to respond to the Compound. His anger at Bob the Annex chief flared.

"Why did he keep telling us to stand down?" Tanto asked rhetorically, then launched into a profanity-laced attack on Bob. He added sarcastically: "He's probably trying to get 17 Feb to come save us right now, too."

D.B. felt the same way. He believed that Sean Smith wouldn't be dead and Chris Stevens wouldn't be missing, if only they'd rushed to the Compound when they first jocked up.

Tanto called quietly to the DS agent, who'd been sitting on his own on the far side of the roof, watching the area beyond the south wall.

"Hey dude," Tanto said. "What happened over there?"

"We're sitting enjoying ourselves," he told the operators, "about ready to go to bed. We're smoking hookahs. And then all of a sudden we hear some chanting and guys are at our gate, and all of a sudden all shit goes to hell and they start firing."

"So you guys had no alert at all?"

"Nope."

"What did your 17 Feb guys do?"

"Man, they weren't even around."

"Where were your Blue Mountain guys?"

"I don't know where they were, either," the DS agent said. "We didn't know, we had no alert. By the time we knew what was going on, they were already on top of us."

Tanto and D.B. apologized to the DS agent for not getting there sooner.

━━━

After the firefight ended, Jack saw cars arriving and people congregating around the north end of Zombieland. Tanto, Tig, and some of the other Annex defenders heard chants coming from the direction of the Fourth Ring Road. Several saw smoke rising over the 17 February barracks building as it continued to burn at the Compound.

Unknown to the Americans at the Annex, looters, curiosity seekers, and perhaps some of the initial attackers roamed unchecked inside the unlit Compound. The burned-out hulk of an armored Land Cruiser sat outside the barracks, its rubber tires melted down to the metal rims. Official papers littered the ransacked TOC and fluttered outside on the trampled grass. One sheet showed Ambassador Stevens's schedule for the week. Bullet shells dotted the brick driveway. A beige upholstered chair with gently curved arms floated in the villa pool alongside a broken umbrella and a flock of red cushions. Patio furniture, appliances, and other debris rested on the pool's blue bottom. Black soot stains and spray-painted Arabic words spread like ivy across the buildings' yellow outer walls. Young men with guns exulted to the sky as photographers captured the scene, with the flames of burning buildings as the backdrop.

The villa's blown-open front doors led to a charred ruin that resembled the inside of a huge fireplace. Paint and wallpaper curled from the scorched walls. The marble floor was cracked like an ancient mosaic, and the thick rugs that once covered it were reduced to ash. Interior wooden doors lay smashed and prone. Broken stone planters spilled their contents like earthen puddles. A chandelier hung improbably from the ceiling, coated with ashy grime. Twisted metal, shattered glass, and splintered remnants of blackened furniture completed the apocalyptic murder scene.

The fire in the villa had burned itself out. The building had cooled enough to allow local men to skitter through the rooms and hallways, including the safe-haven area, which they entered through the open bedroom window. At least some came to strip the villa of any remaining value or respect. Several left with garment bags filled with the Americans' clothing. Somewhere around 1:00 a.m., or ninety minutes after the last Americans left the property, a few local men reached the previously inaccessible back rooms of the villa's safe haven. There they found an unresponsive, middle-aged white male, his lips black with soot, his white T-shirt smeared with ash.

A young Libyan man who made a cell-phone video of the man's motionless form later told CBS News that he heard someone shout in Arabic, "There's a body, a foreigner!" As the man was carried from the villa through the window, the video captured someone yelling in Arabic, "God is great! He's alive, he's alive!" The man who made the video told CBS News that no one knew the man's identity. He said several people called for a doctor but couldn't find one in the crowd.

An official US government review said six unknown men believed to have been acting as Good Samaritans brought the unidentified man to the Benghazi Medical Center, less than two miles from the Compound, between the Second and Third Ring Roads. They arrived there around 1:15 a.m. Although the man showed no signs of life, doctors said they attempted to resuscitate him for roughly forty-five minutes before they pronounced him dead from apparent smoke inhalation.

At 2:00 a.m., the US Embassy in Tripoli received a call from Scott Wickland's cell phone, which he'd given to Chris Stevens when they took refuge in the safe haven. During the call, a man speaking Arabic gave a description fitting the ambassador and said the unidentified man was at a Benghazi hospital. Someone apparently had plucked the phone from the man's pants pocket, and the Arabic-speaking man had been calling stored numbers. But the caller couldn't provide a photograph or other proof that would satisfy the Tripoli diplomats that he was actually with Stevens.

Complicating matters further, at first it wasn't clear which hospital was involved. When embassy officials learned that the man had been taken to Benghazi Medical Center, they feared a trap, according to the official review. Local sources told them that the medical center was allied with, or possibly controlled by, the Ansar al-Sharia militia.

US Embassy officials were suspicious that someone had simply found the phone or had taken it
from a dead or kidnapped Stevens. Claiming that
the phone's owner was at a hospital might be a
devious ruse to draw Americans into the open for
an ambush. The embassy's political attaché, David
McFarland, pressed his Benghazi contacts for
answers.

Even if the caller's claims were true, the possibility existed that any Americans who went to the
hospital to find Stevens would cross paths with
injured attackers from the Compound and their
companions. If American officials were certain
that Stevens was there and alive, they would treat
it as a hostage rescue situation and send operators
loaded for bear. Otherwise, they'd be prudent and
wait. To speed the process, embassy officials sent
a Libyan they trusted to the hospital, to confirm
the man's identity and his condition. The Libyan
was the same man who'd rescued the downed
American F-15 pilot in 2011, and who now ran the
school where Stevens had planned to establish an
American Corner.

Almost simultaneously, word spread through the
Annex radios that the seven-man team from Tripoli
had reached the Benghazi airport. But it didn't look
as though they'd be joining the Annex defenses
anytime soon. Bob the Annex chief and the diplomats in Tripoli were struggling to get the Libyan
government to send transportation and security

to the airport to escort the response team to their destination. None of the new arrivals had ever worked in Benghazi, so they didn't know their way around. Commandeering vehicles wouldn't be an option, especially on a night when it seemed to be open season on Americans.

Sometime after the firefight, D.B. heard the Team Leader say they also might get help from a Special Operations team coming from Italy. D.B. sensed morale rise with news about the Tripoli team and a possible second unit of reinforcements. D.B.'s combat experience had taught him a basic equation of military math: *Anytime you're in a fight, you always want as many of your friends to show up with as many guns as they can.*

Meanwhile, officials in Tripoli and Washington debated whether the Tripoli response team should go to the hospital on a rescue mission, or to the Annex to bolster defenses before all the Americans there evacuated. That decision depended primarily on whether an American man was in fact at the hospital, and if so, whether he was Chris Stevens. The biggest question of all was whether he was still alive.

ELEVEN

Incoming?

———

AFTER THE FIREFIGHT, OZ AND TIG STOOD ON their steel tower trying to decompress. Tig pulled up his vest and lifted his shirt so Oz could look at his side. Angry red welts rose on Tig's skin where the shrapnel hit, but no wounds needed Rone's care. They talked and rested, even as they remained on guard. Both knew they couldn't relax while they still heard voices of men moving in the bushes, some apparently wounded. The operators' muscles ached from standing for so long and crouching behind a sandbag-filled bin at the edge of the tower.

Tig retrieved the water that he'd dropped near the workout area when the bomb hit. Oz drank first while Tig watched beyond the wall, then they switched.

Meanwhile, Rone called Dave Ubben and asked him to come to Building C's roof, so Rone could check the dressing on Ubben's injured forearm.

After Rone patched him up, Ubben remained atop Building C with Rone and the Annex staffer who'd had combat experience in Afghanistan.

The Annex had been quiet for some time after the firefight, and during that time several case officers returned to their rooms to gather their belongings. Tig decided to leave the northeast tower to find the Team Leader, to urge that all the shooters also be allowed to rotate off the roofs and towers to their rooms.

As Tig climbed down the tower ladder, he found himself highlighted by Dave Ubben's flashlight, shining on him from the roof of Building C. Tig threw up his hands in annoyance and Ubben switched off the light. *What the fuck, man?* Tig thought. *We were just in a firefight. Trying to get me killed?*

The T.L. agreed with Tig's suggestion, so Tig went inside the room he shared with Jack and tossed his computer and iPad into a backpack, then he returned to Building C and asked the Team Leader if anyone had seen his helmet. While the T.L. went to find it, Tig ducked inside and saw a maintenance man and the Annex cook, holding a shotgun, sitting silently on a couch with thousand-mile stares.

Tig felt sympathetic toward the non-shooters, but not toward several weapons-qualified men he saw among them. The operators needed as many defenders as they could find on roofs and towers, not on couches. *You're fucking shooters*, Tig thought. *We're fighting for our lives. And you're sitting here on your asses.*

＝＝＝

Atop Building B, Tanto and D.B. continued talking with the DS agent from Tripoli about security gaps at the Compound. In light of what had
happened, especially how easily the attackers
had entered the property, the operators couldn't
understand how requests for added personnel and
security measures were denied or delayed. They
never received a satisfying answer.

Around 2:30 a.m., the men on Building B noticed
cars arriving at the same parking area where the
attackers had assembled earlier. Tanto called the
Team Leader: "Are we expecting friendlies now in
that parking lot? I'm seeing more cars coming."

"I don't expect any," the T.L. replied.

"Has 17 Feb set up any blocking areas, to not
let bad guys near here?"

"I'm not aware of any," the Team Leader said.

"All right," Tanto said. "Just be advised, we got
more people starting to mass in that parking lot."

Over a fifteen-minute period, Tanto counted
eight to ten cars arriving in ones and twos. Several
more pulled in, bringing the total to as many as
fifteen. Tanto watched as men streamed into the
house at the edge of the parking area.

Tanto radioed Oz at the tower: "We got more
people coming up in that building. Get your eyes
open, man. I think we're going to get hit again."
Oz acknowledged the warning and told Tanto that
he saw the cars and men.

Tanto and D.B. exchanged wary looks. Tanto

rose from the lawn chair to deliver a frustrated monologue to no one in particular: "Are they serious? Are they going to do this fucking stuff again? You got to be shitting me. Are they really that dumb?"

Tanto drank some water and strapped on his helmet. Several minutes later, the Team Leader called over the radio: "Be advised, ISR is letting us know that ten cars have amassed in a parking lot to our southeast."

Tanto radioed the T.L.: "Roger that. I already put that out, buddy. Hey, tell those ISR guys they're pretty much worthless. They ain't telling us anything we don't already know." However, Tanto added, it would be useful if the surveillance drone took a wider look to see whether more potential enemies were moving toward the Annex from farther away. The Team Leader agreed to ask.

Around 3:15 a.m., the men on Building B watched a stream of armed men file out of the house near the parking area. The operators resolved to hold their fire, to let the twenty or more approaching men think that the Annex defenders had let down their guard. *Let them come close to us,* Tanto thought. *We've got an ambush set up, and we're just going to wait and get them as close as they need to get. And then we're just going to fucking crush them.*

Several of the exterior lights on the east side of the Annex had been shot out during the first firefight, so the attackers might have imagined that they remained unseen as they approached through the trees in the dark. If so, they didn't appreciate the power of night-vision goggles. As the men crept forward, D.B. and Tanto marveled that their foes hadn't varied tactics from the first fire-fight. Again they moved from tree to tree, bush to bush, from the same point of origin. The DS agent kept watch to the south, and again he saw no one approaching from that direction. The other opera-tors saw no movement from Zombieland to the north or from Smuggler's Alley to the west.

The attackers came within one hundred yards of the east wall of the Annex, then fifty, then forty, and still the operators held their fire.

——

From his post atop the tower, ready to engage, Oz noticed a car parked on the far side of the Jersey barriers near the Annex's back gate, located near the northern corner of the east wall. Oz didn't know when the car had arrived, but he knew that it didn't belong there.

First Oz saw only a shadow, but then he made out the full figure of a man coming around the rear of the car. As the man cocked his arm to throw something toward the back gate, Oz drew a bead on the man and squeezed his trigger. The man crumpled to the dirt. A bright white light flashed and an explosion sounded, but the bomb the man had tried to hurl at the back gate fell harmlessly about six feet short. The operators believed that the man had intended to create an opening for himself and others to rush through.

After that, Oz, D.B., and Tanto held nothing

back. They concentrated rounds at the gun-wielding men in the trees and shrubs, hoping to overwhelm the attackers with superior force. The attackers shot back, more than during the first firefight.

———

As soon as Tig collected his helmet from the Team Leader, he heard an explosion and a burst of gunfire from beyond the east wall. He ran to the tower and rejoined Oz, who'd already taken out the bomber.

In the midst of the second firefight, the Team Leader hailed Oz and Tig on the radio to say he'd received a strange call from a 17 February militia leader. The operators had no idea any friendly militia members were in the vicinity. But now the Team Leader said a commander had called with a complaint.

"The 17 Feb guys say you're shooting at them," the T.L. said.

"Fuck that," Tig replied. "Somebody started shooting at us first, and they're still shooting at us. If that's them, tell them to stop shooting."

After a pause, the Team Leader agreed: "If they're shooting at you, shoot at them."

"Roger that," Tig said. He and Oz had never stopped shooting in the first place.

———

Tig, Oz, Tanto, and D.B. shot at every hostile target they could identify. Tanto even targeted cars in the distant parking area. D.B. and Tanto kept low behind the Building B parapet as they moved left and right, spotting their enemies through their night-vision goggles and opening fire. Tanto took aim at a line of attackers. He watched as his rounds hit one in the head, dropping the man in his tracks.

Oz and Tig switched positions on the tower like dance partners and shot repeatedly into the brush. They didn't know how many attackers they hit, but the diminishing fire from beyond the east wall suggested that their aim was true.

For a second time, the men on Buildings C and D couldn't join in. They had no clear view beyond the wall to where the attackers were hiding. Even if they could see the enemy, they would have endangered the men on the east side of the Annex by firing between them or over their heads.

After a five-minute steady exchange from both sides, with even more lead flying than during the first firefight, the attackers began to fall back. After five more minutes, all shooting from beyond the Annex stopped. Tanto saw several of their enemies drop to the dirt, and he witnessed one man he'd shot being helped into the house at the edge of the parking area. Others ran to their cars and sped away. Although some of the attackers used the house as a refuge, the operators say they never fired at the building because they didn't know whether women and children were inside.

For a second time, the attackers had retreated without reaching the Americans inside the Annex. In two approximately ten-minute firefights, separated by roughly two hours, they'd caused only minor injuries to Tig's ribcage and Oz's nose during the first firefight, and no injuries during the second. The operators had exacted a high price in return, but how many attackers were killed or injured remained unknown.

The contrast with the attack on the Compound was stark, and the operators' optimism rose from having repelled two armed assaults with barely a scratch.

Hours of near-constant watch began to play tricks on Jack's tired eyes. He stared at a point on top of the northwestern wall, perhaps fifty yards from his post on Building D, and grew certain that a man was lying motionless atop the wall. He asked the nearby DS agent if he saw the man, but it was only Jack's imagination.

A half hour or so passed with no new threats, and the two men on Building D traded stories about their military experiences. "If this was back in Iraq," the DS agent told Jack, "we would have had a couple of Blackhawks land and pick us up or help us out."

"Yeah," Jack said. "Don't expect that here. We don't have anything."

Jack had begun to believe that they might be stuck at the Annex for several days before someone could figure out how to evacuate them safely.

During a quiet period, the DS agent spoke on his cell phone to someone who Jack believed was from the State Department. The DS agent said the attack on the Compound was already on the news back home, and the media reports suggested that it escalated from a street protest over an anti-Islamic film. Jack knew there had been no such demonstrations in Benghazi, so he wondered what else was wrong about how the story was being told. But he had bigger worries, so he set that thought aside.

The DS agent also learned from the call that a white male had apparently been found alive in the villa at the Compound, and that he'd been taken to a nearby hospital. Surprised, Jack considered spreading the word over the radio, to raise everyone's spirits, but then he thought better of it.

Jack wanted to believe the ambassador was alive, but the news sounded too good to be true. Maybe it was another mistake, like the reports about spontaneous, Cairo-like protests in Benghazi prior to the attack. On one hand, if the man at the hospital was indeed the ambassador, Jack was glad that Stevens hadn't been kidnapped or murdered by terrorists, as he and Rone had feared. But Jack had been inside the villa multiple times, and he'd pulled Sean Smith through the window. He couldn't imagine how anyone who was inside could have survived after the operators and DS agents left.

As Tig resumed his watch over the northeast area beyond the walls, he spotted two Libyan men walking south toward the Annex down a darkened dirt roadway between the tin-roofed stockyard sheds. He wasn't sure, but they might have been the shepherds he'd seen earlier. Tig set his laser gunsight to display a visible red beam.

"If they keep coming, I'm gonna lase them," Tig told Oz.

In the dark, the operators couldn't tell if the men carried weapons, but Tig wouldn't take any chances. He could still hear chanting from the direction of the Compound, and he couldn't understand why anyone would approach the Annex on foot after two firefights, unless they intended to start a third.

Tig took aim and flashed the laser beam on the chest of one man, then moved it to the other. *If you keep coming*, he thought, *I'm pretty much gonna kill you.*

Each man stopped dead in his tracks when he saw a red dot dancing on his chest. Both abruptly turned west and sat down next to a building separated from the Annex by a stand of trees. They never came back, and Tig never learned who they were.

The sheep in the open pens remained a preoccupation for Oz and Tig. The animals' heads bobbed up and down, like swimmers in a crowded pool, as they jostled for position. As the operators stared at the sheep's long faces in the dark, they began to seem almost human. Making matters worse, rams regularly rose up on their hind legs to mount ewes. Each time it happened, Oz and Tig did a double take to be sure it wasn't a man moving among the sheep toward the wall. Although Tig had retrieved his helmet, his broken night-vision goggles made it particularly hard for him to distinguish between coupling livestock and crouching humans.

He and Oz called on the radio for stun grenades or flash bangs to toss into the pens. The operators thought the noise would rearrange the animals, allowing them to be sure that attackers weren't concealed among the livestock. No noisemakers were available, so Tig and Oz considered shining their flashlights, but that would have exposed their position on the tower.

Finally, Oz had an idea: "Let's just start killing the sheep."

If he and Tig had seen even one man among the animals, they might have done it. But that wasn't the case, so Oz and Tig put their sheep-slaughter thoughts on hold. Part of their hesitation was the knowledge that they'd spark a bureaucratic nightmare of second-guessing when the animals' owner demanded restitution and their bosses demanded explanations. Plus, all that sheep shooting would attract more unwanted attention and aggravate their ringing ears. Despite teasing Oz about the gauze bandages he'd used as earplugs, Tig had followed suit.

They passed the time by joking and talking, telling each other that the United States had gotten its money's worth for teaching them how to be soldiers. They'd both seen action before, but nothing as extended or intense as this. "Finally," Tig said with a sardonic laugh, "we get to put our training to use."

━━━

When Tanto felt certain that the second firefight was over, he returned to his lawn chair and a half eaten candy bar, washing it down with a gulp of water. *We kicked their ass again*, he thought. *We might get out of this, whether we get help or not. We just need to find a way to exit out of here. But shit, things are going good.*

"Looks like we repelled the attackers," Tanto told the Team Leader by radio. "There's nobody out there. They're gone." He could have stopped there, but Tanto took pride in his smart-ass reputation. He couldn't resist needling the T.L. and other base officials about the fact that whoever was watching the video stream from the drone hadn't warned them about the men approaching on foot before the second attack. "Go ahead and tell the ISR guys the same, since obviously they're not seeing what's going on down here."

━━━

Oz left Tig alone at the tower so he could check the other fighting positions, to see if shooters needed water, ammo, a bathroom break, or anything else. Oz climbed the ladder at Building C and joined Rone at a belt-fed machine gun position at the roof's northwest corner, while DS agent Dave Ubben stood watch near the northeast corner. The Annex staffer who'd been in Afghanistan climbed down from the roof to collect his personal belongings.

Rone and Oz stood side by side, scanning Zombieland and the stockyard area for movement. They were silent for long stretches, a product of deep fatigue and not wanting to give away their position. But now and then they spoke in quiet voices. Oz asked Rone how things had gone at the Compound. After walking Oz through the events, Rone told him how proud he was of everyone's actions.

"You know," Rone said, "we've got some frigging hellish warriors here. These guys are as good as any I've ever worked with."

Rone had served tours in Afghanistan and Iraq, and had been honored for valor while among elite Navy SEALs. Hearing that Rone felt so strongly about their Benghazi team filled Oz with pride.

"I think we're all glad that we've got each other," Oz said.

Oz asked Rone how the Team Leader had performed at the Compound. The T.L. hadn't joined the operators at the Annex fighting positions, but Rone had no problem with that or with the T.L.'s work at the Compound. "He did great," Rone said. "He let us do our thing while he handled command and control."

Rone told Oz how he became lost inside the burning villa, and how Tig had led him to safety. "He saved my life because he came back for me," Rone said.

They lapsed into silence and continued to watch beyond the wall, listening for noises and occasionally dropping their night-vision goggles over their eyes for a better look. Rone asked if Oz needed medical care for the cut on his nose, but Oz said he was fine. After another silence, they talked about their wives and children.

Rone told Oz that he was eager to return home to see his family, especially after having extended this trip in Benghazi. Rone found it amusing that he, Oz, and Tig all had infant children, and that Jack's wife was pregnant. He talked about how happy he was to be a father, and how much he looked forward to ending his operator career and raising his newborn son, Kai. He joked that they'd all be senior citizens by the time their youngest graduated from high school.

"I think it's going to be easier for me, having a son," Rone kidded Oz. "You're gonna be old when you're trying to fight off your daughter's boyfriends!"

They stood together as the long night continued, still looking out over Zombieland. The staffer who'd been in Afghanistan returned, but Oz told him that he could go back inside Building C. The rooftop was covered with Rone, Oz, and Dave Ubben.

━━━

Tanto climbed down from Building B and went alone atop Building A, near the front gate, to cover the south wall in case their enemies tried from a new direction. He also wanted to keep watch over the unfinished building across the

street that Jack worried might be a sniper roost.
No chair awaited him, so Tanto stood or took
a knee while fighting exhaustion as the night
dragged on.

An Annex staffer came on the radio and asked
if anyone on the roofs needed anything. No one
answered, so Tanto called out: "You know what,
yeah, I could use some food and some water up on
Building A. And if anybody knows of a big-titty,
blonde-haired stripper, I could use her up here,
too." He looked over to Building B and saw D.B.
shaking his head and smiling.

Tanto's supplies arrived in the hands of a
male, African-American staffer who was a serious weightlifter with bulging pectoral muscles.
"Well," Tanto said, "you've got big titties. You're
not blonde-haired and blue-eyed, but you'll have
to do." The staffer burst out laughing.

He kept Tanto company for about fifteen minutes, making whispered conversation to pass the
time. With his left eardrum blown and his right
ear ringing, Tanto knew he couldn't trust his hearing. For more than an hour, he'd thought he heard
voices coming from a field beyond the south wall.
He stared into the brush but couldn't see anyone
there. Tanto asked the staffer to listen. He told
Tanto that the field was silent. When the staffer
left, Tanto again thought he heard voices.

As quiet settled over the Annex, Rone called
on the radio to ask whether anyone else needed
medical care. Alone again, Tanto took the opportunity to get treated for his injured left arm from

when the wall collapsed outside the Compound. Rone climbed to the roof of Building A, where he cleaned and wrapped Tanto's arm, then rejoined Oz and Dave Ubben atop Building C.

A short time later, Tanto looked over the south wall and saw a car with several young men inside pull up to the Annex's front gate. *God, here it comes,* Tanto thought. *Car bomb. And I'm the closest to it.* He made himself as small as he could behind the Building A parapet, keeping his eyes open even as he felt his butt cheeks clench. But as quickly as the driver had turned toward the closed gate, he put the car in reverse and drove away. Tanto exhaled but didn't relax.

He puzzled over who the men were and what they were doing there in the early morning hours. *Could they have been part of the militia?* he wondered. *A bunch of college kids?* Tanto learned that around the same time, D.B. saw a man walking outside the Annex with a phone. *Phones have GPS readings. Was he getting GPS coordinates of our compound?* Latitude and longitude coordinates could be used for targeting, but Tanto didn't want to get caught up in speculation, and he couldn't do anything about it anyway.

Soon after, D.B. radioed Tanto to say that he was heading to their room. His black polo shirt was drenched with sweat, so he stripped it off and put on a black button-down. When D.B. returned, Tanto asked if he'd heard any news. "Sounds like the guys from Tripoli, our guys, are on their way," D.B. said.

———

At around 4:00 a.m. Benghazi time on September 12, 2012, or 10:00 p.m. the previous night in Washington, Secretary of State Hillary Clinton issued a statement condemning the attack and confirming Sean Smith's death, although he wasn't yet identified publicly. The statement said: "[O]ne of our State Department officers was killed. We are heartbroken by this terrible loss. Our thoughts and prayers are with his family and those who have suffered in this attack."

Clinton's brief statement also suggested a possible motive, or at least a tentative explanation: "Some have sought to justify this vicious behavior as a response to inflammatory material posted on the Internet. The United States deplores any intentional effort to denigrate the religious beliefs of others. Our commitment to religious tolerance goes back to the very beginning of our nation. But let me be clear: There is never any justification for violent acts of this kind."

Later, as controversy erupted over the Obama administration's actions before, during, and after the attack, critics called Clinton's statement a smoking gun. They said it marked the start of a politically motivated conspiracy to mislead the public by falsely implying that the attackers were outraged by the *Innocence of Muslims* video, and that the video had caused Benghazi residents to spontaneously set upon the Compound in protest. The theory behind the Obama critics' allegation was that, in the midst of a reelection campaign, the president didn't want to admit that his administration had failed to anticipate or adequately respond to a terrorist attack timed to coincide with the 9/11 anniversary.

Administration officials rejected those claims as false and politically motivated. They said Clinton's statement reflected the incomplete understanding they had about the attack as it unfolded. They also said that their top priority through the night wasn't untangling claims and counterclaims about the attackers' possible motives, it was finding Chris Stevens and organizing the rescue of Americans under siege. They also pointed out that embassies in Cairo and elsewhere did experience spontaneous attacks sparked by the YouTube clips, and that there continued to be mixed signals about whether the videos played a role in Benghazi, as well. Later reporting by several news organizations, notably *The New York Times*, suggested that the *Innocence of Muslims* video fueled the Compound attacks. But that, too, was hotly disputed, as was the *Times*'s conclusion that al-Qaeda played no direct role in the attack. As one media critic put it, more than a year after the attacks, the events in Benghazi remained shrouded in shades of gray and mired in a "political and ideological maelstrom."

Within an hour of Clinton's statement, the Libyan man sent to the hospital by the US Embassy in Tripoli released American officials from one of their two most pressing tasks. He confirmed that the Arabic caller using Scott Wickland's cell phone had told the truth. The white man pronounced dead at the Benghazi Medical Center at roughly 2:00 a.m. on September 12, 2012, was indeed Ambassador J. Christopher Stevens.

The operators' early speculation that Stevens had been kidnapped was mistaken. He'd been inside the villa since the start of the attack, hidden somewhere deep within the safe haven where the DS agents and operators couldn't locate him through the fire and smoke. The bloody handprint Rone and Jack saw must have come from someone else, possibly Dave Ubben after he injured his forearm during one of his searches. The discovery of Stevens inside the safe-haven area also made it unlikely that the BlackBerry that Tanto gave to Bob belonged to the ambassador.

When they learned that Stevens was inside the villa the entire time, the operators doubted Libyan claims that the ambassador had been alive when found, even if only briefly. Considering the smoky inferno they'd experienced during their searches, the lack of any response when they'd repeatedly called Stevens's name, and how quickly Sean Smith had succumbed, the operators felt certain that Stevens had died of smoke inhalation before they'd left the Compound. None of the video or still images of Stevens that have surfaced since he was found contradict that conclusion.

At his death, Chris Stevens was a fifty-two-year-old career diplomat who had dedicated his life to improving relations between the United States and the Arab world. President Obama eulogized Stevens as having died "in the city he helped to save." Obama would tell the United Nations General Assembly: "He acted with humility, but he also stood up for a set of principles—a belief that individuals should be free to determine their own destiny, and live with liberty, dignity, justice, and opportunity."

━━━

With Stevens confirmed dead, the team of Tripoli operators had no reason to venture into potentially hostile territory around the Benghazi Medical Center. Arrangements would need to be made to retrieve Stevens's remains, but only if that could be accomplished without putting anyone else in danger. With transportation and a security escort finally arranged by the Libyan government, the seven-member Tripoli squad headed from the airport directly toward the Annex. Roughly five hours had passed since they'd left the embassy.

When they reached the Annex, one of the Tripoli operators, Glen "Bub" Doherty, might yet have a chance to enjoy an impromptu reunion with his former SEAL friends Jack and Rone, and his newer friend, Tanto.

Glen was forty-two but looked a decade younger, a divorced, charismatic mix of free spirit and fierce self-discipline, a man who approached hard work and hard partying with equal vigor. A gifted athlete and a voracious reader, Glen was as comfortable among his fellow surf and ski bums as he was alongside elite special operators. In fact, "comfortable" was a word that defined how Glen fit into the world and into his own skin.

Raised in the affluent Boston suburb of Winchester, Massachusetts, Glen was the middle child of a stockbroker/boxing-enthusiast father and a candy-store-owning mother. He learned to fly at Embry-Riddle Aeronautical University in Arizona, but didn't stick around long enough to graduate. For several years he bounced around as a ski instructor and white-water rafting guide. Glen was a ripe twenty-four years old when he met a group of Navy SEALs and found his purpose. With Glen as a paramedic and a sniper, his SEAL team responded to the USS *Cole* attack in Yemen in 2000, among other missions. His plan to leave the service changed with 9/11, after which Glen served two tours during the war in Iraq. His team led some of the first Marine contingents moving north to Baghdad and took control of Saddam Hussein's former palaces.

Glen began working as a contract operator after leaving the SEALs in 2005, traveling from his home in California for trips to Afghanistan, Pakistan, Yemen, and most recently Tripoli, where he'd worked alongside Tanto. In between, he alternated between working out and drinking beer, kicking back and coauthoring an authoritative book on being a sniper. Along the way he collected an astonishing number of people who considered him their best friend. The nickname "Bub" fit a self-assured man who believed that every job was worth doing right and no party should end the same day it began.

To Jack, Glen was a natural, good at everything he did, a guy who drew people to him with magnetic warmth and a megawatt smile. Jack knew plenty of former SEALs who were macho and abrasive. Bub was neither. As Jack kept watch atop Building D, he didn't know if his old SEAL buddy was among the operators en route from the airport. But he hoped so. In a tight spot, Jack could think of few people he'd rather have on his team.

Regardless of what occurred the night before, whether revolutionary or routine, murderous or mundane, a new day in Benghazi always began the same way. As daylight drew near on September 12, 2012, the muezzins switched on the loudspeakers in the minaret crowns of the city's mosques and beckoned the faithful to the *Fajr* prayer. Listening to the amplified chants from atop Building D, Jack grew edgy.

A casual Roman Catholic, Jack considered himself respectful of all cultures and religions. *Everybody has their own idea of who and what God is,* he thought. *Nobody is right, nobody is wrong. The simple truth is, nobody knows, so you have faith. If you grew up in China, your idea of how things happened and how they are is different than if you grew up in South America or in the Middle East. For someone to say that my religion is the right one and everybody else is wrong or naïve, is completely ignorant.*

But it had been a long night. Jack didn't feel tolerant toward the people who'd been trying to kill him, and he wasn't in the mood to hear chanting in Arabic. His muscles ached, his eyes stung, his skin and clothes were caked with sweat and dirt. Two good men were dead, and the ordeal wasn't over. Certain that their attackers were Islamic radicals, Jack blamed all that he and his fellow Americans had endured on terrorists who tried to mask their hunger for power by claiming to be defenders of their religious beliefs.

As the call to prayer continued, Jack's temper rose. *I wonder what they're saying right now*, he thought. *I wonder if it's the normal thing, or are they saying, "Kill the Americans!" Or, are they saying, "Hey, stop fighting!" Either way, I just can't stand to hear it right now.*

Jack wasn't one to wallow in anger, so his thoughts shifted from Benghazans rising to pray, to his wife and children inside the home he hoped to see again. *Here I am, all the way across the world. I've barely survived the night. And my wife is probably at home getting ready to go to bed, completely clueless as to what's going on right now.* That thought led Jack to reflect on the fortunate lives led by many Americans, particularly in contrast to innocent people in places like Benghazi where armed militias roamed the streets, buildings burned, and foreigners huddled inside high-walled compounds awaiting rescue or the next attack. *People in America get up and go to their nine-to-five jobs every day and are oblivious to all these battles and wars and people dying every minute all over the world. This is life. This is how other countries live. This is a daily occurrence in some places.*

———

The Team Leader came on the radio with a heads-up: "Tripoli guys are coming in." He said the operators were spread among a ten-car militia escort, but he had few other details. The T.L. asked Tanto, who remained on Building A near the front gate, to confirm their identities before letting them in. The Annex security leader remained at his post near the front gate, but Tanto would have a better view from above.

Tanto wasn't sure the Tripoli team or their escorts knew the location of the Annex, so he told the Team Leader he'd use his laser to draw a circle in the sky above the gate as they approached, a military technique he called "lassoing" a target. If one of the Tripoli operators wore night-vision goggles, he'd see the laser as clearly as if Tanto had lit up a neon VACANT sign outside a roadside motel. Without goggles, the infrared beam would be invisible.

"Roger that," the T.L. said.

Within minutes, the Team Leader radioed to say the motorcade was heading west on the Fourth Ring Road and would soon drive down Annex Road. Tanto stood atop Building A and twirled his laser above the gate, though it remained unclear whether the Tripoli team got the message to look for the signal. Just in case, D.B. added to the welcome with several discreet flashes of visible light.

At about 5:00 a.m., a line of ten vehicles turned right onto Annex Road. They drove past the suspicious house and the empty parking area where the attackers had massed two hours earlier. Tanto was surprised that the cars looked like police sedans, painted red and white, several with strips of red and blue emergency lights on their roofs. Having been told that a militia was en route, Tanto expected fierce-looking Technicals with big mounted guns, pickup trucks filled with armed men in camouflage, and other intimidating displays. *They're traveling a bit light, considering what we've gotten into so far,* Tanto thought. Still, he was glad to see them, although he kept his gun trained in their direction, just in case.

The cars parked in a row, one behind another, stretched out along a wall on the south side of Annex Road. The Libyan police or militiamen remained inside the vehicles, while seven well-armed, jocked-up, unmistakably American men stepped onto the gravel road and approached the gate on foot. Tanto lowered his weapon and told the Annex security leader it was OK to let them in.

Tanto had worked with most of the new arrivals when he'd been in Tripoli, so as they walked through the gate he called down from the rooftop and greeted several by their radio call signs. "Hey," he said, "it's good to see you. Welcome to the party. We're having a blast over here."

Atop Building D, Jack lowered the barrel of his assault rifle and watched the operators enter the Annex. Four were GRS operators, including the Libya country Team Leader; two were active-duty Delta Force members; and the seventh was an older man serving as their translator. Jack briefly lost track of them as they walked past the olive tree toward Building C, so he moved to the east side of the roof for a better view.

Even in the dim light inside the Annex, Jack immediately recognized one team member: Glen "Bub" Doherty. Jack wouldn't drop his guard and call out to his friend, but he allowed himself a moment of good cheer. The two former SEALs hadn't seen each other in nearly three years, since they'd gone through the GRS training session with Rone. But Jack knew that when the danger passed, they'd catch up and tell stories. Jack would have preferred to have run into Glen at a bar, drinking his favorite IPA craft beer, but this would have to suffice.

The seven Tripoli team members went inside Building C, to work out details of the evacuation with the Annex chief and his deputy. Their main concern was getting assurances that the roads and the airport were clear of enemies, to minimize the chance that they'd be heading into an ambush en route.

Sunrise was still about an hour away, but inside the Annex walls it began to feel as though the worst of the night and the battle might be over. Although the Benghazi operators remained at their rooftop posts along with Dave Ubben and the two DS agents from Tripoli, several said the arrival of reinforcements and a militia escort made them feel as though they'd soon be safely away from Benghazi.

Yet as the minutes continued to tick by, the operators again grew tense. They couldn't afford any more delays. As students of military history, Rone and Oz could rattle off examples through the ages of attacks at first light. Standing together near the northwest corner of Building C's roof, they suspected that as the sun neared the horizon, the attackers would use the dim light to test the mettle of fatigued Americans who'd spent all night defending the Compound and the Annex. Rone and Oz knew that if their enemies timed it right, the operators would lose the advantage of night-vision goggles, and their fighting positions would become visible.

"We need to get the heck out of here," Oz said. "It's getting light."

▬▬

After the Tripoli team spent about ten minutes inside Building C, the door opened and one of the new arrivals strode around to the backyard, to find the ladder leading to the roof. Glen Doherty wanted to say hello to Rone.

As Glen approached the ladder, a call came over the radio telling all Annex residents that they had one last chance to visit their rooms to gather essential belongings before assembling at Building C for departure.

The evacuation plan called for members of the Tripoli team to lead a tightly controlled withdrawal of the five survivors from the Compound and most of the Annex staff. The Americans would be sprinkled among the motorcade of militia police cars that remained parked outside the front gate. They'd retrace their route to the airport, then fly to Tripoli on the small jet that the response team had chartered for the flight to Benghazi.

One complication was that the commercial jet was too small to carry all of the roughly thirty Americans, including the Tripoli team, inside the Annex. As a result, the initial evacuation wouldn't include the Benghazi operators, several other shooters, or the remains of Sean Smith.

Under the plan, rather than wait in the open at the airport, the men left behind would stay in the relative safety of the Annex with Smith's body until they got word that another plane had arrived for them. When the second plane landed, the militia motorcade would return to the Annex to escort the remaining men and Smith's body to the airport.

Attempts also were under way to coordinate with trusted local contacts to retrieve Ambassador Stevens's body from the Benghazi Medical Center, so his remains could fly with the operators and Smith's body to Tripoli. From there, the plan called for the operators to arrange flights home or to Washington, and the two fallen Americans to be received with honors at Andrews Air Force Base in Maryland.

When Tanto learned that he wouldn't be part of the first evacuation, he asked D.B. to cover the south side of the Annex from Building B. Tanto climbed down from Building A for a bathroom break. When he returned up top, he noticed that the militia motorcade had remained stationary since its arrival outside the Annex. Tanto called the Team Leader to ask why the militia hadn't set up blocking positions on surrounding streets, to prevent anyone from attempting a third attack on the Annex.

Tanto had barely released his thumb from the radio's talk button when he heard a strange whooshing sound. He squeezed the button again.

"Incoming?"

TWELVE

Mortars!

———

As the evacuation plans took shape inside Building C, Glen Doherty knew that he'd soon be leaving the Annex and that his friends on the Benghazi security team would remain behind for the second plane. They might connect when they all reached Tripoli, but Glen wasn't the sort of man who passed up an opportunity to see a pal. Rone was directly above his head on the building's roof. Maybe they'd have enough time for a brief visit.

———

Up on the roof, Rone stood in a half crouch, partially shielded by the parapet at the far northwest corner, his helmet and body armor securely in place, a twenty-pound, belt-fed machine gun in his hands. Oz was a foot to Rone's right, similarly jocked up, armed with an assault rifle. At their feet were several thousand rounds of linked ammunition. Their eyes darted left and right as they looked out over Zombieland.

In the event of an attack, the two operators had choreographed a reloading strategy under which one would signal the other before ducking down behind the parapet. While one reloaded, the other would increase his rate of fire, to keep rounds flying and their enemies back on their heels.

The third man on the Building C roof was Dave Ubben, who stood watch with his assault rifle at the far northeast corner, near the top of the ladder. Building C was built on an angle to the Annex's rear wall, so from his post Ubben was less than ten yards from the wall, while Rone and Oz were about twice as far.

Ubben's post was about forty-five feet to the right of Oz. At that distance, Oz and Ubben could barely see each other in the early-morning darkness. But with each passing minute, visibility faintly improved. As 5:00 a.m. passed, more than seven hours into the battle, the twilight before sunrise silhouetted the big DS agent with a faint orange glow when Oz looked in his direction.

Oz heard someone coming up the ladder and looked over to see the outline of a man climbing over the parapet next to Ubben. The man exchanged a few words with the DS agent, and Ubben pointed toward Oz and Rone. Glen walked across the rooftop to the northwest corner, flashing his smile at Rone. The two former SEALs shook hands then pulled each other close for a chest-bumping, arm-around-the-back man hug.

Rone introduced Glen to Oz. "Glen's a sniper, too," Rone said. "We need another good shooter up here."

"Well, hopefully we don't need you," Oz told Glen as they shook hands.

―――

After some small talk, Glen turned to walk south across the roof, to look out over the building's front door. Rone and Oz shifted their attention back north toward Zombieland.

Then everything changed.

A rocket-propelled grenade or a mortar slammed outside the Annex's north wall, exploding in almost a direct line from where Rone and Oz stood. Immediately shots flew at the men on Building C from unseen gunmen hiding in Zombieland. Rone never hesitated. He opened up full bore with the machine gun, swiveling his powerful upper body left and right, flooding bullets and tracers into the attackers' positions. He lay down a withering base of fire, in repeated bursts of five to seven rounds, methodically and lethally shooting across the open area beyond the north wall. If the attackers had thought they'd catch the Americans sleeping at dawn, Rone let them know he was wide awake and ready to fight.

The relentless automatic fire of Rone's gun echoed in Oz's gauze-filled ears, *da-da-da-da-da*, *da-da-da-da-da*. Oz had responded as quickly as Rone, blasting their enemies with steady fire from his assault rifle. He couldn't see the attackers, so he aimed wherever he saw muzzle flashes. Pinpoints of light soon shone from bullet holes in a metal Quonset hut in their line of fire. Rone and Oz kept firing.

Then came a second explosion. A mortar landed almost directly atop the north wall, perhaps thirty feet in front of Dave Ubben's post.

"I'm hit!" Ubben yelled. "I'm hit!"

Between shots, Oz glanced to the right and saw the wounded DS agent sitting on the wooden box they used as a step from the roof over the parapet to the ladder. Ubben had his back to Zombieland, his hands pressed to his head. He didn't look critically wounded, so Oz resolved to help him as soon as the shooting stopped.

———

After a radio call ordered all State Department staffers to assemble for evacuation, Jack walked the DS agent to the ladder on Building D, intending to bid him goodbye. The DS agent had stripped off some of his heavy gear, so Jack helped by carrying it to the ladder. The DS agent swung himself over from the roof onto the highest rungs, and Jack reached out with his gear.

At that moment, the first explosion and shock wave rocked the Annex. Jack was about fifty yards away, and he felt and heard the blast almost as strongly as the men on Building C. A black plume of smoke rose from where the explosion hit. The DS agent scrambled down the ladder at the northeastern corner of Building D, while Jack tried to figure out what was happening. *It could have been an RPG*, he thought. *Or maybe somebody put an explosive next to the northern wall, to breach it and get in here from Zombieland.*

Jack looked to his right, to the roof of Building C. He saw Rone and Oz rocking and rolling, shooting hard into the dirt alleyway that cut north through Zombieland. Jack couldn't see the enemy, but he raised his assault rifle and fired in the same direction, adding his gun to the fight. Jack directed his fire by following Rone's tracer rounds, but soon stopped when he didn't see a clear target.

The second explosion came less than thirty seconds after the first, different and more powerful. Jack recognized that this was unlike the previous two firefights at the Annex. After two thwarted assaults on the Annex from the east with gelatina bombs and AK-47s, the attackers had changed tactics, improved their planning, and increased their firepower. The second bomb's detonation, so close to the first explosion and accompanied by waves of rifle fire from the north part of Zombieland, also suggested a spike in military sophistication and an unsettling level of precision and coordination.

Jack saw and heard the second explosion when it hit atop the Annex wall, followed by a shock wave and black smoke. He saw Rone and Oz still firing into Zombieland. But Jack wanted a better view before he resumed shooting, so he held his fire. The cause of the second explosion didn't immediately register with Jack.

Then his radio crackled and an explanation became clear. One of his fellow operators yelled: "Mortars!"

—————

When Tanto first called out "Incoming?" he did so as a question, because he wasn't sure what he'd heard. Although he'd picked up a disturbing sound in the distance, Tanto thought it might have been caused by something as innocent as one of his fellow operators stepping on a sealed bag of Fritos.

In Iraq, Tanto had grown used to the *shush* or *whoosh* sounds of rockets being fired, and to the *clunk* of mortars being dropped into tubes for launching. Although Tanto had heard something like a *whoosh*, with his compromised hearing it didn't sound like anything he'd heard before in combat.

Still, the sound made him flinch and take a knee on the Building A rooftop. When the shell hit, perhaps twenty seconds after he first heard the *whoosh*, Tanto turned toward Building C and saw the men on the roof engaging the enemy. Their guns sounded like buzz saws cutting through cordwood. He moved to the northern edge of the Building A roof, found a clear line of sight into Zombieland, and added another gun to the battle. But after only a few bursts he stopped.

Wait a second, Tanto thought. *If that was us, we would fire mortars to set up an assault. And if they're going to assault, it's going to come from the field to the south that I'm supposed to be watching.*

He spun around and positioned himself to look out over the south wall. Tanto saw the ten-car militia motorcade speed away from the Annex to points unknown. He hoped that some were trying to locate the source of the mortars, but he considered it just as likely that most or all were fleeing. *Like cockroaches when you turn on the light*, Tanto thought.

Then came another *whoosh*. Even with his damaged ears, before the second explosion Tanto knew what was happening. Someone came over the radio and asked if they were under attack by RPGs. "No, it was a mortar!" Tanto said. When the questioner repeated the inquiry, Tanto came across the radio again, loud and clear:

"Mortars! MORTARS! *MORTARS!!*"

━━━

On Building C, after the second explosion Oz dropped down below the lip of the parapet, to replace the spent magazine on his assault rifle. As they'd planned, Rone never hesitated. He remained upright and fully engaged, increasing his rate of fire to mask the temporary loss of Oz's gun.

Rone gripped the black machine gun with his meaty hands, holding the butt hard against his shoulder. With a deafening growl, the weapon ingested belt-fed rounds and spewed them with deadly intent into Zombieland. Rone's thick biceps flexed as he moved left and right. Bullets and white smoke poured from the barrel. Rone kept shooting as Oz reloaded, defending the men on the buildings and towers to his left, right, and rear, protecting the men and women below his feet inside Building C. Exposing himself to fire, Rone delivered on his promise to "unleash hate" on the enemy attackers who were trying to kill them.

Then another mortar exploded. Rone stopped firing.

After two near misses, the attackers had adjusted their aim with devastating results. The third explosion was a direct mortar hit on the roof of Building C, halfway between Rone and Oz in the northwest corner, and Dave Ubben in the northeast corner.

━━━

When the mortar exploded on the roof, Oz had just finished reloading. He was rising out of his squatting position to resume shooting. The ear-splitting blast threw Oz back and off balance, knocking him to one knee. He somehow caught himself before going down completely. Through a cloud of black smoke Oz glanced left. The blast had hit Rone.

The former SEAL with the King Leonidas beard, who'd extended his stay in Benghazi to help protect Ambassador J. Christopher Stevens, who intended to retire from GRS operator trips to work with his wife, who was eager to raise his infant son and see his two older boys grow into men, who instinctively and compulsively watched over his fellow operators, who led the rescue charge into the Compound, who searched through a burning building for two missing men, and who answered the first two explosions by rising with a machine gun and returning fire, had absorbed the deadly concussive force of the explosion.

Oz saw Rone lying on his side, curled almost in a fetal position, motionless and silent. His machine gun was blown from his hands, broken somewhere on the grassy field below. Rone faced away from Oz, toward the parapet, so Oz couldn't tell if he was conscious. But if Rone wasn't rising to his feet and returning to the fight, Oz knew that he had reason to fear the worst.

Oz looked toward the northeast corner, but through the smoke he couldn't see if Dave Ubben remained on the box near the ladder. Oz heard no sound from that direction. He knew that Glen Doherty was somewhere toward the south side of the roof, but he neither saw nor heard the Tripoli operator he'd met less than five minutes earlier.

Oz collected his bomb-scattered senses and focused on his training. He knew that before he could help anyone else, he needed to make sure they weren't overrun. His first move would be to step up into Rone's place, to prevent their enemies from thinking that the American defenders were beaten and that the Annex was defenseless.

Engage, Oz told himself. *Get your rifle up and get into the fight.*

He glanced again at Rone. *If he's badly hurt, press the fight until we can take care of him. Now get up and engage.*

Oz clenched his assault rifle's pistol grip with his

right hand. But as he lifted his left arm to grab the black metal barrel, nothing happened. He tried again, but his left hand refused to answer his command. Oz looked down and saw his left forearm blown open about four inches from his wrist. He felt no pain, but as Oz held up his arm to inspect the damage, his hand and wrist hung at a gruesome forty-degree angle from the rest of his arm.

Not perceiving how badly he'd been hurt, and determined to resume shooting, Oz tried repeatedly to flip his left hand onto the barrel, but it flopped uselessly back down. Oz stared at it, in shock, not comprehending that the mortar had torn through the flesh of his left arm, blown away two inches of his radial bone, destroyed part of his radial nerve, and fractured his ulna. Blood bathed the pulpy mess.

Before Oz could react, another mortar hit the roof to his right, a fourth explosion in quick succession. It released a blinding white ball of light. Oz looked over his shoulder and caught a brief glimpse of Glen. The Tripoli operator faced the opposite direction, about four or five steps away. When the blast hit, it knocked Glen facedown onto the poured-concrete roof. At first Oz thought that Glen had gone down of his own will, to take cover. But then he realized that Glen hadn't broken his fall. The explosion's concussion had felled him like an ax-cut oak. Based on where Glen fell, it seemed plausible that he'd tried to return to the north parapet to help his fellow operators after the third explosion. He might have heard the incoming next rooftop mortar and turned to the south, in an unsuccessful attempt to avoid its blast.

However it transpired, the former SEAL with the infectious smile and abundant best friends, who served bravely in the Gulf War, who soared airborne on skis, surfboards, and good times, who came eagerly from Tripoli to help his fellow Americans, lay stationary and silent, arms at his sides, atop Building C.

Oz still didn't know what had happened to Dave Ubben.

<hr/>

After the second direct hit on the rooftop, Oz remained hunched over, bleeding but not conscious of pain. He wheeled around to the north, to face Zombieland. Again he told himself that Building C had dropped out of the fight, and it was his job to change that, even before he could try to help Rone, Glen, or himself, or look for Dave Ubben.

Still refusing to accept his injury, Oz tried again to raise his weapon, lifting his left arm and awkwardly flipping up his hand, as though he were playing the child's game of catching a ball on a string in a wooden cup. Each time he failed.

In came another mortar, the fifth explosive in perhaps ninety seconds, and the third to land squarely atop Building C. Oz heard the mortar approaching the roof. He turned away at the sound and caught only a glimpse of the blinding flash. When the flying bomb reached the bottom of its arc and exploded, Oz felt as though he'd been stung all over his body by a thousand metal bees.

Shrapnel cut into the right side of his neck, near the carotid artery. A jagged piece evaded Oz's body armor to embed itself a quarter inch into his chest, between his pectoral muscles. Another piece pierced the left center of Oz's abdomen, cutting into his diaphragm. Shrapnel entered his left side, six inches below the armpit, and more metal struck him in almost the same place on his right side. Eight to ten fragments struck his right leg, one high on his groin near the femoral artery. Four or five pierced his left leg, from his calf up to his thigh. Small, bloody holes dotted both shoulders and arms, as though Oz were a boxer whose opponent had put a nail in the thumb of his glove. One piece of shrapnel struck Oz's right hip, sneaking between his beltline and the cell phone in his front pocket. Five small bits slashed his cheeks, just below his night-vision goggles, three under his right eye, two under his left. A piece sliced off skin from the tip of Oz's nose.

Shocked by pain that seemed to inflame every nerve, oozing blood from more places than he could imagine, Oz dove for cover against the parapet at the northwest corner. He didn't hear shooting from Zombieland, and he'd begun to accept that his hand was hopeless. He stopped trying to raise his gun. Instead, Oz dragged himself up to a sitting position and saw Rone nearby, still curled on his side.

Oz reached out for Rone's leg. He was too weak to pull Rone toward him, so Oz quieted his mind of pain to search for a pulse from Rone's femoral artery. He found none. Rone had made no sounds and no movements since Oz first saw him down on his side.

As he hunted for Rone's pulse, Oz felt wetness all around him.

Oh shit, I'm bleeding out.

Oz reached down to the rooftop with his right hand and noticed to his relief that the wetness was cool to the touch. Fresh blood, he knew, would be warm and sticky. Oz realized that the roof was drenched not with blood but water. The mortars had punched multiple holes in a 250-gallon tank atop the roof. Its water drained around him.

He wasn't bleeding out, but Oz knew that he might be soon. He looked down at the blood flowing from his damaged arm and told himself to staunch it. He remembered that he'd left his go-bag with his primary medical kit on the tower with Tig, but he had a smaller kit attached to the right side of his tactical vest. Inside were a one-piece combat tourniquet, Kerlix gauze, a chest dressing, and a nasal tube to create an open airway. Oz unzipped the kit and tried to apply the tourniquet to his left arm by using only his working right hand. The tourniquet was designed for one-handed application, but Oz was too weak or too deep in shock to use it properly.

Oz saw the dark outline of a man hop over the top of the ladder. Unsure if it was friend or foe, he dropped the tourniquet and looked around in the hazy twilight for his gun. Spotting the assault rifle near his feet, Oz reached out for it.

■■■■

Alone at the northeast tower, Tig had spent much of the previous two hours acting as a remote shepherd, keeping watch over the sheep pens for approaching attackers. He'd also been eyeing the dirt pathways of Zombieland beyond the wall. His back ached. His lungs hurt from his searches inside the villa. His stomach growled from eating nothing all night as he subsisted on Gatorade and water. Tig sat in the lawn chair anticipating the evacuation, which couldn't come soon enough. As he stared toward Zombieland, Tig heard a disturbing *thunk* from somewhere to the south, followed by an equally unnerving *fffuuuvvv*.

Mortar? No way, he thought. *Seventeen Feb must've locked down the city by now. Right?*

Mortars are classic siege weapons, typically projectile shells dropped into hollow metal tubes and launched in high arcs to land on remote targets. Tig had heard them many times in his military career. Others would say the first explosion of the third Annex firefight sounded like an RPG, but Tig felt certain it was a mortar. When it hit, he looked to the west and saw a flash of light silhouette the men atop Building C. Then he saw their fusillade of rounds hammer into Zombieland from the roof. As he prepared to join them, Tig heard a deeper and more ominous sound, something like *fffuuummm*.

Mortars were falling, and when the second explosion hit the top of the wall, Tig got the distinct impression that his tower would be underneath the next one. He knew that D.B. could cover his area of sheep pens and dirt paths from atop Building B. Rather than stay on his tower and risk getting slammed, Tig held tight to his rifle, grabbed Oz's go-bag, and jumped down. He moved in a low crouch toward the workout area, in the direction of Building C.

When the third explosion hit, directly atop the roof, Tig looked up and for an instant saw a blinding flash. Then the entire roof disappeared in a shroud of black smoke. In quick succession, the fourth explosion rocked the roof, and then the fifth.

Rocky debris rained down on Tig and bounced like hailstones on the tin roof covering the prison gym. His thoughts sped to the men he was trying to reach. *Oh shit*. The shooting from Building C had stopped as soon as the first of the three mortars landed on the roof, so he knew that the men up there were hurt or worse. If there was one tiny bit of good news, the shooting also seemed to have stopped from their enemies in Zombieland.

As he ran toward the rear of the building to reach the ladder, Tig called on his radio: "Hey, guys on Building C, you guys OK? You guys OK?"

"Yeah," came the Team Leader's reply, from inside the building. "We're fine in here, we're good."

"Not you!" Tig shouted. "The guys on top of the fucking roof!"

The T.L. didn't respond, and neither did anyone

on the roof. After a pause, Tig heard Jack's voice fill the silence on the radio: "I see no movement."

———

Atop Building D, Jack had been watching the neighboring roof intermittently since the first explosion. When the third, fourth, and fifth explosions hit Building C, he saw black plumes of smoke rise from where Rone and Oz had been firing into Zombieland only seconds earlier.

Jack couldn't see the fallen men, who had dropped below the parapet and were blanketed in smoke. But in the quiet that followed, Jack thought he heard someone groaning in pain. Even that was more promising news than he'd feared. Jack considered it doubtful that anyone on Building C could survive a single direct mortar hit to their location, much less three. His heart had clenched when he saw the last two explosions.

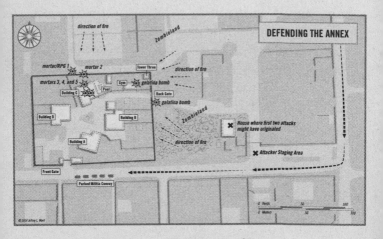

As Tig climbed the ladder to the roof, Jack continued to scan for signs of life, even as he remained on guard for enemy action to the north or west. While Jack waited for word, he stewed over how accurate the mortars were. Three direct hits on a relatively small rooftop were as remarkable as they were lethal. *They had to have somebody spotting them,* he thought. *Somebody was around, probably at an elevated position looking down at us. They hit the wall, and then they corrected and those last three were right on target.*

It also occurred to Jack that the attackers had targeted the single most important and most crowded building inside the walls. Building C housed the Sensitive Compartmented Information Facility and the operators' Team Room, which logically made it the Command Post, and therefore the most likely place for Americans to have taken refuge. *To be that accurate,* Jack thought, *that precise with those mortars, they had to have been very proficient, and they had to have known the exact location of that building.*

Maybe their enemies had done it by dead reckoning, a product of trial and error with help from a concealed spotter. Another possibility was that the attackers had used latitude and longitude coordinates provided by a GPS device, perhaps in a car that drove up to the front gate, or on the smartphone of someone walking outside the Annex. It had occurred to D.B. that the man he'd seen walking outside the Annex might have employed a more primitive approach to target locating: estimating distances by pacing them off on foot.

The more Jack thought about it, the more he felt consumed by dread. Now that the enemy had dialed in the position of the Annex buildings, they might fire twenty or thirty mortars inside the walls. Every rooftop and walkway was vulnerable. Worse, Jack anticipated that the mortars were only the first wave of a full-on assault. As Jack envisioned it, first the attackers would soften up the American defenders by raining mortars on their positions. Then they'd move in on the ground with RPGs and heavy machine guns. Jack knew that he and his fellow operators would put up a ferocious fight, but eventually the Annex walls would give way. The outnumbered, outgunned defenders could hold out only for so long against an overwhelming force.

Considering what had already happened and the various ways the Annex might be overrun, Jack concluded that he'd reached the low point of not only the long night, but of his entire life. He feared that the men atop Building C were dead or dying, adding to the death toll of Chris Stevens and Sean Smith. Having somehow missed the radio call in which the T.L. said that everyone inside Building C was safe, Jack suspected that the mortars had penetrated the roof and killed some or all of them, too. It seemed only a matter of time before he and every other American in Benghazi were dead. He didn't want to imagine what the radicals might do to their bodies.

Jack's thoughts returned to the mortars. He thought about how powerless the Annex fighters were against bombs dropping from above. *You don't know if it's coming*, he thought. *It's not like you can defend against it. You're just out in the open. You can't shoot back towards it. It's basically a lottery. If it's your time, it's your time, and death can come right out of the sky and kill you in an instant.*

He heard the T.L. call on the radio for everyone at fighting positions to check in, by order of location. From Building A. Tanto called: "Roger, all OK." D.B. reported that he was safe on Building B. Everyone waited to hear a voice from Building C. None came.

"Building C, check in." Still nothing. "Building C?"

The silence confirmed in Jack's mind that his worst fears had been realized for Rone, Oz, and Dave Ubben. It was hard to imagine that he could have felt worse, but that would have been the case if Jack had known that a fourth man was on the roof: His friend Glen "Bub" Doherty was up there, too.

Finally, Jack filled the empty radio space. "Building D, roger," he said in a melancholy voice. "I'm OK."

———

Like Jack, D.B. felt as though it was only a matter of time before more mortars hit them. He knew that he needed to cover the area east of the wall, but he also considered abandoning his post if he heard the thumps and whistles of incoming mortars. Then he told himself, *That's actually pretty stupid. Usually the mortar round that hits you is the one you don't hear.*

━━━

After the third mortar hit the roof, Tanto heard the squeal of tires from the area south of the Annex around the dirt racetrack. When no more mortars launched, he believed that some members of the ten-car motorcade had in fact gone in pursuit of the attackers and had chased them off.

At the same time, he wondered when he and the other Benghazi operators would get relief from the Tripoli team, all of whom except Glen remained inside Building C. He called to D.B. on the next rooftop: "Where the fuck are all these guys from Tripoli?"

Tanto returned his focus to a possible ground assault. *Need to get ready*, he told himself. He stared into the unfinished four-story building across the road to the south. Tanto told D.B. that he continued to hear voices in the field near the building, whispering and mumbling from among the weeds. D.B. tossed him a pair of binoculars across the narrow gap between their roofs, to help Tanto scour the building and the grounds nearby.

Between sweeps across his sector, Tanto called the T.L. to say that the ten-car motorcade escort had left. "It doesn't look like they're coming back," Tanto said. "We're gonna need another way to get out of here."

As Tanto remained on watch, he felt as though he'd been prepared for everything that had already happened, and everything yet to come. *You don't have time to feel sorry for yourself*, he thought. *You don't feel sorry for anybody else. You can feel sorry once you're safe and you're sitting back and drinking a beer, and you can howl at the moon. When everything's done, you can feel sorry.*

━━━

With each rung he climbed on the Building C ladder, Tig swiveled his head toward Zombieland, watching for muzzle flashes to see if anyone was about to shoot him in the back. The attackers had stopped shooting after the third mortar struck the roof, but neither Tig nor any of the other Americans knew whether their enemies would resume shooting, launch more mortars, or attempt to breach the walls and invade the Annex. They expected nothing less.

Tig leapt over the parapet and ducked low as he looked around the blackened roof. The sun still hung below the horizon and smoke still swirled, giving Tig only a few feet of visibility. "I need help up here," he called on the radio.

The first man Tig spotted was Dave Ubben, propped against the parapet ten feet from the northeast corner, conscious but dazed, a pistol in his right hand. Tig knelt next to Ubben and grabbed the gun, worried that while in shock and pain the DS agent might mistake Tig for someone who needed to be shot. He tossed the pistol to the side and pulled out a headlamp from Oz's medical bag. Tig flipped down a red lens cover to keep from painting a target for the attackers.

Tig saw that Ubben had suffered major injuries

to his lower left leg and serious wounds to his left arm below the elbow. Tig pulled out both tourniquets from Oz's medical bag. Just as Rone had demonstrated days earlier during the medical refresher course, Tig applied the first tourniquet to Ubben's badly damaged leg. As he worked in the darkness, Tig accidentally raked his hand across the edge of one of Ubben's protruding bones. The razor-sharp bone sliced through Tig's skin, but he'd worry about it later. He moved to Ubben's arm, tightening the second tourniquet just below the armpit. As he worked, Tig offered a steady stream of reassurances.

"Hang in there, dude....You're gonna be OK.... We're gonna get you down....It's gonna be all right....We'll get you out of here." Tig reached back to his days as a Marine and pulled out a motivational nickname for the toughest among them: "Hang in, Devil Dog." Ubben could only mumble a reply.

When both tourniquets were in place, Tig began to move away from the DS agent to see who else needed help. Ubben roused himself: "Hey man, I need my pistol!"

"Roger that," Tig said. He reached to pick up the gun, but with his back turned to Ubben he quickly cleared the mag, unloading it so the wounded man couldn't accidentally shoot him or any others who might come up the ladder to help. After returning Ubben's gun, Tig ducked behind the parapet and looked around.

Off to his left, Tig saw someone lying motionless, facedown near the center of the roof. The man looked to be beyond help, and Tig wanted to prioritize men who might benefit most.

"Anybody else need help?" he called.

Tig heard moaning from the northwest corner. As he hustled that way, Tig passed a hole in the concrete bigger than his fist from where a mortar hit. As he darted toward the moans, he saw the shapes of two men, one moving, one still, next to each other in the northwest corner.

His frustration rising, Tig called again on his radio: "Hey, I got four guys down. I need help up here. Right now!" He began to suspect that no one wanted to leave the relative safety of Building C in case the mortars and gunfire resumed.

D.B. answered from atop Building B, his voice filled with rage: "I need to know if somebody is going up to Building C, because otherwise I've got to get down and get over there." He couldn't imagine why members of the Tripoli team hadn't immediately run to Building C's ladder to help. Tanto knew that D.B. had the best field of fire to protect the Annex, so he told D.B. to stay on Building B and he'd go instead.

Before Tanto could move, someone from inside Building C told everyone to remain at their posts: "We got it. We're coming up."

To Tig, the wait for help felt like an eternity. Through a veil of pain, Oz heard Tig make the calls for more help. Still not fully comprehending that he was one of the four men down, Oz thought about the man lying next to him: *Shit, I've got to help Rone.*

When he reached Oz seconds later, Tig forced him to focus first on his own injuries. "Hey man," Oz told Tig, "look at this." Using his right hand, Oz lifted his lifeless left hand to put it in its proper place. Then he watched as he let go and it flopped back down to an odd angle. "I think I broke it."

"Dude," Tig said, "stop doing that. You're going to fuck it up even more."

Tig grabbed the assault rifle from Oz's lap and set it aside. He picked up the one-piece combat tourniquet that Oz hadn't been able to apply, pulled the band around Oz's upper arm, and twisted it tight to stop the bleeding. Tig knew that Oz needed a lot more care inside Building C and eventually a hospital. He helped him to his feet and asked Oz if he could walk to the ladder.

"I think I can," Oz said as he took tentative steps forward. "I'll make do."

As Oz shuffled away, Tig dropped to his knees and rolled Rone onto his back on the wet rooftop. He ripped off Rone's Rhodesian vest and his other gear, then raised his shirt to look over his bare torso front and back, to check for signs of bleeding. The only injuries Tig noticed were small shrapnel marks on Rone's forehead. Finding no open wounds needing immediate care, Tig pressed his fingers to Rone's thick neck to search for a pulse from the carotid artery. Rone's throat twitched momentarily, but Tig could find no pulse. He flipped up the red lens on his headlamp and shone the white light in Rone's eyes. Rone's pupils didn't react. Tig pressed his ear against

Rone's chest but heard nothing. He put his ear to Rone's mouth and felt no breath.

Tig worked in silence. The attackers who'd been firing from Zombieland apparently had pulled back. The mortars had stopped. Tig knew that that could change at any moment, but at present the only sounds he heard were trickles of water flowing from shrapnel holes in the nearby tank.

It pained him, but Tig knew that there was nothing he could do for Rone. He left his friend and ran to the man lying facedown near the middle of the roof. Tig had never met Glen, and he didn't know that one of the Tripoli operators had climbed up to the roof. He thought the prone man with the scruffy beard was Jack. *What the hell is he doing up here?* Tig thought.

Then Tig remembered that he'd heard Jack's voice on the radio, saying that there was no movement atop Building C. Tig rolled the man onto his back and realized that the fourth person needing help was one of the Tripoli operators.

Glen's assault rifle was still strapped around him, so Tig pulled it off and threw it to one side. He went through the same steps he'd taken with Rone, with the same results. Again he found no sign of major trauma, only a laceration on the left side of the abdomen. Like Rone, Glen was unresponsive, with no pulse, no breath or heart sounds, and no eye movements under the white light.

By then, Tig had company on the roof. Joining him were the Benghazi GRS Team Leader, a Tripoli operator who was a medic, and the two

Delta Force members, known to the operators as D-boys. One D-boy had helped Oz as he walked toward the ladder.

"Can you get down on your own?" the D-boy asked Oz.

"Yeah, I guess I'll have to," Oz answered.

The D-boy helped Oz step up on the box near the ladder. Oz knew that he'd lost a lot of blood, so he hooked his right arm firmly over one of the top rungs, as a precaution. Then Oz swung his right leg over the ledge. *Better be careful*, Oz told himself. *You survived all this, and now you don't want to break your neck getting down.* But just as he feared, Oz's feet slipped out from under him and his body slammed against the ladder. He caught his full weight with his right arm, pulled himself back up, and regained his footing to climb down.

At the bottom, Oz went around the building's northeast corner and past the mossy pool. He ran into one of the operators from Tripoli, a medic who guided Oz the rest of the way into Building C.

━━━

Up on the roof, the D-boys struggled to get big Dave Ubben down the ladder without adding to his injuries. Ultimately, one of the D-boys used a one-inch nylon strap to bind Ubben across his back. He then carried the 250-pound DS agent down the ladder that way. Meanwhile, Tig moved from one rooftop fighting position to the next, collecting weapons and stacking them against the parapet.

When he reached Rone's body, Tig looked around unsuccessfully for the missing machine gun, then grabbed Rone's pistol. Before he moved on, Tig stopped to say an impromptu prayer. He placed his hand on Rone's chest and whispered: "God, watch over him. Guide him to where he needs to be. Take care of his family." He went over to Glen, pressed his hand to Glen's chest, and said the same prayer. Then he collected Glen's weapons.

A case officer inside Building C came on the radio, asking for Rone to come down to help treat Oz's wounds. "Rone, we need you in the CP," he said, using shorthand for the Command Post. No one replied, so he repeated the call. "Rone, we need you in the CP!"

"Hey!" Tig said. "Rone's gone. He's not with us anymore."

Weary and downhearted, but also livid about all that had gone wrong since the start of their ordeal, Tig dragged the bodies of the two former SEALs closer to the ladder, to make it easier to bring them down when it was time to leave.

Tig scooped up the pile of weapons, climbed down the ladder, and jogged around to the front of Building C. He went inside, dumped the weapons onto a couch, and looked over to where several people worked on Oz.

━━━

With a little help from the medic, the blood-drenched Oz had somehow walked into Building C under his own power. The medic applied a dressing on his neck wound and lay him down on a couch. Oz's condition was serious but not immediately life-threatening, so the medic went back to the roof, to see if anyone was worse off. A clutch of case officers and other Annex staffers stood over Oz, none with much medical training. That's when one called for Rone, only to have Tig snap back that Rone was gone.

Oz realized that he'd have to oversee his own care. "I've been hit. I know I'm bleeding," he told them. "Somebody get some shears and cut off my clothes. You need to get me naked and check for bleeds, front and back."

The female case officer he'd escorted to dinner ten long hours earlier ran to the medical area, but she couldn't find shears. When Oz heard her asking for help finding them, somehow he remembered their exact location, on the third shelf of the first set of storage racks, and he called it out to her. The Annex deputy chief had already pulled out a big folding combat knife to start slicing off Oz's clothes.

"Be careful with that," joked Oz. "I don't want to get stabbed, also."

———

When he saw that Oz was in good hands, Tig hurried to the rear of the building. He struggled to raise a steel safety shutter that would allow him to open the back door, enabling the D-boys to bring Ubben inside without carrying him around to the front. But the mortars had damaged the shutter, making it a chore to lift. By the time Tig opened the back door Ubben was already inside, being treated for major wounds to his leg and arm. The Tripoli medic had also started intravenous fluids for both Ubben and Oz.

Tig still held Oz's go-bag, so he went to the medical area to replace the supplies he'd used. The enormity of everything that had happened gripped Tig, and he tore open cabinets and rifled through supplies. When an Annex staffer asked what the hell he was doing, Tig was tempted to raise his fists. Instead he snapped: "I'm looking for tourniquets in case we get more mortars!"

He stormed back outside, intending to return to his tower position. On the way, one of the D-boys told Tig he couldn't go back there because it was too dangerous.

"Fuck you. I've been there all night by myself," Tig said.

The Tripoli-based Team Leader for all GRS operators in Libya stepped in before it turned physical. He told Tig to stay near Building C so everyone could see each other's location. Still boiling, Tig followed the order. *I'm standing here watching a wall*, he thought. *I can't see nothing, can't do nothing, can't react if something happens. Great plan. They've been here five minutes, and they're telling us what to do?*

As he stood in an area he considered a no-man's-land on the east side of Building C, Tig heard over the radio that a fifty-vehicle convoy with Technicals was on its way to the Annex, to guard the evacuation and escort them to the airport. That was quite an upgrade from the lightly armed ten-car motorcade that bugged out when the mortars hit.

Jack heard the radio transmission, too, and he believed that all the remaining Benghazi operators were thinking the same thing: *I hope they're going to escort us to the airport and not attack us. We don't know who's friendly, who's bad. There are militias out there, they all look the same, and some of them are trying to kill us.*

If they had no choice, they'd fight a fifty-vehicle convoy of Technicals, with one hundred or more heavily armed men. But if it came to that, Jack felt certain that the Annex would be remembered as a twenty-first-century Alamo, with no American survivors.

———

Someone drove a white flatbed truck with wooden side rails to the front of Building C, to transport the bodies of Rone and Glen. By coincidence, Rone had used the same truck weeks earlier, on the day when he and another operator collecting supplies from the airport had faced off with a group of hostile militiamen.

Tig moved toward the Building C ladder to help bring down the fallen men. He told the D-boys that he knew where to find a heavy strap that would help them lower the bodies from the roof. The D-boys weren't interested, or they didn't want to take the time. "We got this," one told him. "Don't worry about it."

Tig watched as they climbed the ladder to the roof and lifted Rone's body onto the parapet. Tig knew what would happen next, so he turned away to avoid seeing it. Afterward, Tig couldn't shake the sickening sound of Rone's body hitting the marble patio at the bottom of a fifteen-foot fall.

Jack watched from atop Building D. He'd missed some of the radio calls, so he still didn't know all that had happened. He saw a D-boy lift a limp body, and Jack knew that it was Rone. He recognized Rone's khaki cargo pants and his button-down orange plaid shirt. The King Leonidas beard removed any doubt and extinguished any hope. He turned away.

After Rone, the D-boys took the same approach with Glen. His body hit a bush on the way down, slicing open his abdomen. Disgusted and angry, Tig told himself that both men deserved better. No one was shooting at them, the mortars had stopped, and a huge friendly convoy was supposedly en route.

The most Tig could do for Rone now was to grab his cold hands, while a D-boy took Rone's feet. Together, they carried him to the side of Building C. Two others from the Tripoli team carried Glen.

THIRTEEN

Convoy

━━━━

WITH EACH PASSING MINUTE, THE SUN EDGED closer to the horizon, bathing the Annex in dim light. With the huge convoy en route, the Benghazi GRS Team Leader called for all remaining rooftop defenders to climb down and collect any last personal items. The T.L. stood outside Building C when he made the call. Looking down from the Building D roof, Jack caught his eye. The T.L. nodded, his face etched with sadness. Jack knew that Rone was gone, but he still didn't know about Glen.

Jack climbed down, ran into his room, and rushed to fill a duffel bag with his laptop, cell phone, and everything else he thought might contain personal information. He grabbed the mesh bag with his driver's license and credit cards, but in his haste, exhausted and grieving, Jack overlooked the little box with his wedding ring. It would remain behind in Benghazi, with so much else of Jack.

He went to the Team Room in Building C and filled the remaining space in his duffel with weapons, radios, and other sensitive equipment. Jack walked outside and saw the flatbed truck. Rone's body was there on the ground, so Jack and one of the D-boys lifted it and laid it on the steel bed as gently as they could.

Then Jack saw the second body. His eyes moved from the lacerated abdomen to the unmistakable face: Glen.

Jack fought to keep his knees from buckling. Two men he considered brothers had just been killed on a rooftop a hundred feet from where Jack had stood. Now he was loading their bodies onto the back of a flatbed truck. It pained him more than he could describe that he hadn't even had a chance to greet Glen.

━━━

As the Americans prepared to leave Building C for a final time, the white marble of the living room floor was coated red with blood from Oz and Dave Ubben.

The door to Building C opened and staffers carried out stretchers bearing Oz, who remained alert, and Ubben, who was unconscious. Oz wore only his underwear, but rather than ask for clothes he called for someone to fetch the three things he needed to leave Benghazi behind forever: his wallet, his phone, and his passport.

Jack and several others lifted Dave Ubben's stretcher into the back of a white hatchback. Even with the stretcher pushed all the way in, Ubben's feet hung out the back. The Tripoli medic jumped in the back to care for the injured men during the ride. Before the stretcher-bearers loaded him into the hatchback, Oz looked up and searched for Jack.

"Rone shielded me," Oz told him. "He saved my life."

———

At about 6:00 a.m., the Benghazi GRS Team Leader called Tanto on the radio: "There's another militia coming in, and it's a big one. It's about fifty vehicles and they're Technicals, they're heavy. ID them, to make sure they're the good guys."

Standing atop Building A, overlooking the front gate, Tanto thought about that command for a few seconds. "If they aren't," he answered, "how the fuck am I supposed to stop them?"

A short time later, the promised convoy rumbled down Annex Road, a nearly quarter-mile procession of dirty white Toyota pickups with mounted Dushka heavy machine guns, filled with hard-looking soldiers in hues of gray, brown, and tan camouflage. They bristled with RPGs, AK-47s, and other weapons.

Neither Tanto nor any of the other operators knew which militia they belonged to, or whether they were an official Libyan government force. But that wasn't the Americans' main concern. As long as these soldiers or militiamen were friendly and willing to escort them to the airport, the operators would have no complaints, except for one. As Tig told himself: *If these guys are friendly, why the fuck didn't they get called in to help us at the beginning?*

The moment of truth came, and Tanto lowered his weapon. He welcomed the convoy commander in the lead vehicle with a universal "hang loose" sign, curling the three middle fingers of his left hand and shaking his thumb and pinkie.

The Libyan militia commander smiled and returned the surfer greeting.

Tanto called the T.L. on the radio. "Yep, these are the guys."

As everyone inside the Annex gathered personal belongings, Tanto caught the commander's attention and made another hand gesture. He turned his hand into a finger gun, flipped it upside down, then pointed toward the field across the road. Among American soldiers, the motion signaled an enemy location.

The commander understood. He called up a Technical with a mounted Dushka and told its gunner to cover the field. Then he sent a four-man fire team to search for potential enemies. In short order they pulled out two men who'd been hiding in the brush.

Tanto watched with satisfaction as one of the friendly militiamen tightened flex-cuffs around the men's wrists and marched them to one of the trucks. Tanto didn't know how long the men had been hiding there. He also didn't know if they were mortar spotters, a reconnaissance team, or otherwise linked to a hostile militia. But at least

Tanto hadn't been imagining voices coming from the field all night. He never learned what became of the men.

━━━

Sunrise on September 12, 2012, arrived at 6:22 a.m. in Benghazi, just as the surviving Americans made final preparations to leave the Annex. A half-dozen Annex cars lined up to drive out the front gate to join the big convoy, along with the hatch-back bearing Oz and Dave Ubben. Tig got behind the wheel of the flatbed bearing the bodies of Rone and Glen; Jack rode shotgun. Sean Smith's body remained in the Mercedes for the ride to the airport.

As everyone waited for the signal to move out, Jack watched an argument erupt between Bob the Annex chief and the Benghazi GRS Team Leader. Bob told the T.L. that he wanted to remain behind, to gather information and intelligence from locals about what had happened and who was to blame. The T.L. objected, but Bob held firm, smoking a cigarette outside Building C.

"You are relieved!" the T.L. told Bob. "Get in the fucking vehicle."

Bob snuffed out his cigarette and complied, but he wasn't done arguing.

When the Americans drove through the gate, they filtered in among their armed escorts, who made sure that the pickups with mounted machine guns covered each vehicle from the Annex on all sides. Several Technicals drove out front as a motorized wedge, to block off intersections so the Americans could roll through without stopping. Tanto felt concerned that they might be vulnerable to attack moving toward the airport in daylight, but then he decided that they were part of "the biggest, baddest thing in town." Nobody in his right mind would mess with them.

As Tig steered the flatbed through the gate, Jack saw the gardener whom he'd watched smoking and praying outside his shack during the fire-fight. The gardener turned himself into a one-man honor guard, waving goodbye to his American employers.

Jack looked through the back window of the truck cab, to make sure the sheet-wrapped bodies remained secure. He noticed a perfectly shaped bullet hole through the glass and pointed it out to Tig. Then they returned to the silence of their own thoughts.

Jack thought about Rone's wife, Dorothy, and the infant son who'd never know his father. He felt pangs of sadness as he recalled that Rone had told him Benghazi would be his final job as an operator, and how much Rone looked forward to getting home to be with his family for good. Jack winced as he remembered that Rone had extended this trip twice. One painful thought followed another. He felt crushed by the memory of Rone saying that he planned to surprise his wife with a trip out west to visit Jack and his family. *She doesn't even know he's dead yet*, he thought, *and she won't know about that trip because it's never going to happen now.*

Jack wished that someone else had met him at the airport five weeks earlier, that someone else had slipped the loaded pistol into his hand as a welcome gift, and that someone else had shown him the lay of the land so he'd do good work and stay safe in Benghazi. But Jack also knew that Rone never shied away from protecting others or from doing what he thought was right.

Jack also wished that Glen had never come from Tripoli to help them, and had never climbed the ladder to see Rone. But he knew that Glen wouldn't have wanted anyone to have taken his seat on the plane to Benghazi. He knew that connecting with friends defined Glen's life. And Jack knew that Glen's actions fit the warrior code they all lived by: If his fellow operators were facing danger on rooftops, Glen would be there, too.

Sitting in the passenger seat of the flatbed cab, twisting his head backward to watch over the bodies, Jack felt devastated. His only solace was knowing that Rone and Glen had died as heroes.

When the convoy reached the airport, a militia guard team stationed there prevented it briefly from entering. But soon the convoy rolled through a gate to the noncommercial side of the tarmac and parked near the small jet the Tripoli team had chartered. Several Tripoli operators carried Dave Ubben toward the stairs up to the plane door. The operators had lashed him to the stretcher so they could turn it sideways to get the badly wounded

DS agent through the narrow entrance. Ubben veered in and out of consciousness.

His fellow operators began to lift Oz's stretcher, but he stopped them. "Hell no," he said. "I walked into this country, and I'm going to frigging walk out of this town."

Oz scooted to the edge of the hatchback and raised himself upright. Pushing through the pain, Oz steadied himself. Step by difficult step, he approached the plane with blood dripping down his left arm despite the tourniquet. When the plane's uniformed flight attendants saw Oz coming, they went wide-eyed and ran to spread towels down the carpeted aisle and across a couch near the plane's tail.

Oz climbed the stairs then lay down on the couch. The stretcher-bearers placed Ubben on the floor beside him. The Tripoli medic sat between the injured men for the flight.

Other Americans boarded while their baggage filled the cargo hold. As the loading continued, the militia that apparently controlled the airport challenged the presence of the much larger military convoy that escorted the Americans. Jack watched as dozens of combat-ready men screamed at each other on the tarmac.

This is going to be a complete massacre, Jack thought. *If somebody starts shooting, there's no cover, everyone is just standing around*. He held tight to his assault rifle as the argument raged. Jack said an operator's silent prayer: *Please, nobody shoot*.

Tanto watched the showdown and predicted the

future: *The militia that runs the airport has, like, two cars here. Our militia has fifty cars. There's no diplomatic solution here. Whoever has the biggest guns or the most guns is going to win.*

When tensions seemed highest, a militiaman inadvertently fired his AK-47 into the ground near his feet. The operators braced for action, suspecting that the accidental discharge would trigger jumpy militiamen to start shooting. Instead it seemed to defuse the situation, as though the single careless shot reminded everyone how easily they could all be killed.

As the Americans filed onto the plane, Bob the Annex chief again objected to leaving. He was in Benghazi as an intelligence officer, yet he was being told to evacuate with an endless list of unanswered questions about what had just happened. Bob began a new shouting match, this time with the country GRS Team Leader from Tripoli. The Tripoli T.L. exercised his authority as the ranking American security official in Libya. "You are relieved of duty!" he yelled. "You will get on that plane or I will put you on that plane." Finally Bob complied.

The plane overflowed with Americans eager to take off. But before the pilot started to taxi, the men and women on board began to suspect that they were snakebitten with bad luck: A second accidental discharge cracked loudly, this time somewhere aboard the jet. A further delay followed, as the crew and the operators tried to determine whether the bullet had pierced the hull of the pressurized aircraft, making it unsafe to fly.

Holy shit, Oz thought, *are we ever going to get out of here?* The shock had worn off and so had the morphine he'd been given. He lay on the couch writhing in the worst pain he'd ever experienced. Oz tried to make jokes, to distract himself and ease the mood. But then his arm would cause him a jolt of agony and he'd unleash a torrent of curses before fighting to regain his sense of humor.

As the delay stretched on, Oz's main concern became Ubben. *I'm going to get up with my pistol and frigging tell the captain he's flying one way or the other*, Oz thought. *We got to get Dave to a hospital or he's gonna die.*

Finally someone discovered that the bullet had burrowed harmlessly into the metal frame of a seat. At about 7:30 a.m., the first planeload of survivors from the attacks at the Special Mission Compound and the CIA Annex took flight.

▬▬

Left behind were Jack, Tanto, D.B., Tig, DS agent Alec Henderson, the two D-boys, two of the Tripoli operators, the Tripoli-based linguist, and the country GRS Team Leader, along with the bodies of Rone, Glen, and Sean Smith.

Members of the militia escort understood that the Americans would be abandoning their vehicles, so several asked for the keys. One man with pleading eyes approached Tanto for keys to a four-door BMW, a twin of the sedan with Tig's go-bag that they'd left at the corner of Gunfighter Road.

"Vehicle, sir?" he asked. "Vehicle?"

When the operators felt certain that another plane would be coming, they emptied the vehicles of ammunition, maps, medical kits, and other tools. Tig realized that when the State Department team left in the first plane, they failed to move Sean Smith's body from the Mercedes SUV. He got the keys and, with help, moved Smith's body to the flatbed alongside Rone and Glen. Tanto handed the keys from the Americans' other vehicles to the militia leader. The operators watched as the commander distributed them among his men, who flushed like teenagers with their first cars. The screech of tires as the militiamen peeled out of the airport ended the operators' murky friend-and-foe relationship with the Benghazi militias.

——

Several Benghazans who'd served as local liaisons for the Annex had somehow heard what had happened and came to see the Americans off. One Libyan whom several of the operators liked burst into tears as he apologized.

"This never should have happened," he said. "I'm really sorry."

"It's not your fault," Tanto told him. "You didn't do anything. Just take care of this."

"We will," the man told him. "We'll make sure people pay for this."

"You've got to, or else this'll keep happening," Tanto said. "You got to fix this or else you won't see us here anymore. And if you do, it won't be as friendlies."

Another Libyan in tears was the man who had gone to the hospital to identify Chris Stevens. He understood that there would be no American Corner at his school. The dream of a "friendly, accessible space" where average Benghazans could learn about the United States had died along with the ambassador.

An hour after the first plane left, the operators got word that members of the force that escorted them to the airport had gone to Benghazi Medical Center to retrieve Stevens's body. When the recovery team returned, Henderson peeled back the sheet to officially identify the remains. Stevens was barefoot but fully clothed, with no signs of injury or abuse, his eyes shut in peaceful repose. The operators placed the ambassador's body on the flatbed with the three others.

The Libyan Air Force agreed to send a hulking C-130 cargo plane to take the remaining men and the bodies to Tripoli. While they waited for it to arrive, the exhausted operators stretched out on the tarmac to get some rest, keeping their loaded guns close at hand. They shared their cell phones to call loved ones back home to say they were safe.

Jack didn't know what, if anything, his wife had heard on the news, so he wanted to reassure her. She was not yet three months pregnant, and Jack worried that she might miscarry if she feared that he'd been killed. Jack made sure she was calm, then told her: "Whatever you see on the news, just know that it's over. I'm OK. I'll see you soon."

Jack had told his wife that Rone was with him in Benghazi, so she asked if he was OK, too. Emotions welling for the past few hours overwhelmed Jack. He began to cry. He'd survived, so there was the yang. The loss of his friends was the yin.

"He didn't make it."

"What do you mean, 'He didn't make it'?" she asked, her voice rising.

Jack could barely choke out an answer. "I'll tell you when I get back," he said finally. "But don't talk about it with anybody, because next of kin hasn't been notified. I'll call you soon. I love you."

━━━

Hours of waiting for the plane gave Tanto time to reflect on his fellow operators. *If it had been any other six guys, I don't think any of us would have made it. We lost Rone, we lost Bub, and Oz got hurt, but it could have been worse. We all could have been gone. It was like we were meant to be there together. None of these guys had a panic bone in their body.*

It bothered Tanto that they'd be flying out on a Libyan C-130 instead of a US military plane. The more he thought about it, the more convinced Tanto became: *If we were given what we asked for in the beginning, air support, you name it, we wouldn't have lost Rone and Bub. And if they'd let us leave the Annex at the beginning, the ambassador and Sean would be alive.*

More than two hours after the Americans arrived
at the airport, the Libyan Air Force plane landed
and dropped its cargo ramp. The operators drove
the flatbed to the C-130's tail. They carried aboard
the bodies, two on medical litters and two on canvas stretchers. One of Glen's arms stuck out perpendicular to his body, fixed there by rigor mortis.
Tanto forced down the arm and made sure Glen
was covered.

When all were aboard, the Libyan crew raised
the tail ramp and taxied for takeoff. It was about
10:30 a.m., some thirteen hours after the attack
began at the Compound. They flew in silence to
Tripoli, some dozing, some reflecting, all spent.

When the C-130 landed, embassy staffers met
the last Benghazi evacuees at the airport, greeting them with hugs and tears. One of the D-boys
brought body bags up the cargo ramp, so Jack did
the last thing he could for his fallen friends. He
and the D-boy unfolded the white plastic bags and
spread them on the floor of the plane. They lifted
Rone, then Glen, and placed each inside a bag.

Jack zippered them up and said a final goodbye.

Epilogue

—

WHEN THE LIBYAN C-130 TOOK FLIGHT BEARING the last operators and the four bodies, the Battle of Benghazi ended as a combat engagement between Americans and their enemies. But that was only the beginning. Even before the survivors returned home, controversies exploded over how officials in Washington behaved prior to, during, and after the attack. The acrimony can be divided generally along three fronts:

• Prior to the attack: Who, if anyone, deserves blame and potential punishment for security flaws at the Compound, and did those flaws contribute to the deaths of Ambassador J. Christopher Stevens and Sean Smith? Four State Department employees were placed on paid administrative leave, but all were reinstated and given new jobs at State. Two later retired voluntarily.

• During the attack: Was the US military response appropriate, and if not, why not? A related question is whether more aggressive US military action was possible, and if so, might it have prevented the deaths of Tyrone "Rone" Woods and Glen "Bub" Doherty, and the serious injuries to Mark "Oz" Geist and David Ubben?

• After the attack: Did the Obama administration mislead the public for political reasons, by erroneously linking the attack to protests triggered by clips from the *Innocence of Muslims* movie? A related question was whether the administration downplayed a possible role by al-Qaeda.

Like much else in Washington, most answers have fallen on one side or the other of a partisan divide. Republicans and conservatives have been the harshest critics of President Obama, then–Secretary of State Clinton, and the administration's handling of the Benghazi attacks. Democrats and liberals have been the stoutest defenders of the president, Clinton, and the administration. Media reports have run the gamut on who, if anyone, in Washington deserves blame and punishment, and whether the attacks should be considered a tragedy, a scandal, or both.

However, by early 2014 one conclusion had gained considerable traction across partisan lines: The attacks could have been prevented. That is, if only the State Department had taken appropriate steps to improve security at the Compound

Mark "Oz" Geist on a gurney being transported from Libya to Germany. In the foreground is the flag-draped casket with the body of Ambassador Chris Stevens. *(Courtesy of Mark Geist)*

in response to numerous warnings and incidents during the months prior. That conclusion featured prominently in a bipartisan report by the Senate Intelligence Committee.

That same committee also confronted the controversial issue of a "stand down" order, exploring whether the Annex team was delayed from responding to the attacks at the Compound. Its final report concluded: "Although some members of the security team expressed frustration that they were unable to respond more quickly to the Mission Compound, the Committee found no evidence of intentional delay or obstruction by the Chief of Base or any other party." In a footnote, the committee revealed that "informal notes" obtained from the CIA indicated that the security team left for the Compound without approval from the base chief, Bob. But the committee accepted Bob's testimony, quoting him as saying: "We launched our QRF [Quick Reaction Force] as soon as possible down to the State [Department] Compound." Nevertheless, the Annex security team members stood by their account of being told repeatedly to "stand down" before deciding on their own to leave.

In a memoir of her tenure as secretary of state, published in June 2014, Hillary Clinton gave her most detailed account of her actions to date. She denounced what she called "misinformation, speculation, and flat-out deceit" about the attacks, and wrote that Obama "gave the order to do whatever was necessary to support our people in Libya." She wrote: "Losing these fearless public servants in the line of duty was a crushing blow. As Secretary I was the one ultimately responsible for my people's safety, and I never felt that responsibility more deeply than I did that day." Addressing the controversy over what triggered the attack, and whether the administration misled the public, she maintained that the *Innocence of Muslims* video had played a role, though to what extent wasn't clear. "There were scores of attackers that night, almost certainly with differing motives. It is inaccurate to state that every single one of them was influenced by this hateful video. It is equally inaccurate to state that none of them were." Clinton's account was greeted with praise and condemnation in equal measure.

As Clinton promoted her book, a new investigation was being launched by the House Select Committee on the Events Surrounding the 2012 Terrorist Attack in Benghazi. Chaired by former federal prosecutor Rep. Trey Gowdy, a South Carolina Republican, the committee's creation promised to drive questions about Benghazi into the 2016 presidential campaign and beyond.

***

As explained in "A Note to the Reader," this book is not intended to support or satisfy one side or the other in resolving the controversies that remain. By telling their story, the Benghazi operators hope that the battle and their actions will be understood on their own terms, outside of partisan or political interests.

Another priority for the operators is to see the attackers identified, hunted down, and punished. In August 2013, President Obama confirmed that a sealed indictment had been issued against an undisclosed number of suspects. Several media organizations reported that among those indicted was Ahmed Abu Khattalah, a leader of Ansar al-Sharia of Benghazi. Abu Khattalah acknowledged being at the scene, but denied involvement in the attack. He was captured in a US raid in June 2014 and was being held for trial.

The Ansar al-Sharia militia also denied participating, but praised the attack in a statement read on television on September 12, 2012. In January 2014, the State Department formally designated Ansar al-Sharia of Benghazi and the separate but allied Ansar al-Sharia of Derna as terrorist groups, largely for their alleged involvement in the Compound and Annex attacks. Also designated a terrorist was Sufian bin Qumu, a leader of Ansar al-Sharia of Derna, who spent several years as a Guantanamo Bay detainee; he was identified previously by US officials as a "probable member" of al-Qaeda. Nevertheless, a State Department spokeswoman maintained that "we have no indications…that core al-Qaeda directed or planned the Benghazi attack."

Three days after the attack on the Compound, the bodies of J. Christopher Stevens, Sean Smith, Tyrone "Rone" Woods, and Glen "Bub" Doherty were returned to the United States in flag-draped caskets. President Obama, Vice President Joe Biden, Secretary of State Clinton, and Defense Secretary Leon Panetta were among those present for their repatriation.

After a brief stop in Tripoli, the four uninjured Benghazi operators flew to Ramstein Air Base, a US Air Force facility in Germany, and then to Washington for debriefings. Jack flew commercial and had the surreal experience of sitting across the aisle from someone reading a newspaper account of the Benghazi attacks.

For Mark "Oz" Geist, the return home was delayed by the first of several hospital stays. He eventually faced more than a dozen surgeries and spent time at Walter Reed National Military

Medical Center with Dave Ubben, who also underwent numerous surgeries and significant rehabilitation for his injuries.

Since returning home, all five surviving operators have given sworn congressional testimony behind closed doors about the events described in this book. In December 2013, the United States government honored the operators from Benghazi in secret ceremonies. The State Department gave the operators who responded to the Compound plaques that hailed "[T]he heroism displayed by members of the security team, under fire in the face of extreme risks to their personal safety during the deadly attack against US facilities in Benghazi, Libya, on September 11–12, 2012. The heroic actions of these professionals were selfless, valorous, and representative of the highest standards of bravery in federal service." Hillary Clinton signed the citations. The State Department gave the same men medals bearing the word "Heroism," adorned with blue and silver ribbons. The CIA gave all the operators newly created medals of valor the size of coffee saucers.

Honors also were bestowed posthumously on Rone and Glen, whose family has set up a memorial foundation in his name. Its mission is "to bring education and recreation to those in need." The foundation's website can be found at www .glendohertyfoundation.org. Separately, Stevens' family and friends have created The Ambassador J. Christopher Stevens Memorial Fund for Middle Eastern Studies at his alma mater, the

University of California, Berkeley. Donations can be made at http://givetocal.berkeley.edu/stevens -middle-eastern-studies.

Although the operators fought the battle and by all accounts saved about twenty American lives, because they were neither CIA staffers nor active military personnel they were deemed ineligible for even higher awards, awards that went to other men who played smaller roles and never fired a shot. As an agency staffer, the Benghazi GRS Team Leader received the Distinguished Intelligence Cross, the highest honor bestowed by the CIA. The award goes to clandestine service members for "a voluntary act or acts of extraordinary heroism involving the acceptance of existing dangers with conspicuous fortitude and exemplary courage." Bob, the CIA chief in Benghazi, also reportedly received a prestigious intelligence service medal, according to *The Daily Beast*. One Delta Force member, a Marine, was given the Navy Cross for heroism; the other Delta Force member, an Army master sergeant, was awarded the Distinguished Service Cross, the Army's second-highest honor, according to *The Washington Times*.

———

After Benghazi, the contract operators returned to their homes, their families, and their lives, until now remaining silent as they made decisions about their futures. All have retired from government security contracting for work in the private sector. Mark "Oz" Geist, Kris "Tanto" Paronto, and

In Germany after the attacks (l to r): Dave "D.B." Benton, Kris "Tanto" Paronto, John "Tig" Tiegen, and Jack Silva *(Courtesy of Kris Paronto)*

John "Tig" Tiegen have used their real names in this book. The names Jack Silva and Dave "D.B." Benton are pseudonyms, used to satisfy their hope of preserving their families' privacy and their own. The only other pseudonym was for Henry, the Annex translator. All other information about the pseudonymous characters is true. Names of all other individuals in the book were disclosed previously in congressional testimony and other public forums.

Looking ahead, the surviving Benghazi operators know that the events of those thirteen hours will color the rest of their lives. They remain in close contact, and all wear black aluminum bracelets etched with the names of the two fallen operators, along with the location and date of their deaths.

Above all, the surviving special operators hope that Chris Stevens, Sean Smith, Tyrone Woods, and Glen Doherty, to whom this book is collectively dedicated, will be remembered not as victims or political pawns, but as brave Americans who put themselves in harm's way, who believed in their work and their country, and who died serving others.

A NOTE ON SOURCES

This book could not have been written without the cooperation and candor of the five surviving special operators from Benghazi. Their accounts allowed for a boots-on-the-ground perspective, while also contributing to a virtual drone's-eye view of the thirteen-hour battle. Yet during scores of conversations and interviews, all five men took pains to avoid disclosing information, tradecraft, or techniques that the US government considers classified. For instance, they would not discuss certain details of their employment in Benghazi as security contractors. However, numerous other published and unpublished sources made it clear that the first responders to the Compound attack were employees of the Global Response Staff, as was Glen "Bub" Doherty. Identifying the operators as such was a simple leap of logic by the author.

As a result of the operators' circumspection about certain matters, this book owes a debt to numerous other sources, including many journalists and authors who have spent years covering military affairs and the nation's clandestine services. For instance, in the wake of the battle,

Greg Miller and Julie Tate of *The Washington Post* published an important story detailing the nature and the work of the Global Response Staff, including information about GRS contract operators at the CIA Annex in Benghazi. David Ignatius of the *Post* also made a significant early link between GRS and the events of September 11–12, 2012. They and many others who have written about the battle are cited in the Select Bibliography below. Also cited is the October 2012 congressional testimony of then–Deputy Assistant Secretary of State Charlene Lamb, who discussed the Quick Reaction Force that responded from the Annex. During her testimony, she displayed a map that clearly showed the location of the Annex.

Valuable information about the American presence in Benghazi also came from unexpected sources. One example is the December 2011 issue of *State* magazine, published by the State Department. An article written by Diplomatic Security agent Mario Montoya provided insight and details regarding the establishment of the Special Mission Compound. It also discussed the US government's efforts to collect shoulder-fired anti-aircraft missiles. The makes of vehicles used by the operators came from various sources, including media reports and previous books on Benghazi. One potential source who proved elusive was Bob the Annex chief. Attempts to reach him to hear his version of events were unsuccessful.

Essential elements of the narrative came from the December 2012 report of the State Department's

Accountability Review Board, which investigated the attacks on the Compound and Annex. The ARB report was important in terms of providing details of the Compound attack from the perspective of the DS agents. Also valuable were the Interim Progress Report for the Members of the House Republican Conference on the Events Surrounding the September 11, 2012, Terrorist Attacks in Benghazi, Libya, and the US Senate Select Committee on Intelligence Review of the Terrorist Attacks on US Facilities in Benghazi, Libya, September 11–12, 2012, among others. Several reports from the Congressional Research Service, listed below, were helpful with regard to information about security at US diplomatic facilities abroad, US policy, and relations with Libya.

SELECT BIBLIOGRAPHY

Abbas, Mohammed. "Libya's Benghazi Laments City's Decay Under Gaddafi." Reuters, May 16, 2011, http://www.reuters.com/article/2011/05/16/us -libya-benghazi-idUSTRE74F3ZP20110516.

Blanchard, Christopher M. "Libya: Transition and U.S. Policy." Congressional Research Service, October 18, 2012, https://www.fas.org/sgp/crs/row/RL33142.pdf.

Blanchard, Christopher M., and Jim Zanotti. "Libya: Background and U.S. Relations." Congressional Research Service, February 18, 2011, http://fpc.state.gov/docu ments/organization/157348.pdf.

Booth, William. "Benghazi Doing Better Than Tripoli, Rebels Say." *The Washington Post*, August 14, 2011, http://articles.washingtonpost.com/2011-08-14/ world/35269577_1_benghazi-libyan-rebel-tripoli.

Bosalum, Feras. "T-shirt Store Starts New Fashion Trend in Libya's Benghazi." Reuters, June 30, 2013, http:// www.reuters.com/article/2013/06/30/us-libya -fashion-idUSBRE95T03Z20130630.

Bulugma, Hadi M. *Benghazi Through the Ages*. 1972.

Burton, Fred and Samuel M. Katz. "40 Minutes in Benghazi." *Vanity Fair*, August 2013, http://www.vanity fair.com/politics/2013/08/Benghazi-book-fred-burton -samuel-m-katz.

Burton, Fred, and Samuel M. Katz. *Under Fire: The Untold Story of the Attack in Benghazi*. New York: St. Martin's Press, 2013.

Butters, Andrew Lee. "Dispatch from Libya: Why Benghazi Rebelled." *TIME*, March 3, 2011, http://content.time.com/time/world/article/0,8599,2056521,00.html.

Campagne, Jean-Pierre. "Thousands of Chinese Workers Leave Behind Libyan Ghost Town." *Times of Malta*, June 17, 2011, http://www.timesofmalta.com/articles/view/20110617/world/Thousands-of-Chinese-workers-leave-behind-Libyan-ghost-town.371017.

Campbell, Robert B., LTC (Ret.). "An Adventure in Benghazi: An Episode During the 1967 Arab-Israeli War," *Officer Review*, June 2011: 11–12.

Central Intelligence Agency. "The World Factbook: Libya." https://www.cia.gov/library/publications/the-world-factbook/geos/ly.html.

ClimaTemps.com. "Climate of Benghazi." http://www.benghazi.climatemps.com.

Clinton, Hillary. *Hard Choices*. New York: Simon & Schuster, 2014.

Crisp, Will. "Hanging Out in Benghazi's Car Boot Arms Market." *Vice*, April 30, 2013, http://www.vice.com/en_se/read/benghazis-car-boot-arms-fair.

Doornbos, Harald, and Jenan Moussa. "'Troubling' Surveillance Before Benghazi Attack." *Foreign Policy*, November 1, 2012, http://www.foreignpolicy.com/articles/2012/11/01/troubling_surveillance_before_benghazi_attack#sthash.tHcCp1Ny.dpbs.

Entous, Adam, Siobhan Gorman, and Margaret Coker. "CIA Takes Heat for Role in Libya." *The Wall Street Journal*, November 1, 2012, http://online.wsj.com/news/articles/SB1000142405297020471290457809285362106183.

Federal Bureau of Investigation. "Seeking Information on Benghazi Attacks." http://www.fbi.gov/wanted/seeking-info/seeking-information-on-attacks-in-benghazi/seeking-information-on-attacks-in-benghazi-poster.

Ferran, Lee. "American Killed in Libya Was on Intel Mission to Track Weapons." ABC News, September 13, 2012, http://abcnews.go.com/Blotter/glen-doherty-navy-seal-killed-libya-intel-mission/story?id=17229037.

Ferran, Lee. "Reporter's Notebook: Remembering an Ex-SEAL, Fallen in Libya." ABC News, October 17, 2012, http://abcnews.go.com/Blotter/reporters-notebook-friends-remember-seal-fallen-libya/story?id=17499523.

Flynn, Sean. "Murder of an Idealist." *GQ*, December 2012: 282–286, http://www.gq.com/news-politics/newsmakers/201211/sean-flynn-j-christopher-stevens-benghazi-libya-ambassador.

FoxNews.com. "Transcript: Whistle-blower's Account of Sept. 11 Libya Terror Attack." May 8, 2013, http://www.foxnews.com/politics/2013/05/08/transcript-whistle-blower-account-sept-11-libya-terror-attack/.

Garamone, Jim. "Little Describes Pentagon's Benghazi Decision Process." American Forces Press Service, November 2, 2012, http://www.defense.gov/News/NewsArticle.aspx?ID=118420.

Garcia-Navarro, Lourdes. "Benghazi's Citizens Fill the Libyan Government Gap." *Morning Edition*, NPR, March 9, 2011, http://www.npr.org/2011/03/09/134384820/Benghazi-Update.

Glen Doherty Memorial Foundation. "His Story: Glen Anthony Doherty." http://www.glendohertyfoundation.org/about-glen/.

Griffin, Jennifer. "What Laser Capability Did Benghazi Team Have?" FoxNews.com, November 4, 2012, http://www.foxnews.com/politics/2012/11/04/what-laser-capability-did-benghazi-team-have/.

Gumuchian, Marie-Louise. "Two Years On, Benghazi Threatens 'Another Revolution' in Libya." Reuters, January 31, 2013, http://www.reuters.com/article/2013/02/01/us-libya-benghazi idUSBRE91002N20130201.

Halim, Amr Ben. "A Return to Benghazi Evokes Memories of Libyan in the 1950s." The National, May 14, 2011, http://www.thenational.ae/thenationalconversation/comment/a-return-to-benghazi-evokes-memories-of-libyan-in-the-1950s#full.

Herridge, Catherine. "CIA Moved Swiftly to Scrub, Abandon Libya Facility After Attack, Source Says." FoxNews.com, December 5, 2012, http://www.foxnews.com/politics/2012/12/05/cia-moved-swiftly-scrub-abandon-libya-facility-after-attack-source-says/#ixzz2IE8icKIQ.

Ignatius, David. "In Benghazi Timeline, CIA Errors but No Evidence of Conspiracy." The Washington Post, November 1, 2012, http://www.washingtonpost.com/opinions/david-ignatius-cias-benghazi-timeline-reveals-errors-but-no-evidence-of-conspiracy/2012/11/01/a84c4024-2471-11e2-9313-3c7f59038d93_story.html.

Issa, Rep. Darrell, and Rep. Jason Chaffetz. Letter to President Obama. October 19, 2012, http://oversight.house.gov/wp-content/uploads/2012/10/10.19.12-Issa-and-Chaffetz-to-President.pdf. Also see attachments at http://oversight.house.gov/release/oversight-committee-asks-president-about-white-house-role-in-misguided-libya-normalization-effort/.

Judicial Watch. "Benghazi Aftermath Photos." November 12, 2013, http://www.judicialwatch.org/document -archive/benghazi-foia-response-including-photos/.

Karadsheh, Jomana, and Tim Lister. "Benghazi Tries to Escape its Ghosts, Past and Present." CNN, January 29, 2013, http://www.cnn.com/2013/01/29/ world/africa/libya-benghazi-past-present.

Kelley, Michael, and Geoffrey Ingersoll. "Intrigue Surrounding the Secret CIA Operation in Benghazi Is Not Going Away." *Business Insider*, August 3, 2013, http://www.business insider.com/the-secret-cia-mission -in-benghazi-2013-8.

Kelley, Michael, and Geoffrey Ingersoll. "It's Time to Discuss the Secret CIA Operation at the Heart of the US Mission in Benghazi." *Business Insider*, May 17, 2013, http://www.businessinsider.com/the-secret-cia -mission-in-benghazi-2013-5.

Kiely, Eugene. "Benghazi Timeline: The Long Road from 'Spontaneous Protest' to Premeditated Terrorist Attack." FactCheck.org, October 26, 2012, updated November 6, 2012 and May 9, 2013, http://www .factcheck.org/2012/10/benghazi-timeline.

Kirkpatrick, David D. "A Deadly Mix in Benghazi." *The New York Times*, December 28, 2013, http:// www.nytimes.com/projects/2013/benghazi/?hp#/ ?chapt=0.

Kormann, John G. *Echoes of a Distant Clarion*. Washington, DC: New Academia Publishing, 2007.

Kurtz, Howard. "Benghazi Brawl: The Pundits Take On the New York Times." FoxNews.com, December 31, 2013, http://www.foxnews.com/politics/2013/12/31/ benghazi-brawl-pundits-take-on-new-york times/.

Lake, Eli. "Exclusive: CIA Honored Benghazi Chief in Secret Ceremony." *The Daily Beast*, May 21, 2013, http://www.thedailybeast.com/articles/2013/05/21/exclusive-cia-honored-benghazi-chief-in-secret-ceremony.html.

Lederer, Edith M. "UN Panel: Libyan Weapons Spread at Alarming Rate." AP, April 9, 2011, http://bigstory.ap.org/article/un-panel-libyan-weapons-spread-alarming-rate.

Maxwell, James. "Libya: Why Benghazi Matters." *Think Africa Press*, May 30, 2013, http://thinkafricapress.com/libya/libya-why-benghazi-matters.

McDonnell, Patrick. "Political Football, Benghazi Style." *Winnipeg Free Press*, May 21, 2011, http://www.winnipegfreepress.com/opinion/fyi/political-football-benghazi-style-122381063.html.

McLean, Alan, Sergio Peçanha, Archie Tse, and Lisa Waananen. "The Attack on the American Mission in Benghazi, Libya." *The New York Times*, October 1, 2012, http://www.nytimes.com/interactive/2012/09/20/world/africa/the-attack-on-the-american-mission-in-benghazi-libya.html.

Milbank, Dana. "Letting Us In on a Secret." *The Washington Post*, October 10, 2012, http://www.washingtonpost.com/opinions/dana-milbank-letting-us-in-on-a-secret/2012/10/10/ba3136ca-132b-11e2-ba83-a7a396e6b2a7_print.html.

Miller, Greg, and Julie Tate. "CIA's Global Response Staff Emerging from Shadows After Incidents in Libya and Pakistan." *The Washington Post*, December 26, 2012, http://www.washingtonpost.com/world/national-security/cias-global-response-staff-emerging-from-shadows-after-incidents-in-libya-and-pakistan/2012/12/26/27db2d1c-4b7f-11e2-b709-667035ff9029_story.html.

Mongabay.com. "Population Estimates for Benghazi, Libya, 1950–2015," http://books.mongabay.com/population _estimates/full/Benghazi-Libya.html.

Montoya, Mario. "Mission to a Revolution." *State*, December 2011: 18–23, http://www.state.gov/documents/ organization/178204.pdf.

Morris, Harvey. "In Letter to Friends, Slain U.S. Ambassador Expressed Hope." *The New York Times, IHT Rendezvous* (blog), September 12, 2012, http:// rendezvous.blogs.nytimes.com/2012/09/12/slain -u-s-ambassadors-letter-to-friends-and-family/.

The New York Times. "A Timeline of Events in Benghazi." May 8, 2013, http://www.nytimes.com/interactive/ 2013/05/08/us/benghazi-pentagon-timeline.html.

Nordland, Rob. "In Libyan Rebel Capital, Shouts of Thanks to America and the West." *The New York Times*, May 28, 2011, http://www.nytimes.com/ 2011/05/29/world/africa/29benghazi.html.

Pargeter, Alison. *Libya: The Rise and Fall of Qaddafi*. New Haven: Yale University Press, 2012.

Redmayne, Nick. "Rising from the Revolution: Life in Benghazi." CNN, May 17, 2013, http://travel.cnn .com/benghazi-travel-610366.

Risen, James, Mark Mazzetti, and Michael S. Schmidt. "U.S.-Approved Arms for Libya Rebels Fell into Jihadis' Hands." *The New York Times*, December 5, 2012, http://www.nytimes.com/2012/12/06/world/ africa/weapons-sent-to-libyan-rebels-with-us-approval fell into islamist hands.html.

Rohloff, Florence Hartke. *Flight from Benghazi*. New York: Vantage Press, 1998.

Scarborough, Rowan. "Delta Force Marine Awarded Navy Cross for Fight at CIA Annex in Benghazi." *The*

Washington Times, November 16, 2013, http://p
.washingtontimes.com/news/2013/nov/16/delta
-force-marine-awarded-navy-cross-fight-cia-an/.

Schmitt, Eric, Helene Cooper, and Michael S. Schmidt.
"Deadly Attack in Libya was Major Blow to C.I.A.
Efforts." *The New York Times*, September 23, 2012,
http://www.nytimes.com/2012/09/24/world/africa/
attack-in-libya-was-major-blow-to-cia-efforts.html.

Snapp, Trevor. "The New Libyans." *Vice*, March 31, 2011,
http://www.vice.com/read/the-new-libyans-754
-v18n4.

Stark, Freya. *The Coast of Incense*. London: John Murray,
1953.

Temehu Tourism Services. "Benghazi." August 8, 2013,
http://www.temehu.com/Cities_sites/benghazi.htm.

TheTownTalk.com. "Transcript: Testimony of Gregory
Hicks on Benghazi." May 8, 2013, http://www.thetown
talk.com/article/20130508/NEWS01/130508017/
Transcript-Testimony-Gregory-Hicks-Benghazi.

Thorn Tree Forum. "An Update on Eastern Libya." May
12, 2012, http://www.lonelyplanet.com/thorntree/
thread.jspa?threadID=2199652.

Tiersky, Alex, and Susan B. Epstein. "Securing U.S. Diplomatic Facilities and Personnel Abroad: Background
and Policy Issues." Congressional Research Service,
November 8, 2013, http://www.fas.org/sgp/crs/row/
R42834.pdf.

US Department of State. "Background Briefing on Libya."
Office of the Spokesperson. Washington, DC, October 9, 2012, http://www.state.gov/r/pa/prs/ps/
2012/10/198791.htm.

US Department of State. "Benghazi Weekly Report—
September 11, 2012." September 11, 2012, http://

oversight.house.gov/wp-content/uploads/
2012/10/9-11-12-Memo.pdf.

US House Committee on Oversight and Government
Reform. "Benghazi Attack Pictures." October 2012,
http://oversight.house.gov/wp-content/uploads/
2012/10/2012-10-09-lamb-testimony-final1.pdf.

US House Committee on Oversight and Government
Reform. "Benghazi: Exposing Failure and Recogniz-
ing Courage." Hearing held on May 8, 2013. Washington, DC: US Government Printing Office, 2013,
http://www.gpo.gov/fdsys/pkg/CHRG-113hhrg
81563/html/CHRG-113hhrg81563.htm.

US House Committee on Oversight and Government
Reform. "Deputy Assistant Secretary of State Charlene
Lamb Testimony Before House Oversight Committee; Washington, DC, Wednesday, October 10, 2012,"
http://oversight.house.gov/wp-content/uploads/
2012/10/2012-10-09-lamb-testimony-final1.pdf.

US House of Representatives. "Interim Progress Report for
the Members of the House Republican Conference on
the Events Surrounding the September 11, 2012 Terrorist Attacks in Benghazi, Libya." April 23, 2013, http://
oversight.house.gov/wp-content/uploads/2013/04/
Libya-Progress-Report-Final-1.pdf.

US Senate Select Committee on Intelligence. "Review
of the Terrorist Attacks on U.S. Facilities in Benghazi, Libya, September 11–12, 2012, Together with
Additional Views." January 15, 2014, http://www
.intelligence.senate.gov/benghazi2014/benghazi.pdf.

Vandewalle, Dirk. *A History of Modern Libya*. Cambridge:
Cambridge University Press, 2006.

Von Mittelstaedt, Juliane. "Libya's Soccer Rebellion:
A Revolution Foreshadowed on the Pitch of Benghazi." *Spiegel Online*, July 15, 2011, http://www

.spiegel.de/international/world/libya-s-soccer
-rebellion-a-revolution-foreshadowed-on-the
-pitch-of-benghazi-a-774594.html.

Wainstein, L. "Some Aspects of the U.S. Involvement in the Middle East Crisis, May–June 1967." Institute for Defense Analyses, 1968, http://www.dod.gov/pubs/foi/Science_and_Technology/WSEG/505.pdf.

The Wall Street Journal. "How the Benghazi Attack Unfolded." http://online.wsj.com/news/articles/SB10000872396390444620104578008922056244096.

The Wall Street Journal. "Witness Hicks: How the Benghazi Attack Unfolded." *Washington Wire* (blog), May 8, 2013, http://blogs.wsj.com/washwire/2013/05/08/witness-hicks-how-the-benghazi-attack-unfolded/.

What The Folly?! "Transcript: Testimony of Regional Security Officer Eric Nordstrom on the 'Security Failures in Benghazi.'" October 11, 2012, http://www.whatthefolly.com/2012/10/11/transcript-testimony-of-regional-security-officer-eric-nordstrom-on-the-security-failures-in-benghazi/.

Youssef, Nancy A. "Libyans, Diplomats: CIA's Benghazi Station a Secret—and Quickly Repaired." McClatchy Newspapers, November 12, 2012, http://www.mcclatchydc.com/2012/11/12/174455/libyans-diplomats-cias-benghazi.html.

ACKNOWLEDGMENTS

Heartfelt thanks first and foremost to the families of the Annex security team. Their love and support sustained the operators during their time in Benghazi, especially during the thirteen hours of battle. Deep appreciation also goes to the team members' mentors, friends, and comrades in the US military and elsewhere, who helped to train the operators for what they encountered that night and to prepare the survivors for what came after.

Editor Sean Desmond of Twelve was a steadfast advocate and an insightful collaborator. To borrow Sean's phrase, assistant editor Libby Burton earned her stripes in "special ops, publishing." Special thanks to Jamie Raab, Deb Futter, Brian McLendon, Paul Samuelson, Mari C. Okuda, Rick Ball, Carol Ross, and the team at Twelve and Grand Central for treating this book with such great care.

Agent extraordinaire Richard Abate of 3Arts was like the host of a complex dinner party, pulling together a seemingly incompatible guest list with his signature flair. His assistant Melissa Kahn made sure every course arrived hot.

Dana Hatic created order from chaos, culling details from numerous sources to assemble an invaluable timeline. Nick Lehr crafted a sophisticated dossier on Benghazi, from its history to its idiosyncrasies, that displayed his talent as a researcher and writer. Steve Wylie set land speed records for turning digital recordings of interviews into voluminous, error-free transcripts.

Special thanks to Sid and Gerry Zuckoff, for giving me everything I needed.

Finally, to Suzanne, Isabel, and Eve: Now and always, you're the reason and the reward for everything.

INDEX

ABOUT THE AUTHORS

Writer **Mitchell Zuckoff** is a professor of journalism at Boston University and the author of six previous nonfiction books, including *The New York Times* bestsellers *Lost in Shangri-La* and *Frozen in Time*.

The Annex Security Team consists of five surviving CIA Special Ops contractors who responded to the September 11, 2012, attack on the US diplomatic Compound in Benghazi and fought the battle that repulsed the attackers and saved roughly two dozen American lives.

ABOUT TWELVE

TWELVE was established in August 2005 with the objective of publishing no more than twelve books each year. We strive to publish the singular book, by authors who have a unique perspective and compelling authority. Works that explain our culture; that illuminate, inspire, provoke, and entertain. We seek to establish communities of conversation surrounding our books. Talented authors deserve attention not only from publishers, but from readers as well. To sell the book is only the beginning of our mission. To build avid audiences of readers who are enriched by these works—that is our ultimate purpose.

For more information about forthcoming TWELVE books, please go to www.twelvebooks.com.